1 MONTH OF
FREE
READING

at

www.ForgottenBooks.com

By purchasing this book you are eligible for one month membership to ForgottenBooks.com, giving you unlimited access to our entire collection of over 1,000,000 titles via our web site and mobile apps.

To claim your free month visit:

www.forgottenbooks.com/free145092

ISBN 978-0-267-99657-5
PIBN 10145092

This book is a reproduction of an important historical work. Forgotten Books uses
state-of-the-art technology to digitally reconstruct the work, preserving the original format
whilst repairing imperfections present in the aged copy. In rare cases, an imperfection in
the original, such as a blemish or missing page, may be replicated in our edition. We do,
however, repair the vast majority of imperfections successfully; any imperfections that
remain are intentionally left to preserve the state of such historical works.

Lately Published, in Two Volumes, demy 8vo, 30s. bound.

CONVERSATIONS

WITH M. THIERS, M. GUIZOT,

AND OTHER

DISTINGUISHED PERSONS, DURING THE SECOND EMPIRE.

BY THE LATE NASSAU W. SENIOR.

EDITED BY HIS DAUGHTER, M. C. M. SIMPSON.

Among other persons whose conversations are recorded in these volumes are King Leopold; the Duc de Broglie; Lord Cowley; Counts Arrivabene, Corcelle, Daru, Flahault, Kergolay, Montalembert; Generals Lamoricière and Chrzanowski; Sir Henry Ellis; Messieurs Ampère, Beaumont, Blanchard, Bouffet, Auguste Chevalier, Victor Cousin, De Witt, Duchâtel, Ducpetiaux, Dumon, Dussard, Duvergier de Hauranne, Léon Faucher, Frère-Orban, Grimblot, Guizot, Lafitte, Labaume, Lamartine, Lanjuinais, Mallac, Manin, Mérimée, Mignet, Jules Mohl, Montanelli, Odillon-Barrot, Quételet, Rémusat, Rogier, Rivet, Rossini, Horace Say, Thiers, Trouvé-Chauvel, Villemain, Wolowski; Mesdames Circourt, Cornu, Ristori, &c.

'This new series of Mr. Senior's "Conversations" has been for some years past known in manuscript to his more intimate friends, and it has always been felt that no former series would prove more valuable or important. Mr. Senior had a social position which gave him admission into the best literary and political circles of Paris. He was a cultivated and sensible man, who knew how to take full advantage of such an opening. And above all, he had by long practice so trained his memory as to enable it to recall all the substance, and often the words, of the long conversations which he was always holding. These conversations he wrote down with a surprising accuracy, and then handed the manuscript to his friends, that they might correct or modify his report of what they had said. This book thus contains the opinions of eminent men given in the freedom of conversation, and afterwards carefully revised. Of their value there cannot be a question. The book is one of permanent historical interest. There is scarcely a page without some memorable statement by some memorable man. Politics, and society, and literature—the three great interests that make up life—are all discussed in turn, and there is no discussion which is unproductive of weighty thought or striking fact.'—*Athenæum.*

'The present selection of Mr. Senior's Journals, edited with remarkable skill and judgment by Mrs. Simpson, is extraordinarily full and interesting. Althou h the unreserved and original communications of Thiers are especially fascinating, the book would be abundantly interesting if it consisted only of the reports of conversations with Guizot, Montalembert, Cousin, Lamartine, and other persons of celebrity and eminence.'—*Saturday Review.*

'These conversations extend from the year 1852 to 1860, and will be found to refer to some of the most interesting public events of our time—the Revolution of 1848, the Crimean War, the French Alliance, the attempt on the life of Louis Napoleon, the Indian Mutiny, and the Italian campaign of 1859. Besides these great public occurrences of European celebrity, we have many very curious and piquant anecdotes of a private character, and expressions of opinion on men and things by persons of eminence. All that is said in these volumes of France, England, and Russia, is as interesting now as when it was first uttered.'—*Standard.*

'The two new volumes of the late Mr. Nassau Senior's most interesting conversations give us the ideas of some eminent foreign statesmen on the Eastern Question. They embrace the six eventful years from 1852 to 1858, during which Mr. Senior paid prolonged visits to Paris, and conversed on the most confidential terms with some of the shrewdest men of the time. They set forth the opinions of those who had the best means of informing themselves on Russian objects and English interests. They abound, besides, in most interesting details as to the personal character of the Emperor Nicholas and his successor; as to the relations of Russia and Austria; as to the social condition and resources of the two empires; as to the considerations that govern their policy, and their respective capabilities as fighting powers.'—*Blackwood's Magazine.*

HURST & BLACKETT, PUBLISHERS,
13 GREAT MARLBOROUGH STREET.

CONVERSATIONS.

VOL. I.

CONVERSATIONS

WITH

DISTINGUISHED PERSONS

DURING THE SECOND EMPIRE

FROM 1860 TO 1863.

BY THE LATE

NASSAU WILLIAM SENIOR

MASTER IN CHANCERY, PROFESSOR OF POLITICAL ECONOMY,
MEMBRE CORRESPONDANT DE L'INSTITUT DE FRANCE, ETC.
AUTHOR OF
'CONVERSATIONS WITH M. THIERS, M. GUIZOT, ETC.'
'A TREATISE ON POLITICAL ECONOMY,' 'BIOGRAPHICAL SKETCHES,' 'ESSAYS ON FICTION,'
'HISTORICAL AND PHILOSOPHICAL ESSAYS,'
'JOURNALS KEPT IN TURKEY AND GREECE,' 'JOURNALS KEPT IN IRELAND,'
'JOURNALS KEPT IN FRANCE AND ITALY,'
'CORRESPONDENCE AND CONVERSATIONS WITH ALEXIS DE TOCQUEVILLE,' ETC.

EDITED BY HIS DAUGHTER

M. C. M. SIMPSON.

IN TWO VOLUMES.
–VOL. I.

LONDON:
HURST AND BLACKETT, PUBLISHERS,
13 GREAT MARLBOROUGH STREET.
1880.

LONDON
PRINTED BY JOHN STRANGEWAYS AND SONS,
Tower Street, Upper St. Martin's Lane.

PREFACE.

THE great interest excited by the two volumes of Mr. Senior's Journals, published in 1878, has induced me to accede to the demand for more.

The present series will be found no less instructive and entertaining than the last.

In some cases, where the speakers have not yet retired from public life, I have been forced to give initials instead of their full names; but it is sad to observe how seldom this has been necessary. Two of Mr. Senior's intimate friends have died whilst this book has been going through the press.

It will be a matter of general regret that the Conversations in 1863 form the last of Mr. Senior's Journals. The illness which was to take him from us began in a general feeling of lassitude towards the end of that summer, and early in the following June he passed away.

There are still in MS. his Egyptian and Algerian journals, and many portions of his Contineutal journals. Some of the conversations that have already appeared lose much of their value from the necessity of suppressing the names of the distin-

guished men who took part in them. For instance,
in the 'Journals in France and Italy,' published in
1871, Thiers and Guizot were indicated only by the
initials H. and Z.

The interest in these Conversations, however,
continues to increase so sensibly, that I hope
some day to publish a connected series of the
Journals, containing much that the world has not
yet seen.

It is impossible to help lamenting that Mr.
Senior did not live to arrange and to annotate the
Journals himself, and that there is, comparatively
speaking, so little of his own political opinions in
these volumes. The attentive reader will, however,
find that there is more of Mr. Senior's own mind
brought into play than would appear from a cur-
sory glance, and he will admire the skill with
which the information and peculiarities of the different speakers are brought out, and the sense of
humour with which my father obliged them sometimes to express inconsistent and extreme opinions
of which he wished to expose the fallacy.

He never cared to shine himself. He seems to
have considered that, as Bacon says, 'The Honour-
ablest part of Talke is to give the Occasion, and
again to moderate, and to passe to somewhat else,
for then a Man leads the Dance.'

M. C. M. SIMPSON.

KENSINGTON, *January*, 1880.

CONTENTS

OF

THE FIRST VOLUME.

CONVERSATIONS.

1860.

[THE last volumes published of Mr. Senior's Journal ended with our visit to M. Guizot at Val Richer, in the month of August. Our next visit was to the Count Hervé de Kergorlay.

The war in Italy was at this time at its height, and Garibaldi was in the full tide of victory. Francis II. fled before him to his army at Gaeta, and on the 7th September Garibaldi entered Naples. Pius IX., greatly alarmed by these proceedings, set Lamoricière at the head of an army collected from all countries, ready to fight for the Papacy and to support Francis II., who threatened an invasion of his former dominions from Gaeta, while Austria from Mantua and Verona were preparing to join their cause.

Cavour hesitated no longer ; he determined at once to take possession of the Papal States in Umbria and the Marches (already in open revolt), push forward the army to Naples and Sicily, and wrest from Garibaldi the leadership of the nation. The deputations from these countries demanding immediate annexation were favourably listened to, Antonelli was summoned in the name of Italy to disband his mercenaries, the Sardinian army crossed the frontier,

18th of September, besieged and took Ancona on the 29th, and entered the Kingdom of Naples on the 15th of October, having taken Lamoricière prisoner and scattered his army to the winds.

Garibaldi had meanwhile defeated the Neapolitan troops in the battle of Volturno, and driven them under the guns of Gaeta. The two victorious armies met at Capua, and Garibaldi was the first to salute Victor Emmanuel with the title of King of Italy.—ED.]

Château de Canisy, near St. Lô, September 6.—We reached this place this morning, having slept two nights at Caen and one at Bayeux.

The tapestry of Bayeux and the fine churches at Caen are too well known to require description, and so is the still finer Cathedral of Bayeux. It has been restored, and the walls and pillars and traceries of the interior are perhaps more beautiful than they ever were. All are of the mellow, cream-like colour which the Caen stone possesses when first extracted. The painted glass is wanting, so that the windows are picture-frames without pictures. The inconsistent Italian cupola which, when I saw the Cathedral in 1850, disfigured the central tower, has been removed, and the tower is to be finished in the Decorated Gothic in which it was begun. The exterior, too, has been cleared of the buildings which used to conceal it.

We drove to Arromanches, a village on the seacoast, seven miles from Bayeux, to breakfast with Dr. de Mussy, who is staying there.

There are good sands, the sea and the air are very fine, but there is not a tree.

With increasing wealth, the taste for sea-bathing and marine villas has taken possession of the French. Trouville, twenty years ago a fishing village, has become a flourishing watering-place; and Arromanches, in the midst of one of the richest districts in France, and only seven miles from a railroad, hopes to equal its fortunes.

Miserable little houses, with spiral staircases and closets for bed-rooms, let for 1000 francs a-month; and land, worth 1000 francs an acre three years ago, now sells for 100 francs the perch, which we made out to be about 360l. an acre. Dr. de Mussy seemed to me to be very much inclined to purchase at this price about an acre and a half, running from the road to the sea, and to build a villa for his two months' vacation.

September 6, *Canisy.*—The most modern part of the Château of Canisy belongs to the beginning of the sixteenth century; the oldest to the eleventh. The east front is about 650 feet long; the south about 300. The dining-room and drawing-room are passage rooms, lighted each way. The south front, as far as the south-eastern tower, is the modern part, over it are the rooms occupied by the family, and, as at Val Richer, a corridor runs along the first floor to the north, into which they open.

The south-east tower, about thirty feet in diameter, is now a bed-room, but is to be the drawing-room, and the present drawing-room is to be the library. Our bed-rooms are on the ground-floor, looking east. The two eastern gate-towers and the tower beyond them are covered with ivy, which seems to be the growth of centuries. This last tower, larger than any of the others, and machicolated, is now inhabited.

The walls are about six feet thick ; the roofs lofty, and ending in the acute angle usual in the French mediæval châteaux.

The whole is built of the conglomerate of the country, which, where it is not covered by ivy or creepers, has assumed a fine yellowish red.

Its great size, fine colouring, and grand architecture, make it one of the most imposing buildings that I know. It is in very bad repair, and hewn stone and sand are already collecting for its restoration, which is to be begun in the spring, and is to cost not less than 20,000*l*.

It will never, however,—at least not for 200 years after its restoration,—be so striking as it is now : much of the ivy, and almost all the lichens, must go. I am glad that I have seen it in its picturesque decay.

Kergorlay is a Breton name, and the Kergorlay property was in Brittany. It was confiscated during the Revolution.

The Canisy estate belonged to a Marquis de Faudois, who had two daughters. One married, in 1789, my friend's father ; the young people were absent on a wedding tour on the 14th of July, and did not return to France until 1802.

M. de Faudois and his unmarried daughter resided in the Castle. They were popular, took no part in politics, and were long unmolested. Her portrait, that of a very pretty girl of eighteen, with a bright, gay expression, is in the drawing-room. It was taken in 1793, a few months before her death.

In a letter to a young friend, she said : 'Ma chienne vient de mettre au monde quatre petits citoyens.' The letter was opened at the Paris post office. She and her father were accused of 'incivicisme,' arrested in their castle, carried to Paris, and guillotined.

How the property was saved from confiscation, Kergorlay does not know. An old servant, the concierge, resided in it ; and when the Comte de Kergorlay returned to France, he took possession of it in right of his wife.

The party consists of M.* and Mde. de Kergorlay, their son, a nice boy of nine years old, Mr. Sheldan, his tutor, and a nephew, a young man studying his '*droit*.' The hours are the same as those of Val Richer.

September 7. — We drove over to St. Lô, the capital of the department of La Manche.

The Church, in the Early Pointed style, as are

---

* M. de Kergorlay's family was Legitimist, and he was an hereditary 'pair de France.' During the Empire he accepted a place in the Senate, for which he was rather coldly looked on by the Irreconcilables. He was a kind, and constant, and most obliging friend. He died about five years ago.—ED.

almost all that I have seen in Normandy, is remarkable for its great width and its fine towers. Near to it is a small church dedicated to St. Thomas à Becket, at his own suggestion. He was passing when it was nearly completed. The founder asked him to say to whom it ought to be dedicated. 'To the next saint,' answered Becket, 'who shall shed his blood for the Church.' He himself was the next.

An intelligent man, a M. du Bose, showed us the archives of the departments. We saw charters signed by the Conqueror; by his son, Beauclerc; by his father, Robert le Diable, who calls himself 'Dux Normanorum;' by Lanfranc, by the contemporary bishops of Hereford, of Worcester, of York, of Coutances and of Bayeux, by Bohun, by Mowbray, by Percie, and by other great Anglo-Norman names.

They all sign by a cross. ✠ This is a copy of the Conqueror's cross, which is larger than any of the others: underneath is written, 'Signum Gulielmi Ducis Normanorum et Regis Angliæ.'

The charters of a later date have pendent seals, but are not signed. The seals of the bishops are often representations of their cathedrals. On that of a Bishop of Worcester is his cathedral in front, and on the back the impression from an antique ring, of Venus and Cupid, whom he seems to have taken for the Virgin and Bambino.

M. du Bosc has to travel in the department in search of ancient documents, and sees much of the clergy.

I asked him what was their feeling towards the Emperor ?

Du Bosc.—Hostile, since the quarrel with the Pope ; but that is not injurious to him. The clergy are so unpopular that their friendship or their hatred is a minus quantity. Their favour would do him harm, their dislike does him good.

Senior.—What are the causes of their unpopularity ?

Du Bosc.—Their narrow education, which, begun in the cottage and the village school, and carried on in the seminary, turns them into the world having never talked to anyone but a peasant, a child, or a priest.

Their opinions are the ascetic, anti-social prejudices in which they have been steeped in the seminary, and which have been still more strongly incrusted on them by their ecclesiastical superiors. In this diocese they forbid the girls to dance. They insist on observances which the people despise, they make the wife unhappy if her husband will not confess, they interfere in the management of children, and even in the expenses of the household. They are petty, vexatious, ignorant tyrants—all the more so because they are sincere.

On our return I repeated all this to Kergorlay, and asked him how far he agreed with it.

Kergorlay.—It is much too highly coloured. Without doubt the quarrel with the Pope has offended the clergy, who are generally Ultramontane, and have no loyalty except to the Pope. In fact, that is the only loyalty now remaining, except among some old Legitimists of the Faubourg. The Orleanists think that the restoration of the Comte de Paris would be useful to the country ; the Imperialists had rather keep the present dynasty than encounter the risks of a revolution ; but neither of these parties is loyal in the old sense of the term,—neither of them has the personal devotion which you have towards your Queen. This devotion the priests have to the Pope : but they prefer their own interests to his. Now the Emperor has favoured those interests. He has augmented their salaries, he helps to build their churches, he treats them with respect, and has forced all the subordinate authorities to respect them. The bishops are greater men than they have been since 1830. The clergy would prefer the Branche Ainèe to the Bonapartes, but they prefer the Bonapartes to the Branche Cadette, and still more, to the Republic.

Again, though the inferior clergy are not *gens du monde*, they are not ignorant ot the world in which they live. The years spent in the seminary are indeed worse than wasted. They learn there legendary theology and ascetic morals and prejudices, but their earlier education, in the college or farmhouse, and the village school, is not effaced in the seminary, and the feelings produced by it revive when they emerge into the life of a secular priest. Confession, too, gives them a great insight into human nature. So far from being a minus quantity, I believe their influence, even in olitics, to be considerable.

At the last election, our Bishop selected as a candidate for one of the *arrondissements* of this department a young man of some property, but little known. He directed all his clergy to support him, and he was brought in triumphantly.

Senior.—Do any persons belonging to the higher classes take orders ?

Kergorlay.—Very rarely ; only enthusiasts. The seminaries are recruited partly from the farmers, and partly from the very lowest labouring families. The best priests come from the latter. A farmer, if he wishes to make a son a priest, always takes the dunce of the family—the one who has not brains enough to carry on a farm, or push his way in a town.

But the children of the very poor families look to the priesthood as an object of the highest ambition. They have not the means of preparing their children for it, but they send them at their own expense, or at that of the *Commune*, to school ; the curé recommends the best of them to the bishop ; they are taken, perhaps, as *enfans de chœur ;* sent by the bishop, or through his influence, to the seminary, and, being chosen for their talent and industry, and having nothing else to depend on, distinguish themselves in the field which is open to a clergyman. It is not wide, but it is long. Many portions of human knowledge are fenced off against him, but he may be a great theologian, a great casuist, a great orator, and even a great writer.

Religious questions are as important with us as they are with you : what was called the Congregation, that is, the ultra-religious party, overthrew the Restoration. The favour shown to hypocrisy, the disgrace in which men of independent opinions found themselves, the law of sacrilege, the general ultra-religious tone of the Administrator, which even Villèle—a man of the world, knowing its mischief and its danger—was forced to assent to, and even to join in, were the real causes of the Revolution of 1830.

The anti-religious, or at least the anti-Catholic, character of Louis-Philippe's reign, the placing a Protestant on the steps of the throne, and a Protestant at the head of the ministry, had much to do with that of 1848.

The ambition, the superstition, and the ignorance of the world of churchmen, make the Church a dangerous friend. It drives those who try to please it into language and conduct which disgust the liberal party. It arms against those who offend it the prejudices and superstitions of a party, not so active as the liberal party, but enthusiastic and well disciplined. It is a mischievous ally and a mischievous enemy.

If the Emperor were to die, the Empress would be Regent. She is in the hands of the Jesuits. She has all the superstitions of a devout Spaniard. If her confessor were a wise man, he might put her into the hands of an honest and able minister—if such a one is to be found—and things might go well. But an unwise confessor might attempt to govern himself in her name. A suspicion that such was the case, would be fatal to a dynasty so weakly rooted as our dynasties are.

Again, if the Regency, or the Empire, fell to Prince Napoleon, his fanatical irreligion would drive the religious party mad, and there is no saying what a large party, restrained by no scruples, believing every means of serving the Church to be lawful, might effect.

Have you heard of Prince Napoleon's conduct at the death of King Jèrôme?

Senior.—I have heard that the Prince was anxious to see him; that Dr. Rayer said that it was useless, as the King was too far gone to recognise him; that the Prince insisted, and that he forced his way into the room.

Kergorlay.—And that the King said, ' *Te voilà, mon brave,*' and that Rayer's remark was, ' *Je vous ai bien dit qu'il ne vous reconnaîtrait pas.*'

Well, that story is an invention; the real story is this :—The Empress and the Princess Clotilde were anxious that the King should not die without receiving the sacraments of the Church. But they knew that his son would try to prevent it, and were of course afraid of a scene. They almost lived in the King's apartments and had a priest within call. Just as the King was dying, the Prince happened to be absent. The priest was introduced, and the Eucharist was taken, and extreme unction was being administered when Prince Napoleon came in. The Empress was kneeling. She rose on his entrance, and said, ' *N'en voulez pas à Clotilde, c'est moi et*

l'Empereur qui l'avons voulu.' The Prince turned
round, kicked the door, slammed it violently after him
as he went out, and did not see his father alive
again, for in a few minutes he was dead.

We talked at dinner of Madame Rècamier, with
whom Kergorlay was intimate.

Kergorlay.—The best thing that has been written
on her is Madame Mohl's article in the *National
Review.* Madame L—— knew her well, but her
jealousy made her hostile to many of Madame
Rècamier's friends. Some she has left out altogether;
others, such as Châteaubriand, she has made as disagreeable as she could.

Châteaubriand in society was simple, unobtrusive,
rather a listener than a talker. It was in his letters
and in his political conduct that his vanity and
jealousy showed themselves.

As soon as he entered Villêle's cabinet, though a
mere *homme de lettres*, inexperienced in government,
he thought himself entitled to be its master, and
when the attempt to be so failed, he became its bitter
enemy. He was no debater; he could not improvise,
and therefore could not reply. He was of little use
as member of a government, but most formidable as
member of an opposition.

Senior.—His speeches were written and read?

Kergorlay.—Always.

Senior.—How, then, could they be effective?

Kergorlay.—Effective they were, and eminently
so. The were well written and admirabl delivered.

I have known many written speeches influence power-
fully an assembly ; Royer Collard's, for instance.

Among the philosophers in the Chamber, Guizot
was the only really great speaker. Not only his
matter but his look, his voice, and his action, were
superb. Sauzet* was a wonderful oratorical machine ;
his speeches are nothing when read, but were irresistible when delivered. I was present when he
defended Chantelauze, one of the ministers of Charles
X. I was then, as I hope I am now, a Liberal.
I abhorred the *ordonnances*,† and I abhorred their
authors. But Sauzet had not spoken for five minutes
before I was in tears.

There are four or five men the misconduct of each
of whom was necessary to the success of the Revolution. Sauzet was one. He was President on the
24th of February. He sent verbal orders to the
troops to repel the *émeutiers* who were threatening
the Chamber of Deputies. The general in command
refused to act without a written order. Sauzet
refused to give one, and 1500 ruffians were allowed

---

* Paul Jean Pierre Sauzet was the son of a physician at Lyons.
He became a distinguished advocate. After the downfall of
Charles X. he embraced political life, and attached himself successively to Lamartine and to Thiers. He was appointed Minister of
Justice by Thiers. When his party ceased to be in power, he
became one of the most violent opposers of the Molé cabinet. From
1839 to 1848 he was President of the Chamber of Deputies.—ED.

† The first *ordonnance* was to suspend the liberty of the press,
the second to dissolve the Parliament, and the third to set aside
the charters which the king had sworn to observe.—ED.

to dissolve a Chamber in the face of a guard of 5000 men.

Another was Molè. He wasted thirty-six hours in trying to form a ministry. During that interregnum the *émeute* was strengthening itself and the army was becoming demoralised. If he had given up the attempt as soon as its impracticability became evident, that is, after the first hour or two, Guizot might have been recalled, and the *émeute*, which was irresistible on the 24th, might have been stifled on the 23rd.

Lamartine is a third. My relation, Mornay, had obtained the assent of the leaders of the revolution to the regency of the Duchess of Orleans, provided that Lamartine consented. He feared that the Duchess would be under the influence of Thiers, and in the interest of his own miserable vanity destroyed our last chance of constitutional monarchy.

September 8*th.*—We drove this morning into St. Lô, to see the Imperial Haras, or stud. On our road we talked of the Emperor.

Kergorlay.—I can tell you a piece of diplomatic news, little known, but which reached me from an authentic source. Not long ago Montemolin* had an interview with the Emperor and Empress. The Emperor expressed great sympathy, but urged him not to be in a hurry. 'If you will only wait patiently,' he said, 'you will get all that you wish.

---

* The eldest son of Don Carlos. He died in 1861.—ED.

Policy consists in watching for an opportunity. *Il ne faut rien brusquer.'*

Senior.—I recognise a favourite maxim of the Emperor's.

Kergorlay.—Montemolin, perhaps as an excuse for having made an apparently inopportune attempt, complained that he had been ill supported by the Spanish Legitimists. 'Faithful subjects,' he said, 'ought to be always ready to sacrifice their lives in their sovereign's cause.' 'Yes,' said the Emperor, 'but on one condition : that he is ready to sacrifice his. There are no privileges amongst revolutionists.' 'I did,' said Montemolin, 'all that prudence permitted.' ' There are occasions,' replied the Emperor, ' when one must do more. "*Quand le vin est tiré il faut le boire.*" ' I do not know the details of what followed, but it is certain that they parted *avec de l'aigreur.*

I do not like this Russian news. We are told that Alexander and the Prince Regent of Prussia are to meet at Warsaw. Europe seems to be drawing a *cordon* round us.

Senior.—It is merely a defensive *cordon.*

Kergorlay.—I am not sure of that. Merely defensive armaments cannot be continued indefinitely. They cost too much. Austria professed to be merely on the defensive in May 1859. But she found the expense and anxiety intolerable and attacked. So may the present coalition. What I fear is a general feeling that economy, tranquillity, and improvement are impossible while a Bonaparte reigns in France. Leopold fancies that he is going to annex Belgium,

Prussia that he wants her Rhenish provinces, Austria thinks that he is intriguing against her in Hungary, Spain that he wishes to rectify his southern frontier, Sardinia was indignant at the peace of Villa Franca,, and has been quarrelling with him ever since. I believe that most of these fears are groundless, and that the others are exaggerated, but you must admit that the existence of such feelings endangers peace.

Senior.—We shall not attack you, and I do not think that the Continent will move while we stand aloof.

Kergorlay.—There are ways of overthrowing a dynasty without war. You cannot but know that many of your friends believe that it was you who overthrew Louis Philippe.

Senior.—I know that they think so, and I have always told them that their belief was absurd. I differ from you, however, as to the danger to which peace is exposed by our mutual fears. I believe that they will preserve peace. Nothing but fear will make us arm. Nothing but fear will keep you quiet.

Kergorlay.—My own opinion as to Louis Napoleon is that he does not wish for war. He knows that it would not be popular. The Corps Législatif warned him, in terms which he understood, that they would disapprove a war. I do not believe that they would refuse a war budget, but they would criticise it, and they might refuse to extend the conscription ; they might, and I believe that they would, seriously

fatal to his commercial policy, which is a child of his own, and a favourite child. He believes in its success, and is anxious that that success should convince the world that he was right and all his advisers wrong.

Senior.—Does he understand the subject ?

Kergorlay.—Perfectly. Any man of strong sense, unwarped by private interests or prejudices, and uncommitted by previous expressions of opinion, must understand it. The proofs are all on the surface ; and I have heard him discuss and explain them. The conversation at his dinners is free.

During the session I dined with him, with a large party of members of the Corps Législatif. After dinner there was a little knot in the corner, to which somebody was talking protectionism. The Emperor joined it, and explained as clearly as Michel Chevalier could have done that protectionism is the sacrifice of the future to the present, and of the many to the few, and urged, too, that free trade was the best preservative of peace.

There are a hundred stallions in the Haras, some of them gifts from foreign sovereigns. Four Persian horses, large and finely formed, were a present from the Shah. Many were bought in England : Assault, for 98,000 francs ; Flying Dutchman, for 105,000— more than 8000*l.* The price charged for the use of a stallion of mixed blood is 10 francs, for a thoroughbred 100. A stallion does not cover on an average

more than fifty or sixty times in a season, the young
and the old not more than forty times, the middle-
aged seventy or eighty.   The thorough-breds live to
twenty-five or twenty-six, the others to about twenty.
There are twenty-six of these Haras ; they are expensive but very useful.   The use of geldings is
increasing in France.   I remarked that the horses in
the diligences in Paris are all stallions.

Kergorlay.—Yes, and principally for this reason.
The coats of geldings are much thicker in winter than
those of stallions.   It is necessary to clip them.   To
clip a horse costs ten francs.   The Company of the
Diligences of Paris has 10,000 horses ; to clip them
would cost 100,000 francs a-year.

In the evening the magnates of the town dined at
the Castle.   Among them were the Préfet, the Sous-
Préfet, the Procureur Gènéral, the Maire, the Juge
d'Instruction, the Superintendent of the Haras, and
others whose names I did not hear.   There was not,
as there would have been in England, a clergyman.
The conversation was local, without any mixture of
politics.   I got tired and went to bed before they
broke up.

September 9th.—We drove to Coutances.   The
country is pretty, the inclosures small and surrounded
by fossés.   A fossé is a mound five or six feet high,
and four or five broad, planted with a single or
double row of trees, thickly placed, so as to make a

gigantic hedge. The frame of fossés surrounding a field often occupies as much ground as the field itself.

Kergorlay.—It is a deplorable waste of land, besides the injury done by the roots and the shade ; but in this country and in Brittany the practice has existed for centuries. Forced partitions increase it. The co-heirs, in their mutual jealousy, often require each field to be divided. If partitions were managed as they are with you, and the whole property were divided into only as many lots as there are heirs, there would not be much ' *morcellement.*' But according to the practice of our peasants an estate of twenty fields may be divided by two co-heirs into forty fields, and in the next generation into eighty, without any increase of population.

Senior.—Cannot it be sold?

Kergorlay.— Not without a lawsuit. The expenses of a sale, including the tax to the State, are above ten per cent of the value, or more than three years' income, to which must be added the expenses of a suit to decide whether a sale shall take place or not, which is at the discretion of the tribunal. The rent of the best land—and the land here is very good —is from twenty to thirty francs an acre, according to its situation ; the capital is small, and the return under sixteen bushels an acre.

Coutances is a small town, with a fine cathedral in the simple Pointed style of the beginning of the

thirteenth century. The roof of the choir is 100 feet
(French) high, that of the central tower is 220, or
about 240 English feet. We ascended it. The
country, from the abundance of hedge-row trees,
resembles a forest. Almost all are lopped; the
heads, therefore, expand. The high roofs and lofty
chimneys are like Milton's ' towers and battlements,
bosomed high in tufted trees.'

At dinner Madame de Kergorlay talked of her
mother's castle near Péronne, in Picardy.

'It is a fine place,' she said, ' but during the
Empire there was an objection to it. It lies directly
on the road between Paris and Brussels, and about
half way. It was a road frequently travelled by the
Imperial family. Caffarelli, who is a relation of
ours, told them that they would find themselves
more comfortable at our house than at an inn. That
family *ne se gênait pas*, and at last they got into
the habit of making us their half-way house. Once
the Princess Borghese wrote to my mother to say
that she was coming the next day, and begged that
she might put them to no inconvenience as she
wanted only twenty-six beds. Another time, my
mother, returning from a short absence, was informed as she approached the castle that some of
the Imperial family had established themselves in it.
She turned her horses' heads and left them in possession.

This is the last da of our leasant visit to

Canisy ; to-morrow we go to Corcelle's* château, Beaux Fossés, near Alençon.

Monday, September 10th. Château Beaux Fossés. —We reached this place in the afternoon. The château is a modern house, an enlargement of one which formerly belonged to the Marquis de Puysy, who took the Royalist side in the Vendèan rebellion. It stands in a small park, with fine trees, in a pretty country. As is the case in almost all the parts of Normandy that I have seen, pasture much predominates. The hedgerow trees, the small inclosures, the comparative absence of tillage, the deep lanes, and the scattered cottages, each with its garden and orchard, and the forest-like appearance of all the distant prospects, put me in mind of Devonshire. Our party consists of the Comte and Comtesse de Corcelle, their daughter, the Marquise de Chambrun, and her husband, and a charming little boy about ten years old—Corcelle's only surviving son. They lost another boy, who was between him and Madame de Chambrun. ' *Une perte,*' said Madame de Corcelle,

---

* Count François de Corcelle shared the opinions of Tocqueville before the Revolution of 1848, but after that time his ardent Catholicism drew him nearer to Montalembert. In 1849 he represented France at the Vatican, and assisted the Pope in restoring the Papal government. It was said that Pius IX. entreated him to remain, and be his Prime Minister ; but M. de Corcelle refused to forsake his own country. After the Franco-German war he again became ambassador to the Vatican. He has now entirely given up public life.—ED.

'*qui a été le malheur de notre vie.*' She is a daughter
of Madame de Lasteyrie, who was a daughter of the
General Lafayette ; George Lafayette was her uncle,
Mesdames de Rémusat and Gustave de Beaumont are
her sister and first cousin.

The Château is full of interesting memorials.
There is a Sèvres service, given by Louis XVI. to
Washington, and by Washington to Lafayette, an
onyx of the twelfth century, given by the Pope to
Corcelle, and portrait after portrait with its history.

I took a long walk with Corcelle before breakfast.
We passed through the village, pretty and neat, and
ascended a rocky eminence surrounded by ancient
fortifications. It was for thirty-eight years the
extreme outpost of the Anglo-Norman territory, and
after defying open attack was surprised while the
garrison were catching their Good Friday's dinner
in the brook at its foot. He asked me whether
Guizot and Thiers expected peace or war.

Senior.—Peace.

Corcelle.—So do I, but only for the present.
Louis Napoleon believes himself to be the type of
the French nation. He thinks that his feelings and
wishes are also theirs. To a considerable extent he
is right ; the great majority of the French are eager
for war, and glory, and conquest, and extension of
territory. These feelings, originally excited by
Louis XIV., exaggerated by Napoleon, and kept
alive, or rather resuscitated, by the Opposition in
their blind eagerness to discredit Louis Philippe,
have taken possession of the uneducated and ill-

educated masses. In no mind are they stronger than in that of Louis Napoleon; that is the secret of what is called his knowledge of the French character. He knows it, because it is his own. He thinks, with truth, that those masses prefer the Bonaparte policy to that of the Bourbons, war to peace, intimidation to conciliation, glory to prosperity, equality to liberty, and he is anxious to show himself a Bonaparte. But he is dilatory and irresolute; he is easily checked, easily turned aside; he is alarmed by the attitude of Europe; and I really believe that his present wish is to sit down under his laurels and enjoy uncontrolled expenditure, shameless adulation, and all the vulgar pleasures of mind and body. But events seem to be preparing which, whether he like it or not, will force him to action. Italy is in the hands of Garibaldi.* He is not a statesman, he is not a prudent, he is not even an honest man.

Senior.—I thought him an enthusiast, but honest. He is incorruptible; *il est prêt à faire tous les sacrifices pour l'unité Italienne.*

Corcelle.—Instead of '*faire tous les sacrifices,*' you should say, '*à sacrifier tout,*' not only his own life, but the lives of all who stand in his way, or whose deaths he may think useful. Like Mazzini, he is utterly unscrupulous. Look at the people whom he employs. Orsini, whose title to favour is that he is the brother of an assassin; Zambianchi, who murdered twelve men, many of them innocent, all untried, during the

---

* Garibaldi entered Naples on the 7th September.—ED.

siege of Rome. I knew one of them, the priest of the Minerve, an old, inoffensive man. They were seized by Zambianchi, and as they passed the church of San Calixte on their way, as they thought, to trial, Zambianchi stopped them, gave them five minutes for prayer, and shot them. I was then with Oudinot before Rome; the story was told to me when we entered the town, not many days after.

I said that Italy is in the hands of Garibaldi, but Garibaldi is also in the hands of Italy.

Your Government seem to believe in a constitutional peaceful kingdom for Italy. It is impossible; Italy is unfit for constitutional monarchy. Even Piedmont, the wisest portion of it, submits to it only as a means of aggrandisement. If Charles Albert or Victor Emanuel had remained at peace, Piedmont would have become despotic or revolutionary.

Senior.—The Tuscans are quiet, sensible people.

Corcelle.—The educated Tuscans are sensible, but you have called the populace to power, and they are carried away by the revolutionary torrent. Do you suppose that Italian mobs can calculate chances? Do you suppose that even if Garibaldi were wise enough to wish to keep his hands off Venice they would let him do so? If he attacks Venice, he is beaten. Can Louis Napoleon allow Austria to re-establish her influence below the Po?

Senior.—He threatens Piedmont that he will do so.

Corcelle.—And will he allow Austria to regain Lombard ? If the Piedmontese troo s or Piedmontese volunteers from Milan, cross the Mincio, and Austria repels them, will she not follow them into Lombardy? Can Louis Napoleon suffer all the results of his Italian campaign to vanish? His threats to Piedmont are mere threats; he will not venture to act on them. To do so would be against all his policy, personal and national. He would be again exposed to the Italian daggers, he would lose his prestige of success, he would have allowed his friends to be ruined, and his enemy to become stronger than ever. He cannot do this. If Garibaldi is beaten, Louis Napoleon must rescue him, and then we shall have a German war. We shall beat the Germans at first—we always do so. Will you permit us to reap the fruits of victory?

Senior.—If France were to make an aggressive war, if Piedmont, having annexed Southern Italy, were to leave Austria undisturbed, and Louis Napoleon were to declare the balance of power to be so altered that Rhenish Prussia or Belgium must be thrown into his scale, I have no doubt that we should try, even by war, to prevent such an annexation; but I am not sure how we should act if war were forced on Louis Napoleon in defence of his ally, and in defence of Italian liberty.

Corcelle.—Your supposition that Italy may leave Austria undisturbed is a very improbable one. Still its consequences are worth considering. I believe that the only bond among Italians is war; that peace, instead of a cement, would become a solvent; that left to themselves they would crumble into dust.

Mais ce serait une poussière révolutionnaire. I believe that their conspiracies, their Carbonarism, and their Socialism, would infect other countries, even yours at last, for in England, as well as on the Continent, these elements exist, together with others almost equally noxious which have an affinity to them. But if Italy were to remain united and monarchical, I feel that not merely Louis Napoleon, but, what is more important, France, would have a right to ask for an extension of territory. She might ask for it on the south, on the west, or to the north. She might take Belgium and the Rhine, or Catalonia, or the Riviera and Genoa. Would you permit her to do any one of those things?

Senior.—I have already said that we should resist the annexation to France of Belgium or of the German provinces on either bank of the Rhine. I was not aware that you coveted the Riviera or Catalonia.

Corcelle.—All that was arranged at Plombières was, that if Piedmont were raised to ten millions, as she would be by the annexation of Lombardy and Venetia, she should give Savoy to France. It seems a natural consequence that if she is raised to fourteen millions by the annexation of Modena, Parma, Tuscany, and the Romagna, she must . pay something more ; and that if she gets nine millions more by incorporating the Two Sicilies, she must cede still more. She cannot give us Turin, but Genoa would be very convenient to us. As to Catalonia, I can tell you something more precise. I know that in May last an offer was made by Louis Napoleon to Queen Isabella to enter into an intimate alliance with her— to renew, in short, the family compact, and to assist her in obtaining Portugal if she would cede Catalonia to France. That was the meaning. The words used were, ' That the Emperor would see with pleasure the annexation of Portugal to Spain, if Spain would consent to a rectification of the French frontier to the south.'

Senior.—This explains his proposal to promote Spain to the rank of a great power, and also, when Queen Isabella refused these offers, his return to Montemolin.

Corcelle.—Well, may we take Catalonia, if Spain will give it?

Senior.—Not at the expense of Portugal.

Corcelle.—Will you fight for Portugal?

Senior.—If she is attacked we shall. We have guaranteed her independence.

Corcelle.—If it comes to a general war, a gulf is opened to which I see no bottom. If we succeed, we destroy the liberties of Europe ; if we are beaten, national humiliation will unchain passions as mad as those of 1793. A revolutionary force will be generated which will carry away certainly the throne, and probably the altar. It may enable us to throw down the thrones and altars of our neighbours. Instead of destroying the liberties of Europe, we may destroy its securities. Instead of spreading despotism, we may spread anarchy. Europe can never be safe until France is constitutional.

We talked at breakfast of Lamoricière. He is Corcelle's cousin and intimate friend.

Senior.—Was it at your suggestion that he went to Rome?

Corcelle.—It was. I saw that the Pope was in danger, though I did not perceive the extent or the imminence of the danger. I deeply distrusted Louis Napoleon, and, even if he were the sincerest of friends, I felt that he would be still more friendly if he thought that the Pope could do without him.

I examined the state of the papal army, and found it utterly worthless. There were about 16,000 men, dispersed in little garrisons of a couple of hundred each, incapable of communication in cousequence of the absence of roads, ignorant, undisciplined, even undrilled. The officers were perhaps worse than the privates, for no man of any spirit, or real military feeling, would enter the childish service of the Pope. The stupidest of the cardinals was always chosen to be minister of war.

Senior.—I was acquainted with one papal minister of war, Cardinal Piccolomini, and he justified your statement.

Corcelle.—I knew Lamoricière's talents, not only as a general, but as an administrator. I thought him the man in the whole world most fit to create a papal army, and, I might almost say providentially, he was unemployed.

I easily persuaded the Pope to invite him. He was ashamed, indeed, of having to show to a French soldier the nakedness of the land, but he has too much sense to yield to the feeling. I carried the invitation myself to Lamoricière. With him I had great difficulty. He is not young, he is rich, he is fond of his family, he has a high reputation, he had not served for ten years. He was not willing to risk health, fortune, and fame. A letter from the Pope, imploring his aid, decided him.

We left Paris at the same time; but as I travelled directly, and he went round by Trieste and Ancona, I got to Rome a few days before him.

I found our minister the Duc de Grammont, in great excitement.

'It is intolerable,' he said, 'that the Pope, who exists only by French protection, should put his army under a French *mécontent*, without consulting us. If Lamoricière comes, I shall ask for my passports.'

'The Pope,' I answered, 'does *not* exist by French protection. You are here for your own pleasure, not for his. He has often told you, and he is ready to repeat to you, that you may go whenever you like.'

'Why did he not consult us?' said the Duc.

'Because,' I answered, 'he is an independent sovereign.'

'At least,' he said, 'Lamoricière might have asked the Emperor's permission. *He* is not a sovereign.'

'Nor,' I replied, 'does he admit that he is a subject of the Emperor. His sovereign is not at the Tuileries. *You* may propose to him to ask the

Emperor's permission. *I* will not, and I do not think that *you* will succeed.'

Next day the *Moniteur* stated that the Emperor had granted to General Lamoricière permission to take the command of the Papal troops.

I was present at the first interview betweén him and the Pope. They were mutually pleased.

' *C'est une âme toute pure,*' said Lamoricière ; ' *on y voit jusqu'au fond.*'

The Pope was amused by Lamoricière's military frankness.

The Duchess of Parma had presented to the Pope ten guns.

' That will be enough, I suppose? ' he said.

' Ten! ' said Lamoricière ; ' I shall want fifty.'

' Bah! ' said the Pope; ' no pope ever had twenty.'

' I can't help that,' said Lamoricière ; ' I must have fifty.'

' I suppose,' said the Pope, ' that we must buy horses in Austria? '

' *N'allez pas faire cette bêtise,*' said Lamoricière ; ' your own are better and cheaper.'

Senior.—We have been told that there has been some jarring between the Pope and Lamoricière.

Corcelle.—None whatever. There is perfect mutual confidence. Lamoricière has had his own way as far as the Papal revenue has been able to answer his wants. He has created a good army of 25,000 men : 8000 are Romans, 6000 are Swiss, and the rest are French, Germans, and Irish. The Irish are among the very best. Some mistakes were made at the beginning. One of the recruiting agents made promises of pay and privileges which were totally unauthorised and incapable of fulfilment. Some of them were despatched without officers, and misconducted themselves on the road. Those who were dissatisfied were sent home, and they told, as discharged servants do, all sorts of lies. But there is now an Irish battalion of 1200 men, well disciplined and well disposed. Many are old soldiers. Some served under Lord Clyde at Lucknow. There were scarcely any lateral communications in the Roman States. To go from Viterbo to Spoleto you had to pass through Rome. Lamoricière has made cross-roads, which are necessary for military purposes, and will be useful commercially.

I believe that Lamoricière, with his 25,000 men, could beat 50,000 Garibaldians or Piedmontese, such as the Piedmontese now are. But if he is attacked by 80,000, if Garibaldi menace him on the south, and Piedmont on the north, he will scarcely be able to do more than keep Ancona and the Comarca.

Senior.—Is Antonelli an able man?

Corcelle.—He is a diplomatist of the Italian school. He knows how to elude, and delay, and retract; but he knows nothing of the art of government, or of the sciences from which that art draws its maxims. He is no political economist, he is no legist, he is no statistician. His knowledge and his experience are purely Roman. He has never

travelled farther than to Gaeta, and what he saw
there was not much better than what he had left
behind, or indeed very different. He has vague,
imperfect ideas as to what constitutes a good or a bad
administration.

Senior.—Do you believe that the secularisation of
the Papal administration is possible and advisable?

Corcelle.—It certainly is advisable, so far as it is
possible. Ecclesiastics, from the narrowness of their
education, from their celibacy, from the peculiar
nature of their intercourse with the world, from the
tendency to consider government as an institution
rather to prevent sin than crime, from the asceticism
which renders them, if sincere, indifferent to progress
and to worldly prosperity, are more unfit to be administrators than perhaps any other class whatever.
Soldiers, country gentlemen, lawyers, men of letters,
and men of the world, have all furnished good
administrators. Ecclesiastics never. But there are
great difficulties. The first is the want of good laymen. All the higher offices having been for centuries
closed against laymen, no laymen have been educated
for them.

Senior.—Is it true that the Pope wished you to
become his Home Minister?

Corcelle.—He said something of the kind; but he
knew too well the impossibility of my accepting the
offer to make it seriously.

Much, however, might be done. At present the
Prélature, whether in Holy Orders or not, all wear

the ecclesiastical dress and enjoy ecclesiastical privileges; and though they do not all take the vow of celibacy, scarcely any of them marry. All this might be put an end to. The Monsignori might be encouraged to marry, to remain lay, to dress as laymen. The most distinguished of the lay Monsignori might be employed in high offices. Without any sudden or violent change, lay administration might be gradually introduced.

We took a long walk to a neighbouring forest to see what are called the finest trees in the country. They are tall—many of them 120 feet high, and 80 to the first bough. A celebrated oak, which bears the name of the oak of St. Louis, is probably 30 feet higher. The forest is thickly planted on a gentle slope and looks magnificent from a slight distance, but the beauty is gone when you enter it and find yourself among lofty, smooth, naked poles, with bushy heads.

We talked of the relations between France and the Papal Government.

Corcelle.—We entered Rome in 1849, as the restorers of order and public safety. The predominant feeling of the Roman delegates who came to negotiate with me was fear of the excesses which Garibaldi's volunteers might commit in their last struggles. They were anxious to finish the capitulation, and let our troops enter as quickly as possible. I had inserted some words expressing the confidence of the

Romans and of the French that the Pope would grant to his people liberal institutions. They struck them out. 'We don't care,' they said to me, 'about institutions, if we are to remain the subjects of the Pope. We want to be a part of a great nation. We want to be the subjects of the King of Italy.'

This is the feeling of all ambitious men. They wish their country to be great, not that it may be happy, but that they themselves may be great. They wish for large power, large patronage, and large salaries ; and those are to be had only in a large empire.

Louis Napoleon's celebrated letter to Edgar Ney * produced little effect. The Romans did not wish for the Code Napoléon ; and he soon forgot it himself. For many years his great object was to be *sacré* by the Pope. The Pope temporised. He did not refuse, but he raised difficulties. At last he said it might have been done some years before, but that he was now too old to travel ; that the Emperor must come to Rome. From that time Louis Napoleon's friendship for the Pope cooled. The occupation was prolonged, but rather to gratify the vanity of France than the interests of the Pope.

After the peace of Villa Franca, he wished to please all parties : to please the Carbonari by inducing the Pope to secularise his administration ; to

---

* A private letter expressing his high approval of the expedition to Rome.—ED.

please Austria by restoring at least Tuscany to its
Grand Duke ; to please the Piedmontese by securing
to them Parma and Modena, and by giving them
hopes of keeping Romagna.

Here is a copy of the proposals which he made to
the Pope in last March :—

'PROPOSITIONS FAITES AU MOIS DE MARS, 1860.

'La question des Romagnes demeurant exclue de
la discussion, les Plénipotentiaires de la France, de
l'Autriche, de l'Espagne, du Portugal, de la Bavière,
de la Belgique, des deux Siciles, et de la Sardaigne,
se réuniront en conférence avec un réprésentant du
Saint Siège pour procéder à la signature d'un protocol,
ou d'une convention dont les termes seraient acceptés
d'avance, et qui arrêteraient les points suivants.

'1°. Le Saint Siège annoncerait son intention de
proclamer les réformes décidées en principe, ou, ce
qui vaudrait mieux, le fait de leur publication
préalable.

'2°. Les puissances Catholiques sus designées
auxquelles le Brésil serait invité à se joindre, garan-
tiraient au Saint Siège la possession des provinces
restées sous sa domination.

'3°. Les mêmes puissances, chacune au proratâ de
la population Catholique, inscriveraient en téte du
gros livre de la dette publique, une somme fixe qui
serait versée aux échéances d'usage entre les mains
du représentant du Saint Siège.

' 4°. Il serait convenu qu'à l'exception de la
France, de l'Autriche, des deux Siciles, et de la
Sardaigne, les autres puissances catholiques de
l'Europe, c'est à dire, la Bavière, la Belgique,
l'Espagne, le Portugal, fourniraient successivement,
et pour une période de 3 ans un contingent de 2000
hommes d' infanterie, et de 500 hommes de cavalerie
destinés à participer à la garnison de Rome, sans
pouvoir être employés à aucun autre usage.

' 5°. La France et l'Autriche s'offriraient pour
faciliter le transport, par mer, du contingent des puissances qui leur en adresseraient la demande.'

He tried a remarkable means to forward his nego-
tiations.

Louis Napoleon likes indirect paths, and knows
so little of Rome that he thought that a young French
lady, living in Rome, with whom he had been on
terms of intimacy, could influence the Papal Government. He wrote to her a letter which I saw, but
could not copy. Its substance was—that he writes
in very bad spirits, that the Italians are ungrateful,
that Piedmont opposes him, that Rome seems un-
willing to help him, that he fears that the glories
of the war may be obscured by the ill-success of
the peace. That, in the name of past friendship,
he entreats her, and if it be necessary he orders her,
to exert herself to obtain the consent of the Pope to
his terms. If they are refused, he must throw himself into the arms of the King of Sardinia.

Senior.—Had he any success?

Corcelle.—Not the slightest. '*Elle fut éconduite sans cérémonie.*' And he has, as he threatened, played the game of Sardinia. I believe that now he will play the game of Garibaldi.

He made the Tuscan revolution. M. de la Ferrière, our minister in Florence in 1859, is my cousin. The instructions which he received from Walewski, and his own honour and good sense, made him anxious to support the Grand Duke, if he would restore the Constitution. Such was also the wish of all the wisest and best of the Tuscans. But when Prince Napoleon came, with 30,000 men at his back, he overruled Walewski, told La Ferrière that the Emperor had resolved to dethrone the Grand Duke, and set the Revolution going.

Senior.—Do you believe that Prince Napoleon wished to take the Grand Duke's place?

Corcelle.—He has always disclaimed any such intention. He says that nothing will induce him to leave Paris. And I believe him to be sincere.

September 12th.—The news of the Piedmontese demands on Rome reached us this morning.

Corcelle.—They must be made in concert with Louis Napoleon. If so, the Pope will have to quit Rome. If Providence should permit his absence to be permanent, the effects on religion—even on civilisation—will be disastrous.

A Pope, the subject, or even the guest, of a

foreign sovereign, would lose his independence, and with his independence the respect of the Catholic clergy.

The time is past when the Catholic bishops were men of birth and station, supported by their own revenues, able and willing to resist the temporal power. They are now men of humble origin, trained to look to the Government for their salaries and their promotion, and trained to respect the noblesse as their natural superiors. All that keeps up their heads, all that gives them any backbone, is the support of the Pope. If the Pope be degraded, if they be no longer able to lean on him, they will fall at the feet of the Government. If the bishops be subservient, so will be the clergy. And if the clergy be the slaves of the Government, they will lose the respect of the people. They will be considered as ' *l'ombre de la police.*'

Now the people take their religion on trust. They must do so. They have neither time, nor knowledge, nor intelligence, to inquire into its evidences. If they distrust their clergy, they will not become Protestants,—they will become infidels. France has already lost its loyalty. It fears authority, but neither loves nor respects it. It has lost its respect for its aristocracy. If it loses its respect for religion, what will there be to restrain it? You may say with Lucretius :

> ' Suave mari magno, turbantibus æquora ventis
> E terrâ alterius magnum spectare laborem.'

It is an insular feeling. But are you sure that the land will be firm under you ?

Senior.—To what extent does the Pope now influence your clergy ?

Corcelle.—To a considerable extent. They are subject not only to his moral and religious influence, but also to his temporal power. He can refuse to make them bishops.

Senior.—And does he exercise that power ?

Corcelle.—Certainly he does ; but we do not hear of it, for a prudent Government always asks his consent before it nominates. A case, however, occurred not long ago, in which his consent was publicly refused. The Emperor nominated a certain Abbé to a bishopric, and the nomination was inserted in the *Moniteur.* The Pope knew the man to be a servile Imperialist : and, besides, he was deaf, which is a canonical impediment. A negotiation followed, in which one of the curés of Paris took part. He wrote long letters to me and to the Duc de Grammont, urging the danger to the Pope if he publicly affronted the Emperor. The Pope was firm. He refused his sanction. The Abbé is still only an abbé, but the curé has been rewarded by the Cross of the Legion of Honour.

Thursday, September 13th. Chartres.—We left Beaux Fossés this morning, and on our road to Paris spent a couple of hours in the Cathedral of Chartres.

It is the finest that we have seen. The ordinary fault of French cathedrals is the want of breadth corresponding to their length and height. This is eminently the case in the Church of St. Ouen; but in that of Chartres, length, breadth, and height, are all in proportion. It produces a feeling of uniform vastness. All that is fine, at least, in the interior, belongs to the thirteenth century. In the seventeenth century, a screen, partly stone and partly iron, was drawn between the choir and the nave, and a huge virgin, raised up on marble clouds, was squeezed in behind the high altar, and allowed to shut out the Lady Chapel. I hope that the good taste which has restored Bayeux, and left the whole magnificent vista, from the western front to the apse, and through the arches of the apse in the Lady Chapel, free, may be allowed to remove these barbarous obstructions from the choir of Chartres.

Saturday, September 15th.—I spent the day with A. B. C., in his pretty villa near Paris.

A. B. C.—All that is going on, on the part of the Emperor, is a comedy; though, if the species to which a drama belongs is decided by its catastrophe, it may be a tragedy. No one who knows anything of Louis Napoleon can believe that Cavour and Garibaldi are acting in opposition to his wishes. As he could crush both of them by a stroke of his paw, he could stop both of them by merely lifting up his paw.

And no one who knows anything of France can believe that we shall suffer a new Prussia to be constructed. at our gates, without requiring an accession of strength in proportion to the increased force that may be turned against us—and what increase can we have, except the Rhine from Strasburg to Rotterdam?

Senior.—I am told that he has been coquetting with Spain for the Ebro?

A. B. C.—I know that he has. But a man must be as bad a politician as he is, to think of trying to extend our empire to the south-west, over a people who hate us, who are eminently formidable in defensive war, and who could not be annexed without having been subdued.

No ; the Walloons and the Flemings, who speak our language, who have similar institutions, whose commercial and manufacturing interests would profit by the change of masters, and who have no historical connexion with their present sovereigns, and no traditional vanity to be irritated by it, are the new Frenchmen whom we must make, if the union of Italy should require the balance of power to be re-adjusted.

This, I believe that he feels, though among the wild projects that pass through his ill-regulated fancy, the annexation of Catalonia was one.

I further believe that the acquisition of the Rhine has been his object for the last thirty years, ever since the death of his elder brother made him believe himself destined to govern France. But he has pursued it, and is pursuing it, in his peculiar style, slowly, indirectly, circuitously. He never makes a direct bound, his spring is always sideways. He never meant the treaty of Villa Franca, or the treaty of Zurich, to be executed. He intended Sardinia to annex Parma, and Modena, and Tuscany, and the Romagna, and Sicily, and Naples. He intends her to annex Rome. Lamoricière is cut off from Ancona, and must concentrate himself in Rome. Garibaldi will not attack him there. But the Sardinian party will seduce and demoralise his troops. Revolutionary crowds will assemble under the windows of the Quirinal. There will be cries against the Pope's person ; perhaps assassinations of his ministers. Guyon* will ask for a written order to disperse them by force. The Pope will refuse. Guyon will be instructed to say, that unless he be allowed to act, he cannot guarantee the safety of Rome or of the Pope. He will suggest a retreat to Civita Vecchia. The Pope, perhaps, may prefer Ostia ; but when once he has quitted Rome all is over. Rome becomes the capital of the kingdom of Italy, and then Louis Napoleon asks for the Rhine. His case will be plausible. Every public act, down to the recall of Talleyrand from Turin, has been a protest against Sardinian aggrandisement. He will say to England, ' All this is your doing ; *you* sympathised with

---

* The French general in Rome.—ED.

Ricasoli and Garibaldi; *you* forbade me to interfere with the wishes of the Italians; *you* urged me to tie the hands of Austria; *you* held up to Europe, and especially to the Romans and to the Neapolitans, every Italian government except that of Piedmont, as oppressive, as infamous, as intolerable. When I was forced to take Savoy, you must have seen the obligations which the further progress of Piedmont would impose on me. I yield to necessity, to a necessity which you yourselves have created.'

All this I say rather from an attentive study of his character during three whole years, than from actual information. But some information I have. I know that when the Italian deputies, Farini and Cialdini, saw him the other day at Chambéry, he said to them, 'Whatever you do, do it as quickly as you can.' He wishes it to be done during his pleasure tour, and he takes his pleasure tour at this instant, in order that it may be done in his absence.

I know, too, that one of his inmost feelings is hatred of the Pope. As a Carbonaro, he hates him. As a revolutionist, he hates him. He hates him for having refused the *Sacre*. He hates him as the possessor of a spiritual power which his own temporal power cannot break or elude. His ambition, or rather his vanity, is beyond all description, beyond all comparison, except among the Cæsars. He is a mixture of Augustus and Nero—as anxious for power as Augustus, as anxious for admiration as Nero. He would like, like Augustus, to be Pontifex Maximus, as well as Imperator ; and like Nero, to be the first of flute-players. Hence his jealousy of all eminence. If he heard that a great dancer had come to Paris, his first idea would be to rival him ; and if he thought that he could do so, he would like to collect all Paris in the Place Vendôme, and exhibit his activity and grace from the top of the Column. I have no doubt that one of his motives for wishing to merge all Italy in Sardinia is his jealousy of Garibaldi. Garibaldi is more picturesque than he is, a better soldier, a greater conqueror. He hopes that when Italy is quiet under a real king, a man born in the purple, Garibaldi's *rôle* will be over. On the whole, therefore, the chances of peace seem to be almost desperate. If Sardinia succeeds, he claims the Rhine, and he would not get it without a war. If Sardinia is beaten, he must come to her assistance. His army is good and large ; his finances, for four or five years to come, are inexhaustible ; his subjects are homogeneous. Austria has a dispirited army, a ruined exchequer, and an empire composed of nine or ten different nations, disliking one another, and detesting their central government. Nothing but the aid of the rest of Europe can save her. And I believe that that aid will be given. I believe that Prussia will give it, that Belgium will give it, that Holland will give it, that Russia will give it, and that you will give it. If you do not, you deserve to be trampled on one after another.

Even if war can be avoided, even if Europe consent to grant to France what she will ask, or if France consent to the aggrandisement of Sardinia without asking for any equivalent; even in either of these improbable good fortunes, I still foresee great calamities. The Pope will lose his temporal power. That is one of the few things which seem to be certain. Whether his spiritual power do, or do not quit him with his temporal power, the couse-quences, in either alternative, will be disastrous to the Catholic world. If it do quit him, it will, in most kingdoms, fall to the sovereigns. Napoleon used to say, that if he were king of England, he would also be Archbishop of Canterbury. It is the instinct of power.

Of all centralisation this is the worst. We see its consequences in Russia. The little resistance to power that is made in Catholic countries is made by the clergy. They make it, because their allegiance is to the Pope. Monseigneur Dupanloup and M. de Montalembert brave the temporal authority, because they acknowledge the spiritual one. Transfer the allegiance of the clergy to an emperor or to a king, and they will become slaves, and rivet the chains of their fellow-subjects. Ou the other hand, if the Pope, deprived of his territory, were to retain his influence, he would have much more power than he has now, and be much less fit to exercise it. He will have much more power, because it will be uncontrolled. The temporal power of the Pope is necessary in two opposite ways. It gives him independence, and it

limits that independence.   It gives him independence,
because he ceases to be a subject.   It limits that
independence, because his interests as a temporal
prince are a security for his moderation as a spiritual
one.   It gives his fellow sovereigns a hold on
him.

You have broken with him : you give him no
help : you have not even direct diplomatic relations
with him.   And look at the consequences.   He thwarts
all your policy in Ireland ; he opposes your united
education ; he sends you firebrands for bishops, and
keeps the majority of your Irish subjects in a state of
chronic disaffection.   What keeps the Curè of A——
in order ?   That he depends on the Municipality for
his *presbytère*, on the parishioners for his *casuel*, on
the Prefect for the repairs of his church, on the
Ministre des Cultes for his promotion, and on the
State for his salary.   The catholic sovereigns of
Europe are the municipality of the Pope, he not
only fears their power, but respects their opinion,
he is proud to think himself one of them.   Himself
an administrator and a politician, he sympathises with
them.   He knows their wants, and understands their
arguments.   Deprive him of these temporal interests
and of this temporal experience, and he becomes a
monk : that is to say, a superstitious ascetic.   How did
the Pope employ himself at Gaeta ?   In defining the
Immaculate Conception.   It is quite true that the
temporal power of the Pope is inconsistent with the
good government of the Roman people.   As I have

already said, the union in one hand of spiritual and temporal power is the worst of despotisms. But I think that I have shown that in order to keep those powers separate elsewhere, they must be united in Rome. I am sorry for the Roman people, but I prefer the interests of the Catholic world to those of the Roman people,—the interests of two hundred millions to those of three millions.

September 16th, Les Bruyères.—We spent to-day at Les Bruyères, the pretty villa of M. de Circourt,* in the forest of La Celle, between Versailles and St. Germains. Before dinner we went over the château of La Celle, once the country retreat of the monks of St. Germains, afterwards the residence of Madame de Pompadour, and now inhabited by the widow of an eminent tobacconist. She is still handsome, and her manners are agreeable.

The Circourts gave an amusing account of the society of *nouveaux riches.* The P——s used to send invitations to their neighbours, and to Parisians whom they supposed to be desirable guests. Some came, some sent excuses, and some did not answer at

---

* Count Adolphe de Circourt was a member of the Orleanist party. Under the administration of Tocqueville, in 1849, he was appointed ambassador at the court of Berlin. He is a man of extraordinary information and vivacity. His wife, who died in 1863, was also a brilliant converser, and had one of the most agreeable *salons* in Paris. M. de Circourt has long given up public affairs.—ED.

all. But as the P——s did not know the faces of
their friends, when the company came they often
could not tell who had accepted and who had refused;
so that they were continually making mistakes, and
dropping those who were ready to come to them,
and importuning those who had resolved to keep
away.

The park is not extensive, but is well situated
on the slope of a hill, and finely wooded. The
house is of the Louis XIV. age—a centre with two
pavilions. The principal rooms are, as is usual in
French châteaux, passage-rooms with double lights.
Byron's Giaour, and a portrait of Mme. P—— when
young, both by Scheffer, are the best pictures.

On a neighbouring hill we saw Beaux Regards,
the château of Mrs. Trelawny, the Marquise de Beaux
Regards,* with the national flag flying over it, to the
great scandal of the neighbours.

At dinner we met an intelligent Russian, M.
Tchihatchef. We talked of Russia.

Tchihatchef.—She is busied about her own social
revolution; but even if it were convenient to her to
take an active part in international affairs, I doubt
whether she would wish to do so. Since the beginning of the war, which was the folly of a proud,
obstinate old man, she has had to complain of everybody. The peace of 1856 imposed on her restrictions

---

* Mrs. Howard, formerly Louis Napoleon's mistress.—ED.

to which she cannot permanently submit. She hates England and France as open enemies; she hates much more bitterly Austria as a faithless friend. She hates Louis Napoleon for having deceived her, for having pretended friendship, and deserted her when she asked for a congress. She cannot attack Austria, lest an Hungarian or Gallican insurrection should extend to Poland. She cannot attack Piedmont, or even Garibaldi, because that would be assisting Austria. She will look on and enjoy the quarrels of her enemies.

Circourt.—Our Emperor is nearly in the same position. He, too, hates everybody.

Senior.—What is his quarrel with Spain?

Circourt.—It has several motives. One is, that Queen Isabella is a Bourbon; another, that she rejected his alliance; and a third, and the most important, that she declined a visit from the Empress. 'I never,' she said, 'will receive as Empress a woman whom I refused to make one of my ladies-in-waiting.' So you see that when the Emperor and Empress landed at Mahon they found that the Queen had left it the same morning. Louis Napoleon is as implacable as he is grateful. He never forgets a kindness or an offence.

I heard a curious anecdote respecting the Baden conferences. A friend of mine, immediately after Louis Napoleon's departure, went over the house which he had occupied. Behind the sofa on which he used to sit, and therefore in face of all those who

conversed with him, was a closet containing a bed, a
chair, and a writing-table. A large hole had been
cut in the wall between this closet and the sofa, and
concealed by being papered over. A person in the
closet could hear all that was said near the sofa.
There can be no doubt that a stenographer was kept
there by the Emperor night and day, to record all
that passed.

I asked Mme. de Circourt if she had heard lately
from Cavour.

Mme. de Circourt.—About ten days ago I received
a letter from him, in which he announced his intention to resign. 'Victor Emanuel,' he said, 'is going
too fast for me. I do not like to play double or quits
when my country is one of the stakes.'

Tchihatchef.—I do not wonder that Cavour fears
to be driven into another war with Austria. The
Piedmontese army was bad at its best. Benedec
beat it easily at Solferino; the Savoy brigade alone
resisted him; and now, filled as it is with revolutionary foreigners, it is worth nothing.

September 17th, 1860, Héry, Cher.—We reached
this place, the château of M. Duvergier de Hauranne,*

---

* M. Duvergier de Hauranne was early initiated into political
life. He was co-editor of the *Globe* with Guizot and Rémusat from
1824. In 1831 he was elected a deputy, and he supported by every
means in his power the Liberal party in the Chamber. He was a
warm adherent of Thiers in 1840, and an opponent of Guizot when

this evening.* Our road, after quitting Orleans, lay through the Sologne,† one of the parts of France in which the population decreases. It consists of extensive plains of sand, or coarse gravel, covering a clay subsoil. The water arrested by the clay spreads itself into marshes and shallow lakes, or is drained by straight cuts. The thin soil is covered chiefly by brushwood, birch, fir, or dwarf heath or rushy pasture.

To the south-west of the Sologne is Berri, less flat, and with a better soil and climate, but still low in wealth and population. The forests are extensive, and contain, as those of the Sologne do, wild deer, wild swine, and even wolves.

These are the advantages that made Sologne and Berri popular three hundred years ago among the

---

the latter, on his return from the post of ambassador in London, became Prime Minister, and encouraged the reactionary policy of the King. M. Duvergier was one of the chief promoters of the political banquets which had a great share in overturning Louis Philippe. After the revolution he was elected member of the Constituent Assembly, and afterwards of the Corps Législatif; and on the 2nd December, 1851, he was imprisoned, with the other victims of despotism, until the 9th January, 1852. Since that time he has given up politics, and has been chiefly engaged in writing a parliamentary history of France.—ED.

* The conversations at Héry, except a small portion, which could not be copied in time, were read and corrected by M. Duvergier.—N. W. SENIOR.

† All this country has been celebrated and idealised in the writings of George Sand.—ED.

French aristocracy. They were vast hunting grounds. When the seigneurs deserted the provinces for Paris and Versailles, their great châteaux fell into ruin. Forests were cut for sale, and not replanted. Drainage was neglected, the country became unhealthy, and the population sank so low that it does not amount to more than three hundred persons to the square mile, about half the average of France. This has preserved it from the *morcellement* of the Revolution. The great estates were not sold, because the land was not worth having in small portions, and the purchasers of confiscated property have not capital enough to cultivate, much less to reclaim, it on a great scale. The old proprietors remained in their houses, or returned to them when the *émigrés* were recalled. The estates, therefore, and the farms, are very large, but they are ill cultivated. The *métayer* system is common, perhaps more common than *fermage*.

Towards the east of Berri, on the banks of the Loire, are M. Duvergier's château and park.

The park is large, the largest that I have seen in France. It is about three miles round, and well wooded. The house is a Louis XIII. château, a centre with two wings. The principal rooms are passage-rooms, and fill the whole of the centre, looking east and west.

As at Guizot's, the books spread over the house, filling three libraries, and extending in double rows into the passages. The English library, taken alone, is considerable.

We found here Gen. Changarnier,* Odillon Barrot,†

---

* Born in 1793, General Changarnier first distinguished himself in 1823, in the Spanish war. In 1830 he became an officer of the Royal Guard ; but he was soon afterwards sent to Algeria, where he justified a rapid rise in his profession by a series of brilliant exploits. In 1847 he was appointed general-in-chief of the French army in Africa. When, a year later, Cavaignac was appointed governor and general-in-chief of Algiers, Changarnier returned to Paris, set himself at the head of the forces assembled by the Party of Order, and succeeded in putting down the insurgents in April 1848. He continued in command of the National Guard, and on two occasions commanded all the troops in Paris. He supported successively the authority of Cavaignac and of Louis Napoleon, until he saw that the rule of the latter was degenerating into despotism. Perceiving that he could not use Changarnier as a tool, Louis Napoleon deprived him of his functions, and on the 2nd December, 1851, imprisoned him. For some years afterwards he lived in exile at Malines, and had not long returned to his native land when we met him at Héry. He lived to a great age, and in August 1870, forgetting the wrongs he had suffered at the Emperor's hands, put his sword at the disposal of Louis Napoleon. He was shut up in Metz with Marshal Bazaine, and took an active part in the defence of that fortress. On October 24th, he was granted an interview with Prince Frederick Charles, in which he endeavoured to obtain the free departure of Bazaine's army to Algeria. It was refused ; the town capitulated on the 27th and Changarnier was taken prisoner. He was liberated on parole, and retired to Brussels. After the adjustment of the terms of peace, he returned to France (1871), was elected a member of the Assembly, and gave his constant support to the Government of M. Thiers, whom he greatly assisted with his advice with regard to the re-organization of the army. In person he was tall and distinguished, very polite to ladies, and extremely well dressed. He was an interesting converser, but he spoke indistinctly, and when at a loss for words finished his sentences with gestures. He died in 1877.—ED.

† Odillon Barrot, born in 1791, inherited liberal principles from his father. He was appointed *avocat du Roi* in 1814 ; but on

Lanjuinais,* M. and Mme. Target,† and two or three other persons whose names I have not discovered.

---

finding the principles of the Restoration were not as liberal as he expected, he joined the National party, and in 1830 took an active part in promoting the revolution of July. He was named prefect of the Seine under Louis Philippe. The new monarchy was far from answering his expectations, and in a few months he was again in opposition. He offered himself as a liberal candidate to the Department de l'Eure, and spoke in the Chamber in which he was destined to obtain such brilliant triumphs for the first time at the age of forty, in answer to Guizot. He became one of the most influential members of the *Coté Gauche*, but he would not allow himself to drift into Republicanism. He advocated the cause of a liberal constitutional monarchy, and spoke always in defence of any liberties which he thought threatened by the abuse of power. In 1840 he joined M. Thiers against Guizot, and in the struggle of principles which followed he was called, 'if not the chief, the standard-bearer, of the party,' and the 'hero of the banquets.' Believing thoroughly in the power of the party to effect the reforms which he desired, the revolution of February took him by surprise. His own account of the part he played in it will be found a few pages hence.

Barrot received the portfolio of Justice and the presidency of the Council in Louis Napoleon's first selection of ministers; but he was far too liberal for the President, and was one of the first to be dismissed. Again in opposition, he agitated, as formerly, for the reforms which he deemed expedient, and again without success: for the *coup d'état*, in 1851, proved the death-blow to his political life. He was tall, strong, and rosy, and looked more like a substantial farmer than a politician. His manner was frank and genial, and he was a delightful converser. He died in 1873.—ED.

* Son of the well-known member of the Convention during the First Empire. He was a deputy in the reign of Louis Philippe, and joined the party of the Left. He was again elected as deputy in 1848, and accepted the portfolio of Agriculture and Commerce in the ministry of M. Dufaure. After the *coup d'état* he retired from public life. He died some years ago.—ED.

† M. Target, M. Duvergier's son-in-law, was French minister

Duvergier asked me what were A. B. C.'s expectations.

Senior.—Warlike. He thinks that what is going on is concerted between the Emperor and Cavour, and that Sardinia is to be allowed to annex all Italy, in order to give France a right to seize the Rhine as a counterpoise.

Duvergier.—I do not believe that Louis Napoleon has any such projects. I believe that he lives *au jour le jour*, thinking of politics only among the intervals of pleasure, and changing his plans every morning after he has read the papers. The interest of France, as well as of Europe, is to keep him at peace. War will please our vanity if successful, rouse our anti-national hatreds if it fail, and in either event distract our attention. It is only in peace that we think of ourselves, that we feel our degradation, that we discuss the characters of the wretches to whom we are sold, that we resolve to shake off this despotism of rogues and pimps. The Napoleonic throne cannot stand five years of peace.

Senior.—I hope that your opinions are correct ; but if they are, is it not to be supposed that he shares them?

Duvergier.—If you draw round him a sufficiently strong cordon—such a cordon as Prussia, Austria, Holland, Belgium, and England can furnish—he will not attempt to break through. He dreads hostile

at the Hague in 1877, when the Duc de Broglie was Prime Minister.—ED.

coalitions. His condition of existence is successful war. It is your business to make that impossible. I know that this is frightfully expensive; but it is less expensive than actual war. It retards the accumulation of capital, but it does not destroy existing capital, it does not interfere with commerce; and though a slow and expensive policy, I am convinced that it will be a successful one.

Senior.—You say that the throne cannot stand five years of peace. How is it to be overturned?

Duvergier.—That is a question which I cannot answer. I foresee the event : I do not foresee the means. The most probable one is an *émeute.*

September 18*th.*—In the drawing-room hangs a portrait of Madame de Maintenon. We were looking at it before breakfast this morning, and the conversation passed to the château which bears her name.

Odillon Barrot.—I once spent a long day in its neighbourhood, but I was too busy to visit it. It was when I was escorting Charles X. to Cherbourg in 1830. He had established himself at Rambouillet with a considerable force, and Marshal Maison and I were sent by Louis Philippe to persuade him to retire. A mob grotesquely armed accompanied us. As we approached the château, and saw the numbers of the infantry, cavalry, and artillery, that surrounded it, we felt that if the troops were faithful there was the nucleus of a civil war.

The King received us sulkily.

'What do you want?' he asked. 'I have sent my orders to the Chambers; I have sacrificed myself, and reserved only the rights of my grandson.'

'We are grieved,' we answered, 'to have to say to your Majesty that further sacrifice is necessary. We believe that your Majesty's continued residence in France is unadvisable.'

'*Retirez-vous*,' he replied; 'I will consider what answer is to be given to you.'

As we were going he called back Maison.

'You are a soldier,' he said; 'you will tell me the truth. How many people have you with you?'

'Sixty thousand,' replied Maison.

There were about ten thousand.

In about an hour he recalled us.

'I will retire to the coast,' he said.

'It will be our duty,' we answered, 'to accompany your Majesty.'

'Why so?' he replied. 'The police will protect me.'

'The police,' we answered, 'is powerless. While we are with your Majesty there is no danger; but we cannot answer for the consequences if we leave you.'

He submitted, and we began our long, slow, anxious journey to Cherbourg.

Charles X. soon saw the necessity for our presence. In all the towns, and even in the villages, the populace turned out, shouting, '*À bas les ministres! À bas les ordonnances!* Turn Polignac out of the carriages. We know that he is in one of them.'

Senior.—Would not the King have been protected if he had taken a guard with him?

Barrot.—The guard would scarcely have been faithful. It might have saved him from being torn to pieces; but if the people had insisted on treating him as they did his brother at Varennes, and on forcing him back to Paris, the guard would not have prevented them.

Maison was the general who received Louis XVIII. at Dover in 1814. His was the hand which Louis XVIII. grasped to assist him as he landed. His hand was the last which Charles X. touched as he embarked.

Charles X. had made him marshal. He said at parting that he trusted that the King would believe that his only motive for accepting the office of escorting him had been the hope of being useful to his Majesty.

'*Ne parlons pas de ça,*' answered the King.

I slept at St. Lô on my return. Polignac was in the prison. He sent for me. I never saw so pitiable a countenance. It was that of an old child. It had neither dignity nor intelligence, nor even the grace which when he was all powerful used to be ascribed to him.

'I am detained here,' he said, 'most illegally. I

cannot be reproached with the shadow of an offence. I merely did my duty. I merely obeyed the King's orders. What could I do but sign the *ordonnances* when I received the King's express positive commands?'

'If,' I replied, 'you knew what is the feeling of the people outside, you would rejoice that the prison-door is between you and them. As for your offence, I should deceive you if I did not warn you that the tribunals will have to decide on it. I recommend you to think of your defence.'

'Will *you* defend me, M. Barrot?' he asked.

'I cannot,' I answered, 'for I am a public functionary. What do you think of Berryer?'

'Oh, no,' he replied, 'not Berryer.'

'Then,' I said, 'I recommend to you Martignac.'

He applied to Martignac, who conducted his defence admirably.

M. Barrot and M. Target went out to shoot. Duvergier, Changarnier, and I took a long walk.

'Pray tell me,' I said to Changarnier, 'the real story of the 29th of January, 1849. Was the armed force that on that morning surrounded the Assembly collected by the Garde Mobile or by the President? Was it an attempt at a rouge insurrection, or an attempt at a *coup d'état*?'

Changarnier.—It was something of all of them. The Garde Mobile and the Garde Républicaine,

Caussidière's troops, were the active agents. They intended a rouge revolution. The President knew of their plans, wished them to begin, and intended to turn their attempt into a *coup d'état*.

On the morning of the 28th, going to the Elysée, I found the court full of the Garde Mobile. I asked them what they wanted.

'We want,' they said, 'to see the President. We are told that we are to be disbanded. We are sentinels appointed by the Republic. We will not allow ourselves to be driven from our posts.'

'It is quite true,' I said to them, 'that some of you who are not fit for service are to be discharged, and that the rest are to be subjected to a discipline which you appear, many of you, to want. But you have no business here. Go home to your quarters. I am going to the President, and I will tell him what you say.'

There was much excitement. Some cried, 'À bas Changarnier!' others seemed inclined to threaten violence. I left them in the court, and in about an hour they dispersed.

The President confessed to me that he had allowed them to enter the court, and that he intended to see one or two of them. I pointed out to him the impropriety of his doing so, and he acquiesced. I saw that something serious was intended; and when I got home I sent orders to the corps d'armèc near Paris, and ordered the regiments and the officers on whom I could best depend to come immediately to Paris, and to rendezvous in the Place de la Concorde, the Quai d'Orsay, and the Place des Invalides.

The next morning the Garde Mobile and the Garde Républicaine met in great numbers near the Palais de l'Assemblée and on the Quai d'Orsay, and, finding the troops there, they remained quiet, but without dispersing.

I received a summons to a meeting of the ministers at ten. Soon after we had assembled the President came in, and took his seat. After a few minutes' silence he addressed us in his slow, soft voice :

'Gentlemen,' he said, 'you see that the constitution is impracticable. I have something to propose as a substitute for it.'

He took a paper from his pocket, and began to read it.

He was interrupted by Passy, the Minister of Finance, who said :

'You seem to be preparing a *coup d'état*. Do you not know that another revolution will destroy our finances, and undo all the good that three years of peace have done?'

'Do you talk to me,' said the President, 'of your miserable finances, *quand je joue ma tête?*'

'*Parbleu!*' said Rullière, the Minister of War, '*ce n'est pas seulement votre tête que vous jouez, mais toutes les notres.*'

Barrot said a few words, *très dignement*, and the

President put the paper unread into his pocket, and left us.

We did not wish for an impeachment which might have brought on another revolution ; so we resolved to say nothing about the incident.

The Garde Mobile and the Garde Républicaine gradually dispersed, and I sent the troops home to their quarters, with an order to be ready if I wanted them.

In the afternoon the President left the Elysèe on horseback, and rode slowly along the Rue Faubourg St. Honoré as far as the Rue Royale. He was coldly received, saw that the insurrectionary army had left the Quai d'Orsay, and turned suddenly back to the Elysèe.

Senior.—Do you think that he intended on that occasion to make an attempt?

Changarnier.—I think that he intended to feel the public pulse. If he had found a considerable number of the Garde Mobile and the Garde Républicaine collected, and had been well *acclamé* by them and by the crowd, he might have ridden on to the Tuileries, have been proclaimed Emperor by the mob, and have thanked them from the balcony.

Senior.—Do you know the contents of that paper?

Changarnier.—He showed it to me afterwards. It resembled his proclamation of the deux Décembre : universal suffrage re-established, the existing constitution abolished, and the people were to say how and by whom a new one was to be created.

I never—at least not until the end of 1851—could persuade him that I did not intend to make him Emperor. Persigny persecuted me with offers.

Duvergier.—Persigny persecuted everybody. As he has little tact, and at that time knew nothing of the influential persons in Paris, he used to make ludicrous blunders. He, and Bènoist d'Azy, and Jules de Lasteyrie were together.

'You know,' he said to them, 'that this government cannot last. Why not help to create the one which is to succeed it? Money,' he added, turning to Bénoist d'Azy,—'and rank,' turning to Lasteyrie, 'will be showered on those who show themselves its early friends.'

'You have mistaken your men,' answered Lasteyrie. 'Bènoist is as rich as Crœsus: I am a marquis, and I have not a farthing.'

Changarnier.—Once, as I was leaving his cabinet, I took the wrong door. 'When this house is your own,' he said to me, 'you will know it better.'

On the 13th of June, 1849, after the attempt of Ledru Rollin and Louis Blanc and the other fools who met at the Conservatoire, and had to escape by the window—had been defeated, I asked him to ride with me along the Boulevards. I thought that after an event which had excited some alarm his appearance with me in public might be useful. We had six aides-de-camp with us, four of his, two of mine. We were well received till we came to the Porte St. Denys. There we found groups of sinister-

looking people, who cried, ' *Vive la République!* ' and
seemed inclined to ill-treat us. Never in my life did
I see more degraded or more ferocious faces.

The President was very much affected. He could
scarcely sit his horse. His aides-de-camp said to
mine, ' *Mais on a mené le Prince ici, pour le faire
égorger.*'

I took some of the cross streets, which led us
to the Quais, the Place Vendôme, and thence to the
Rue Castiglione. As we approached the end of the
Rue Castiglione, and saw the Tuileries, the President's agitation increased. He is always sallow,
but he was then livid. I turned to the right, and
took him through the Place de la Concorde back
to the Elysèe. There I took leave of him at the
door. During the whole ride, which lasted five hours,
for we rode slowly, and even when we parted, he
was absolutely silent.

The next day he said to one of my aides-de-camp,
' *Votre général m'a fait tourner très court près des
Tuileries.*' I have not the slightest doubt that he
believed that when I sent to him I intended to carry
him to the Tuileries, and to proclaim him Emperor.

Senior.—Could it have been done?

Changarnier.—With the utmost ease. The Assemblée Constituante had become unpopular. It was
accused of illegally prolonging its reign from ambition or from avarice. The twenty-five francs* a-day,

---

* Each member received twenty-five francs a-day.—ED.

which it had voted to itself, was a constant grievance.
The Parisian mob, like all other mobs, is always
ready to impute the vilest motives to public servants.
The army and the National Guard were under my
command. The people might have been conciliated
by the promise of new elections and universal suffrage. I do not believe that there would have been
any serious opposition.

Duvergier.—He ought to have been '*mis en ac-
cusation*,' and arrested after the Satóry reviews, in
1850. He was taken in *flagrant délit*. There was
no doubt that he had suggested the treasonable cry of
'*Vive l'Empereur!*' that he had rewarded those who
uttered it, and punished those who refused. There
were other still stronger proofs of his conspiracy
against the Republic. The Permanent Committee of
the Assembly had the evidence in its own hands. It
possessed all the rights of the Assembly. It ought to
have exercised the least questionable of all rights—the
right of self-defence.

Senior.—I have no doubt that that would have
been right, if it had been practicable.

Changarnier.—Not only practicable, but easy.
The Legislative Assembly was still popular. Louis
Napoleon had not become so. He depended on nothing but his name. The Republican party, which
always applies the torch to our explosions, was
deeply irritated and alarmed by his despotic pretensions.
If the Assembly had ordered his arrest, I could have
taken him to Vincennes with a corporal's guard. I

was among those who were anxious that it should be done.

Duvergier.—Those who opposed the attack on the part of the Assembly—if a movement really defensive can be called an attack—of whom the Duc de Broglie was the chief, warned us not to drive him to extremities. 'Even a timid beast,' they said, 'will fight, and fight formidably, *s'il est acculé dans un coin.*' They forgot that he was *acculé* by the approach of the term of his Presidentship. The framers of our absurd Constitution dismissed him from the Elysèe to a debtors' prison.

A year later resistance had become almost impossible.

His Socialism and his profusion had made him popular with the lower classes in Paris. The Assembly had become unpopular with them. It was accused of aristocracy,—it had restricted the suffrage. It was believed by them to be conspiring to bring back the Bourbons. In the provinces the state of feeling was different. There, the expectation of a Rouge revolution had made Louis Napoleon popular among all classes,—with the higher, as their protector against the Rouges ; with the lower, as their protector against the Bourgeoisie.

In 1851, the Bourgeoisie of Paris behaved admirably : if the working classes had supported them, as they did in 1830, the army, which wavered much at the beginning, would have joined them, and all would have been saved. But the *ouvriers* almost everywhere answered, ' We will not fight for the Assembly, we will not fight for the *vingt-cinq francs.*'

' You shall see,' said Baudin, one of the Montague deputies, ' how the *vingt-cinq francs* fight for themselves.' He went behind a barricade and was shot.

It was on the Bourgeoisie, therefore, that the massacres of the 5th of December fell. The orders given to the soldiers were to fire at all the windows, and down all the streets. The objects were, first, to terrify, and, secondly, to create a feud between the soldiers and the people of Paris. Louis Napoleon succeeded in both.

Senior.—I walked down the Boulevards on the 21st of December, 1851. There was not a single house, from the Place de la Bastile to the Boulevard des Italiens which was not covered with the marks of balls. The soldiers must have fired indiscriminately at every window.

A shower drove us into a summer-house.

We talked of the Presidential election.

Duvergier.—Cavaignac was the proper man. He would have been sincere. Republican government would have had a fair trial.

Senior.—It was to prevent that that Louis Napoleon was elected. He was elected for the express purpose of destroying the Republic.

Duvergier.—Without doubt many votes were given to him as the enemy of the Republic. When I visited this department, before my election in 1849, many of the farmers and peasants, especially the women, said to me, ' We are tired of these Assemblies. *Il nous faut un maître.*'

Senior.—Thiers told me that one of his own motives for voting against Cavaignac was his revolutionary foreign policy,—that he would not engage to withdraw his support from the party in Piedmont, which was opposed to Monàrchy, and which in fact betrayed the royal troops in the battle of Novara.

Changarnier.—I do not know what was Cavaignac's policy in Italy. He opposed the Revolutionary, and the Unionist party in Germany. He said that he would use every means by diplomacy, and if necessary by war, to prevent the consolidation of Germany into one State.

While we were endeavouring to agree on a candidate, Thiers came to me and said, ' Mignet is returned from a tour in the provinces. He says that my name is on the lips of everyone. If I should stand for the Presidentship, can I hope for your support?'

' Consult Molè,' I answered ; ' if he will support you, I will.'

About the same time—I am not sure whether before or after—Molè asked for my support. ' Consult Thiers,' I answered. ' If he will vote for you, I will.'

I heard no more on that subject from either of them.

We talked after dinner of the battle of Solferino.

Changarnier.—There was no generalship on either

side. We had excellent regimental officers and generals of division, but there was no commander. The Austrians twice surprised us—before the battle and after it. They crossed the Mincio and established themselves within three miles of us, without our suspecting their proximity. They crossed it again, after the battle, without our knowing what they were doing. Though defeated they did not leave behind, on their retreat, a prisoner or a gun, except some heavy artillery from Verona, which were in position and could not be drawn away.

Louis Napoleon did not ask for the armistice an hour too soon. They might have attacked us with a fair chance of success, and we could do little against them.

Duvergier.—The young Emperor is scarcely fit to follow Metternich's dying advice:—'If you are beaten before Milan,—do not yield. If you are beaten before Verona,—do not yield. If you are driven across the Isonzo,—do not yield. If you are driven across the Brenner,—do not yield. If the French are in Verona,—do not yield.'

The conversation passed to French affairs.

Senior.—What was the impression produced by Louis Napoleon's letters to Persigny?

Duvergier.—Deplorable. We thought it humiliating to him and humiliating to us.

One of the qualities which render him dangerous, is his power of sacrificing his vanity to his interest.

He wanted to please, or at least to deceive, the
English, so he wrote to you a letter of apology, protestation, and excuse. If you had asked him to stand
in a white sheet in Notre Dame, he would have done
it. In fact he has done it, for that letter is the most
penitential of sheets.

Thursday, September 20*th.*—We generally meet
in M. Duvergier's study, about ten, and stay there
till breakfast time, at half-past eleven.

We talked this morning of 1848.

Duvergier.—Louis Philippe and Guizot differ as
to their mode of separation on the 22nd. Guizot
says the King would not give him carte-blanche.
The King affirmed that Guizot said that there were
two things, neither of which he could do. He could
not grant reform, nor could he fire on the National
Guard. The King maintained, therefore, that there
could be no question about giving carte-blanche to a
man obstinately opposed to two lines of action, one of
which must necessarily be adopted. I do not think,
however, that the retirement of Guizot, or the inde-
cision of Molè, were the main causes of the disaster.

The first mistake made by the King, was, the
uniting in the same cabinet Barrot and Bugeaud.
Barrot personified concession, Bugeaud resistance.
They neutralised one another. The liberals did not
believe in Barrot, coupled as he was with Bugeaud.
The conservatives had no faith in Bugeaud, con-
trolled, as they supposed him to be, by Barrot.

Senior.—Lavergne showed me a letter from Bugeaud,* in which he imputes the failure of the resistance to orders given to him by the new ministers.

Duvergier.—I have seen that letter. It is full, not of mistakes, but of absolute falsehoods,—of statements which are pure inventions by Bugeaud, in the hope of assisting his candidature for the Presidentship. We never gave an order. We never had the power to do so.

Our ministry was an embryo, which, after about three hours of gestation, expired.

We all believed, or at least hoped, that the *émeute* would be stopped by the announcement of the formation of a new ministry of liberals and reformers ; and that until the result of that announcement was known, it was not advisable to act offensively. But no express order to that effect was given. It was the general feeling, in which Bugeaud joined. His story, therefore, that his hands were tied by an order from the ministry to suspend operations and to send the troops to their quarters, is totally unfounded.

Thiers received his commission to form a ministry at about 2 a.m. on the 24th of February. He spent what remained of the night in selecting colleagues and obtaining their consent.

Lamoricière was to be his Minister of War,

---

* See *Conversations with Thiers, Guizot, &c.,* vol. i., for this letter.—ED.

Barrot of the Interior, Rémusat of Justice, and I of Finance. We met at his house at about half-past seven on the morning of the 24th of February.

Thiers was shaving with the conscientiousness which, as you have often attended his levée, must be familiar to you.

A note from Bugeaud was brought to him. As his hands were employed about his chin and his razor, he told the servant to lay it on the table.

'It may be important,' I said : 'I wish you would leave that beard of yours and read it.'

As he delayed, I took it and opened it. It contained a few lines, in which Bugeaud complained of the want of ammunition ; he had, he said, only ten cartridges per man : and three pages, in which he told Thiers the history of a M. Magne, and begged that he might be kept in his place.

'I knew,' said Thiers, 'that it would contain *des bêtises*, which was why I did not want to read it before you.'

We were to be at the Tuileries at nine. We arrived there at half-past eight. The King was still in his bed-chamber. After some delay, he received us in his cabinet.

Thiers, as provisional Premier, since he had been desired to form a ministry, spoke for us.

'It is necessary,' he said, 'that the outline of the new administration should be clearly defined.'

'Well,' said the King, *avec un air, comme il me*

paraissait, un peu goguenard, 'You have reform. What can you wish for more?'

'Your Majesty is aware,' answered Thiers, 'that we are a minority. With the assistance of your Majesty's friends in the Chambers, we might carry reform, but we should be in a minority on all other questions. On such conditions we can scarcely carry on the Government. We must ask your Majesty for a dissolution.'

'Never!' said the King; 'a reform you shall have, but no dissolution.' And he went back into a room behind his cabinet and shut the door in Thiers' face. I am very short-sighted, and could not see who were in that room; but some of my companions distinguished there the Queen and Guizot.

We now debated what was to be done. The Guizot ministry had resigned. Molé's attempt to form a ministry had failed. *We* had accepted, but were not nominated; and now the condition which we thought with truth essential to our Government was refused. It was between eight and nine o'clock. We could hear the tumult of the *émeute* increasing and approaching.

In any ordinary times, we should have taken our hats and returned to our breakfasts. But if we did so, the only hope of averting a sanguinary struggle was abandoned; for nothing but either force, or the announcement of a reforming ministry, could stop the *émeute*.

We could ask neither help nor advice from the

King, for he had left us, and was probably then listening to other counsellors. So we resolved to consider ourselves a ministry, and to issue a manifesto declaring that the King had formed a liberal ministry for the express purpose of proposing and carrying electoral reform. Some time was spent in drawing it up,—more in getting it printed. We had to use the press of the *Journal des Débats*. Thiers and Barrot then proposed to go out to the people, explain to them what had happened, and distribute the manifesto. But we could not spare Thiers, so Barrot went alone. He never returned.

The commander of the National Guard was not to be found. It was proposed that Lamoricière, though Minister of War, should also take the command, but be under orders for the present of Bugeaud. This scheme was adopted.

In the meantime the news became worse and worse. We heard that the ammunition from Vincennes, carried through the Faubourg St. Antoine, instead of by the river, had fallen into the hands of the insurgents, that the name of Thiers was ill received by the people, and that that of Bugeaud was execrated.

Il était a-peu-près midi et demie, et les choses allaient fort mal, quand M. Crémieux demanda à être introduit auprès du Roi. On le fit entrer, et je le vois encore, au-devant du Roi immobile sur son fauteuil, faisant une harangue à la fois familière et respectueuse, mais débitée d'un ton singulier. 'Sire,' lui dit-il, 'la révolution marche à grands pas, et, je regrette de le dire, le nom de M. Thiers n'est pas suffisant pour l'arrêter : mais si Votre Majesté consentait à nommer M. Odillon Barrot président du Conseil, je crois pouvoir répondre de tout.'

Le Roi alors se retourna vers Thiers, qui était à son coté, et d'une voix assez bienveillante, ' Eh bien, mon cher ministre,' lui dit-il, ' vous entendez, vous voilà à votre tour impopulaire, que me conseillez-vous ? '

' Sans contredit, Sire,' lui répondit Thiers, ' de nommer M. Odillon Barrot président du Conseil.'

An ordinance naming Barrot President of the Council was drawn up. General Trèzel, one of the former ministers, was sent for ; it was signed by the King, and countersigned by Trézel. So that Barrot became legally minister ; and this was in fact the only appointment completed.

The King was then advised to go down into the Carousel and review the National Guards, who were assembled there. He was received by the cry of *' La Réforme ! La Réforme ! '*

' Mais vous avez la Réforme,' he answered. *' Barrot est chargé de la préparer.'* Still the cries continued. He left the Carousel and returned to the cabinet. It was then the cry of abdication was heard. Bugeaud says that he protested against it. It is false. He was not in the room ; he was below with the troops. The King had lost his presence of mind. He was deeply grieved and alarmed at the conduct of the National Guard,—men with whom he had been shaking hands for years.

He took the cry, '*La Réforme*,' as intended to insult him, and he consented to abdicate.

Such is the history of the 24th of February, as far as I took part in it.

The real cause of the Revolution was the King's obstinate resolution to grant no electoral reform. In the debate on the address in January, 1848, an amendment was proposed by M. Sallandrouze, recommending the Government to take the initiative in proposing a moderate reform.

Guizot defended it by a speech, in which he promised that the subject should be examined in that year, and gave hopes of something being done in the next year.

One of the King's aides-de-camp, Chabaud-Latour, whom you must have known in Algiers, went from the Chamber to the King to announce the defeat of the amendment.

He heard it with great pleasure, but when Chabaud-Latour gave him an outline of Guizot's speech, he broke out against it with indignation.

'Guizot,' he said, 'may have promised a reform, but *I* have not. I will never let in the wedge. The Peers, however, will reject it.'

Chabaud-Latour ventured to suggest some doubts as to the conduct of the peers. '*Ça m'est égal*,' replied the King. 'I will use my veto.'

We had a party at dinner. Among them was the

Marquis de Vogué.* He is a large proprietor in Berri, and has also extensive iron-works.

We talked of the *métayer* system.

Vogué.—I defend it in such a country as this,—a country in which there is little capital, little population, and much land. Of course, I prefer *fermage*, where good *fermage* is practicable. If I could get such a farmer as one of Duvergier's farmers, M. Vaillant, who is now sitting at the other end of the table, a man with large capital, intelligence, and knowledge, I should prefer it, but such men are rare here— indeed, everywhere. Here we have, in general, to chose between *fermage* by a tenant with little capital, *exploitation* by the proprietor himself, and *métayage.* In the first case, the land is unproductive, yet exhausted; in the second, you must employ a bailiff, on whom you seldom can depend, or you must personally superintend these details—a business for which a gentleman is seldom fit, and which in our large estates is, in fact, impracticable. Under the *métayer* system you have a tenant whose interest is yours, who, having studied nothing but agriculture, knows

---

* M. de Vogué entered the army in 1823, served in the African campaign, and was present at the siege of Algiers. In 1830 he quitted the service rather than swear allegiance to Louis Philippe, retired to his estates, and took an active part in all provincial questions. He was elected member of the Constituent Assembly in 1848, and afterwards of the Legislative Assembly. After the *coup d'état* he once more retired into the country. In 1871 he was elected a member of the National Assembly, and took his place on the Right.—ED.

it well, who, what is equally important, knows the specialities of every field, and who is not above seeing that the day-labourer works, or above higgling with purchasers and sellers in the market.

Your English ironmasters hope much from the treaty ; they will be disappointed. We shall reduce the price of our iron just enough to exclude them.

Senior.—French agriculture, then, will be the gainer ; nothing keeps it down so much as the high price of iron.

Vogué.—The tiller will gain a little, but it will be very little. A duty of thirty per cent and expenses of carriage, amounting to ten per cent, will require only a slight reduction of price to exclude you. And that reduction will be made at the expense of another species of agriculture—that of forests. You, Emmanuel,* will have to reduce the price of your wood. You are at the mercy of the ironmasters. The greater part of your forest land is fit for nothing else. To clear it, and plough it, and drain it, would cost more than it is worth. We shall be forced to offer you a lower price and you will be forced to take it.

After dinner we talked of Talleyrand. I mentioned Tocqueville's high praise of his despatches to Louis XVIII. from the Congress of Vienna.

---

* M. Emmanuel Duvergier, now the only son of M. Duvergier de Hauranne.—ED.

Duvergier.—I have read them. The Duc de Broglie, when Minister of Foreign Affairs, had them copied, and showed them to me. They are very good, but scarcely merit Tocqueville's encomiums.

Talleyrand was always able and sometimes energetic. He saved the monarchy in 1814; he almost ruined it by introducing Fouché* into the cabinet in 1815. He thought that Fouché would be a screen to himself, a sort of *paratonnerre*, on whom the public hatred against the men of the Revolution and of the Empire would exhaust itself. It fell on Fouché, but it did not stop there; it extended itself to Talleyrand, and he had to bear not only his own burden, but Fouché's.

He was too much a man of pleasure, too much a pococurante. He could work ably, and energetically for a time, as he did in 1814, but he relapsed into indolence and indifference, and let things take their course. The greatest mistake that he made was his joining in the plot to overthrow the Melbourne Ministry in 1834.

Senior.—I was not aware that he had anything to do with it. I always supposed it was a *coup de tête* of William IV.

Duvergier.—William IV. was the active agent, but he had been *travaillé* by a Tory conspiracy for months before. They knew that he had turned round on the Reform question, and was as much

---

* The first Napoleon's Minister of Police.—ED.

alarmed by it as he had once been favourable to it. The Lievens, the Austrian Minister, and the Corps Diplomatique, thought everything justifiable that would deliver them from Palmerston. Talleyrand was unwise enough to join in the plot. It broke out on Lord Spencer's death, and when the Peel ministry fell, after its short existence, Talleyrand had to leave England and never could return.

Friday, September 21st.—The news of Lamoricière's defeat arrived this morning, and spread a gloom over the society.

General Pimoden was a relation and intimate friend of M. de Voguè. And Lamoricière himself is known to almost all the party, and beloved by them. They feel, too, a national interest in his military reputation.

Senior.—It can scarcely be injured by the defeat of newly-raised heterogeneous levies by superior numbers.

Changarnier.—It does not appear that, at least, until the Neapolitans had come up, the numbers need have been superior. Fanti and Cialdini entered the Roman states in separate corps, with a spur of the Apennines and fifteen leagues of country between them. If Lamoricière had centralised his force, and fallen upon one of them alone, he might have been successful, and perhaps have afterwards beaten the other. Instead of doing so he let his men be dispersed, 4000 in little garrisons to the north, and

4000 more in Ancona, so that his army in the field was only 12,000 men. The small detached garrisons were cut off one by one; the Papal army was dispirited, the Sardinian encouraged. Cialdini got between the Papal army and Ancona; Lamoriciére attempted to cut his way through, and was defeated. Such at least is the appearance which the little that we know of the campaign presents. I estimate so highly Lamoricière's talents, skill, and décision, that I suspect that there were insurmountable obstacles to the manœuvres which seem to me to have been the right ones. Lamoricière's military reputation is a national property. I lament that it was exposed in such a service. I know that he was influenced by religious motives, that he accepted the command against his will, in obedience to the entreaties of the Pope, that he had not at that time to expect any thing so strange as the conquest of Naples by Garibaldi, nor so monstrous as the invasion of Umbria by the Sardinians. But public opinion is the slave of success. He has failed, and you will see him abused and ridiculed by the ignorant foreign press, and by the servile French press.

Senior.—You expect the French press to attack him.

Changarnier.—Certainly; *ils auront le mot d'ordre.* Fanti and Cialdini are merely the instruments of the Emperor. You know that he said to Cialdini at Chambéry, ' *Faites, et faites vite.*'

Senior.—Can Ancona resist long?

Changarnier.—I could tell you if I knew where

the Sardinian siege artillery is. It cannot resist long after that comes up. Four thousand dispirited troops are very few to defend works so extensive, and to keep down a disaffected population. Lamoricière will have to sign a capitulation or to escape by sea.

Senior.—Will he return to Rome?

Changarnier.—I hope not; the cardinals are his enemies. They will accuse him of having wasted the last resources of Rome; there is no calumny against him that they will not invent. The Pope is too weak to defend him.

Senior.—The Pope will scarcely remain in Rome.

Duvergier.—Certainly not, if he have any sense of dignity. He cannot remain a French *protégé*.

Senior.—Will Guyon allow him to choose his retreat?

Duvergier.—Guyon may use strong language, but will shrink from actual violence. Whatever the Pope chooses to do he will be allowed to do.

Barrot.—I fear that all this may end in a schism, or perhaps in several schisms. In 1848, when the Papal troops joined the revolutionary army that marched on the Rhine, Austria threatened a schism. It will be a great calamity. The Catholic priesthood will become the slaves of their governments, and the governments uniting temporal and spiritual power will be omnipotent.

We walked with Duvergier, Changarnier, and Barrot, in the avenues of pines in the park.

I asked Changarnier his opinion as to the courage of Louis Napoleon.

Changarnier.—It is great in theory, small in practice. He forms schemes to which great personal danger is incidental. But when the danger comes he quails before it.

At Strasbourg, when the regiment on which he depended refused its support, he ran, and was found in a state of abject terror, hiding under a carriage. In the Boulogne attempt, when he had got half-way across the Channel, he became alarmed, and wished to turn back. The people about him called for champagne, and kept him to his purpose by making him half drunk. As he approached the town and no friends appeared, his alarm returned. The first troops that met him were under the command of a sensible old officer, who, when he saw the strange procession, accompanied by the tame eagle, and was told that Louis Napoleon was at its head, instead of joining him summoned him to surrender.

Vaudreuil had said that at Strasbourg Louis Napoleon had not dared even to fire a pistol in his own defence. Louis Napoleon recollected this *mot*, kept a pistol in his hand, and fired at the officer, but his hand shook so, that though the man was not five paces off he missed him and wounded a poor cook, who in his white apron was standing at a door to see what was going on. Louis Napoleon turned, ran towards the sea, and got into a boat. A boat from the shore pulled after him. He gave himself up, begged them not to hurt him, and said that he had 200,000 francs in his pocket, which he would give to them. He was landed, and begged M. Adam the Maire to take the 200,000 francs.

Adam said that he would take care of them, but, with business-like habits, chose to count them first. It was lucky for him, for when they were counted in the presence of the crowd, there were found to be only 120,000. These 120,000 francs, when he was on his trial before the peers, he claimed, and the *cruel* government of Louis Philippe let him have them.

Senior.—Did he not show courage at Magenta?

Changarnier.—He never crossed the Ticino. He was smoking in a house during the whole time. At Solferino he did not move or give an order, but he smoked fifty-three cigars. We know this, as he always carries with him little boxes, each of which contains fifty cigars. One was quite exhausted, and three had been taken out of the other. Once a spent ball came near him, but that is the only occasion on which he could be considered as under fire. I saw a letter from one of the Cent Suisses to his mother. ' You need be under no anxiety,' he said, ' about me. I am with the Emperor, and therefore out of danger.' In fact none of them were ever hit.

Senior.—Is it true that he admits that war is not his *métier?*

Changarnier.—Quite true; and that is one of our hopes of peace. If a war should break out on our frontiers, he will not like to engage his person, and will scarcely venture to stay at home.

Barrot.—I hear that he has now become haughty, irritable, and inaccessible: that was not his character when I knew him. He was then mild, accessible, and always ready to listen. So little effect was generally produced by one's arguments, that I sometimes doubted whether he really heard them. When he made me his minister, he sent for me, and said that he wished to talk over with me his system of government. I said that nothing could be more satisfactory to me.

'When a man,' he said, 'is at the head of such a nation as this, he is bound to do great things.'

I bowed.

'You have read,' he said, 'my book on pauperism?'

I was forced to admit that I had not.

'I will give you then,' he said, 'an outline of it. I propose to take all the common lands, and to divide them among the poor families which want relief.'

'In the first place,' I answered, 'you have no right to take them; and if you do take them, if you take the land on which the peasant feeds his cow, you will create more paupers than you will relieve. And how do you intend that the paupers shall cultivate these lands? Who is to supply them with capital? Who is to supply them with industry and with skill?'

'Well,' he replied, 'what is to be done? How am I to provide for the poor?'

'You are not,' I said, 'to provide for them at all. All that you have to do is, to give them peace at home and abroad, and they will provide for themselves. This is not a brilliant policy; it produces no sudden results; but it is a safe one; and if you follow it, you will go down to posterity as one of the benefactors of France.'

Senior.—Do you believe that his Italian policy is a deep-laid scheme in order to have a pretence for taking the Rhine?

Barrot.—I do not. I do not believe that any of his schemes are deep-laid. I do not believe that he has any Italian policy. He hates the Austrians and the Pope. He is not sorry, perhaps, to see them upset. He hates the King of Sardinia, too; but is afraid to stop him. He hates Garibaldi, but he fears him still more. He would like to extend our frontiers to the Rhine. It would remove the stain on the Bonapartes, that they lost all that the Republicans had gained. But I do not believe that he sees his way. In fact, he does not *see*, he *feels*. He is a man in the dark, il *tâtonne*.

We talked of Prince Napoleon, and I mentioned his appearance at a meeting of Republicans on the 3rd of December.

Barrot.—I do not think that he ever got into the room. The meeting was held in the apartment of a baker, named Ladrin. Madame Ladrin was posted at the door to prevent intrusion. She ran in to say that Emile de Girardin and Prince Napoleon were coming. Five or six persons ran to the door to stop them. Prince Napoleon announced that he was come to cast his lot with the Republicans, to live or die with them. But they refused to let him in.

Senior.—On what terms is he with the Emperor ?'

Changarnier.—On terms of intimacy, but not of confidence.

We talked in the evening of the proposal of the Questors to enable the Assembly to protect itself by a permanent guard.

Duvergier.—It was rather a declaratory law than a new enactment. The Assembly had that power by the law of the 11th of May, 1848. But some doubt existed, or was pretended, as to its continuance. Our legislation had been so voluminous, and often so inconsistent, that such doubts can be raised against any law. We, the Constitutionalists, thought it advisable therefore to re-enact it. We had obtained the adhesion of the Legitimists, of the Orleanists, and, as we thought, of the Montague, in which case we had an ample majority.

Senior.—If you had passed your law, could you have executed it ?

Duvergier.—Certainly. We should have declared ourselves *en permanence*, and have called to our aid a sufficient guard. A single regiment would have been enough to protect us against the President's troops, just as a single regiment would have been enough to protect the President against ours. The red trousers will not fire on the red trousers.

Before we came to a vote, we asked St. Arnaud, the Minister of War, whether it were true that the copies of the law of the 11th May, 1848, requiring the President of the Assembly to watch over the safety of the Assembly, and the military force to obey orders proceeding directly from him, had been torn from the walls of the guard-houses. As respected the fact, St. Arnaud's answer was confused and evasive, and, what was more important, he denied the validity of the supposed law, and protested against any law whatever, enabling the President of the Assembly, or any one except the Minister of War, and his subordinates, to give direct orders to the military force. Even the Duc de Broglie now admitted the necessity for the proposed law. As we were proceeding to vote, St. Arnaud made a signal to Magnan, the commander of the garrison of Paris, who was sitting in a tribune, and they, and Morny, left the house. They expected the law to pass, and had resolved to anticipate us by attacking the Assembly that very evening. We saw the members of the Montagne break into knots and deliberate, and to our astonishment they voted in a mass against us, and rejected the motion. St. Arnaud, Morny, and Magnan, were with the President when the failure of the motion was announced to him. He rubbed his hands, and said, 'Now, gentlemen, as there is nothing which must be done this evening, we will go to dinner.'

Senior.—What was the motive of the Montagne?

Duvergier.—They were silly enough to fancy that if the President overturned the Constitution, they could overturn the President, and introduce the Red Republic. '*C'était un calcul de fous. Mais ils sont fous.*'

September 22nd.—M. Chambol, formerly editor of the *Siècle*, and M. Forgues, who writes much in the *Revue des deux Mondes*, arrived last night. I sat for some time before breakfast with Odillon Barrot. We talked of Mehemet Ali, of whom he saw much in Egypt in the last years of his reign. Mehemet Ali said to him,—

'For the first fortnight you are my property; you must breakfast and dine at Shubra; afterwards you are your own master.'

Barrot.—He showed great and intelligent curiosity; and once complained to me that thinking over our conversations prevented his sleeping.

He asked me to tell him my opinion on slavery.

'As respects the slaves,' I answered, 'you treat them well, better than Europeans would do. You intermarry with them, they rise to the highest employments. But the effect on the masters of uncontrolled power, and of associating with persons who have no will but yours, seems to me very mischievous. You complain to me that you have no men ; that you fail in half the things that you undertake for want of instruments. Is not slavery, and the sort of education that slavery produces, the cause of this ?'

Artim Bey, who was present, listened in silence, with his hands crossed before him. Every one, indeed, seemed to approach him, I will not say with terror, but with a submission which much resembles terror. Artim said to me, as we left him,—

'If I had said half what you have said, my skin would have adorned one of the gates of Shubra.'

Senior.—The rule of Said Pasha, though arbitrary, is not tyrannical. I am inclined to prefer it to this.

Barrot.—So am I. Property is safer here ; but persons are safer there. In 1852, lists were drawn up in every department by the Préfet, the Procureur Imperial, and the Military Commandant, of the persons believed to be hostile to the government. Every person whose name is on one of those lists, is con- sidered as a *condamné*, and under the *loi de sûreté générale*, may be sent, *administrativement*, to Cayenne or to Lambressa. No one was tried, or even heard, or even informed, before his name was inserted in a list. The lists themselves have been kept secret, many are believed to be lost. It is held, however, sufficient when a man is arrested, or *interné*, or *exilé*, or *deporté*, to say to him, ' *Votre nom est sur une liste.*' He is not allowed to see the list, or to know whether his name is really on it, or on whose denunciation,

or on what grounds. It is principally on the bourgeois, the ouvriers, the medical men, the higher middle
classes, that this tyranny falls. He fears the higher
classes, especially those whose names are known. He
allows the salons to say what they like.

Duvergier.—But he keeps spies on them. We
have been forced to dismiss two servants for making
reports to the police. I believe that they told only
who visited us, but we could not tolerate such an
intercourse. Among the peasants he retains his
popularity. My relation, the Marquis de Joubert, a
liberal, that is to say, a monarchist, though he has
done much for his neighbours, for their church, for
their schools, for their roads, and indeed for themselves, is ill-treated by a Bonapartist municipality.
Among other petty vexations, they have just driven
a road through his meadows, useless for all purposes,
except teasing him. He threatened to appeal.

'We don't care about your appeal,' they answered.
'*L'Empereur aime le peuple, et il nous donnera raison
contre un bourgeois comme vous.*'

September 23rd.—We drove with Duvergier,
Changarnier, and Chambol, to the, Loire, and afterwards along the embankment to M. Duvergier's
largest farm, the one occupied by M. Vaillant. He
pays 800*l.* a-year, and employs a capital of 6000*l.*
His house, however, is very poor, and the yard in the
usual slovenliness of French farm-yards. In the
sitting-room were two beds. His wife, though very

decent in appearance, was not much superior in
manner or conversation to the wife of one of our
smallest farmers.

The embankment is kept up by the State. We
saw two places in which it was carried away by the
floods of 1851. It has been repaired, but with a
narrower basis. Being therefore much weaker than
it was in 1851, it will fall before a less formidable
flood than that was. The Loire is fed by two
streams, the Loire proper and the Allier. In general,
they swell at different times. If they rise simul-
taneously, and high, there is a disastrous flood.

Duvergier.—Our master was exceedingly dis-
pleased by the flood of 1851. He said that he
would confine the rivers of France, like her revolutions, within proper bounds. Ever since, the
engineers *des ponts et chausseés* have been preparing a vast plan of drainage and embankment;
but as nothing but paper has come of it, the next
flood will find us worse prepared than the last
did.

He showed us a rising ground about a mile from
the river.

Duvergier.—The Préfet of Le Cher came in his
carriage as far as this place. He could see from
hence a vast extent of water. We wanted him to
go farther and look at the breaches by which the
inundation had entered, but he said that he had seen
enough, and returned. A few days after, the *Journal*

du Département glorified him for the diligence with which he had examined ; for the dangers which he had run ; in short, for '*un courage et un dévouement, approchants de ceux de l'Empereur,*' which was true, for the Emperor did just the same, looked at the inundation from a safe distance, and drove back again.

I talked with Changarnier about the chances of war.

Changarnier.—I think them less now than they were two years ago. Then you were unprepared. Austria and Prussia had quarrelled. Russia was hostile to both. If Louis Napoleon had turned towards the Rhine instead of the Po, he had a fair chance of success. But he preferred making his spring on Austria, as the weaker enemy, and one against whom he could arm his favourite allies, the Revolutionary party in Italy and in Hungary. The alarm which this has created in Germany, the alliances which it has produced there, and, above all, the extraordinary military spirit which has shown itself in England, have checked him. Probably his schemes of aggrandisement to the North are not abandoned, but they are adjourned. That is his temper. He abandons nothing ; he adjourns everything.

I asked him what he expected to be the effect of new weapons.

To diminish the use of infantry charges, and to increase cavalry ones. Cavalry crossing the ground more rapidly, will be a shorter time exposed to fire. *On les tiendra couverts par un pli de terrain, et on les lancera.* There will be less bloodshed. The Romans conquered the world with a sword two feet long. The beaten army was so close to the conquerors that it was destroyed. *Now* it will be so distant that the bayonet will not be able to catch it.

Senior.—In sieges, will the attack or the defence gain most ?

Changarnier.—The attack, at least as respects fortified towns. It will be necessary to carry the works to such a distance from the town that they will require an army to defend them. Most of the present town fortifications will be found useless.

Senior.—Will the Maximilian system, which requires fewer men, be adopted ?

Changarnier.—Certainly not. It is good for nothing. The Austrians have wasted on it enormous sums. The stone towers will be destroyed by the new artillery. The system will be what is called the Montalembert system, which was used at Sebastopol, the substitution, as far as possible, of earth for stone. The objection to that system is, that it is more subject to escalade, especially if the attack be made by French troops with the *furia francese.* The turf affords footing, and the inclination must be considerable. Still it is better than stone, of which the splinters are as destructive as grapeshot.

At dinner I sat next to Chambol. We talked of the Provisional Government.

Chambol.—Its ministers were *des drôles de gens.* Lebel was *Ministre de l'Instruction publique et des Cultes.* A schoolmaster was complained of to him. He was described in general terms as unfit for his place.

'But what are his precise faults?' said Lebel.

'Why,' it was answered, 'he is in holy orders, and yet has a family by his housekeeper.'

'Give me,' he replied, 'his name in writing, that I may make him a bishop.'

The *Siècle* was mentioned.

Senior.—You were long its editor?

Chambol.—For years; in fact, until it was bought by the Government. While editor I had an opportunity of conferring a favour on Louis Napoleon. He was in prison in Ham, and was brutally attacked by one of the Royalist journals. I said nothing of Strasbourg or of Boulogne, but I defended him for the part which he took in 1831 against the Pope, and I deprecated insults to a prisoner. He was grateful, and sent to me a little ancient statue which he had brought from Italy. I would not accept it; and he then sent me a ring, with his name on it. 'This,' he said, 'M. Chambol cannot refuse, as it is of no pecuniary value; and the time will come when he will find it useful. When he shows me this ring, I will do for him anything that he asks.'

I have the ring still. I might have used it on the 2nd of December, for I had the honour to be among those for whom he provided lodging in Mont Valèrien ; and, perhaps, if he had proposed to send me further, I should have done so.

We had a large dinner-party—among them M. and Mme. Bènoist d'Azy. She is one of the few very handsome women whom I have seen in France. It was the first fine warm evening since we reached Héry. After coffee, Odillon Barrot, who is an habitual smoker, took me into the verandah, and spent an hour and a half and three cigars in relating to me his share in the events of the 24th of February.

Barrot.—After the King, while submitting to reform, had refused us a dissolution, and retreated from his cabinet into the room containing his un-official advisers, shutting the door in Thiers' face, we thought it necessary to send to the barricades to announce the creation of a reforming ministry. I offered to go, and Thiers wished to go with me.

Senior.—It was a service of danger. Had he nerve enough for it?

Barrot.—Sometimes, in moments of great danger, *il se trouble.* His vivid imagination presents to him too many objects at once. He does not know which to select as principally to be pursued or principally to be avoided. He sees too much. Duller men see only one thing at a time, and are calm. This has made his courage doubted. But what he wants is not courage, but rapid decision. He is morally brave. He is always ready to expose himself to danger, if he thinks that the objects to be attained are worth the risk. In this case I thought that as far as he was concerned they were not ; so I begged him to remain in the château.

Beaumont and one or two others accompanied me. We were joined as we went out by Horace Vernet in his uniform as colonel of a regiment of National Guards.

At the first barricade, which was in the Rue de l'Échelle, we were well received. I told them that Thiers and I were ministers, that reform was granted, and that the barricades were now useless. They cried, '*Vive Barrot! Vive la reforme!*' and pulled down the barricade. So it was till we got to the Boulevards. There the people were less satisfied. They cried out, '*On te trompe Barrot! On te trompe! Il n'y aura pas de réforme avec Bugeaud!*' Still they quitted the barricades. Farther on we met some of the troops. The people had got among them, had given them wine, and in some cases had got hold of their arms. Farther still we met with the fourgons of the artillery, which had been sent with ammunition from Vincennes, and were now being plundered by the mob, while the troops looked on, and the officers turned away their heads. Farther still, a little beyond the Porte St. Denys, we found an enormous barricade, crossing the whole

boulevard. The men behind it were silent. I told
them my story; I read to them the manifesto which
we had drawn up, and begged them to pull down the
barricade. They would not answer me. I did not
think it advisable to leave them in my rear, so I
turned back. I was too exhausted to walk. Some
of the mob put me on a horse, and supported me.
As I returned along the Boulevards the barricades
were all down. .The only cry was ' *Vive la réforme!* '
There was no anarchical, or even republican, mani-
festations. As we reached the Place de la Madeleine,
there was a sudden cry, '*Aux Tuileries! aux Tuileries!*' I wish to God that I had gone with them.
The mob that surrounded me was monarchical. They
wished only for reform, and they had got it. They
would have filled all the avenues to the château and
to the Palais Bourbon, and have prevented the subsequent attacks on each. But I undervalued the
danger. The members of the secret societies, the
Rouges, had not yet shown themselves. I did not
suspect that they were ready, and that within an
hour they would rush from their ambuscade. When
I recollected what were the terms on which I had
parted from the King—the words, ' You shall have
no dissolution,' ringing in my ears—it seemed to me
that if, two hours afterwards, I returned to him at
the head of 100,000 *émeutiers*, and there were not
less in my suite, I should return rather as a revolutionary dictator than as a constitutional minister.
So I explained to my followers that I was really too

exhausted to remain with them any longer, that they must lead my horse to my house in the Rue la Ferme des Mathurins, and let me get half-an-hour's rest. They took me home, carried me upstairs, and laid me on a bed.

But in a few minutes messengers came from the Hotel of the Minister of the Interior to say that my presence was necessary there to dictate the telegrams which were to be sent to the provinces. They were known to be in great excitement, and it was feared that armed bodies might march on Paris, if they were not stopped by news of the appointment of a reforming ministry. I went thither in my carriage, for I could not walk or ride. The Pont de la Concorde was filled by a dense mass, which opened to let me through, with cries of '*Vive Barrot! Vive la réforme!*'

I spent about half-an-hour dictating messages, and then proceeded to join my colleagues at the Tuileries. I tried to get into the Carousel, under the arch; but instead of the troops whom I had left there, it was filled by a mob, and I saw the rear of the soldiers marching out under the Tour de l'Horloge.

Then I was told the news — that the King had named me the President of the Council; that he had abdicated, having appointed the Duchess of Orleans regent; that she had been sending everywhere in search of me; and that I should find her in her pavilion at the end of the *terrasse du bord de l'eau*.

It was a sort of summer-house, built for her by the King, on the spot now occupied by the orangery.

I went thither as fast as the crowd would permit me, and searched it all over in vain. This lost me twenty minutes. At last I was told that she was gone to the Chamber of Deputies. I followed her thither, and as I was entering I was pulled aside by some of the revolutionary party, who told me that a provisional government was to be proposed, and urged me to be its president. I refused, of course, with the utmost indignation, and found the Duchess pale, but composed, with her sons and her brother-in-law, the Duc de Nemours, sitting at the foot of the tribune. A mob had entered the Chamber, but seemed rather curious than revolutionary.

M. Dupin had announced the abdication, and the regency of the Duchess.

M. Marie had objected, that by law the regency belonged to the Duc de Nemours, and proposed a provisional government, under whose direction the question as to the person of the regent should be settled.

I said a few words, in which I assumed the regency of the Duchess, and asked the support of the Chamber to a liberal ministry. She herself rose once or twice to speak, but was very unwisely, very unfortunately, held down by those around her.

At length Lamartine got into the tribune. I had no doubt that he would move the immediate recognition of the Duchess as regent, and that I should be able to accompany her to the Hôtel de Ville. To my astonishment, and to that of the Assembly, he declared that the days of monarchy were over, that a solid basis of government must be sought in the lowest depths of society, and that a provisional government must be formed, to act until the people had expressed its will.

A different mob, the mob of the secret societies, armed and furious from the sack of the Tuileries, now rushed into the Chamber. It yelled out its acceptance of Lamartine's proposal. The Duchess and her party were forced to leave the Chamber. Laroche Jaquelin, with the perverse folly of a true Legitimist, cried out that, as the people had declared its will, the powers of the Assembly were at an end.

The deputies, some frightened, some astounded, broke up. The provisional government was proclaimed from the tribune, and enthroned itself in the Hôtel de Ville. I accompanied the Duchess to the Invalides.

'How unfortunate it is,' I said to her, 'that I did not find you at the pavilion! If we had reached the Chamber half-an-hour sooner, you would have been proclaimed as regent before the republican mob arrived, and carried to the Hôtel de Ville.'

'Alas!' she answered, 'I was sitting quietly in my own apartments. Nobody came to me, nobody advised me, until I was told to go to the Chamber.'

We, the friends of Reform, have been accused of creating the Revolution of 1848. It was created by

the enemies of Reform. They taunted us with the
absence of any popular demonstration in favour of it.
The Reform banquets were our answer to that taunt.
At every banquet which I attended, and I presided
at twenty or thirty, I required that the first toast
should be ' The King,' and the second ' The Constitution.' When we found that the minds of the
people were becoming dangerously excited we gave
them up. The King rubbed his hands, and said to
Duchâtel, ' I always told you that this agitation
would come to nothing.' He ought to have known
that a great party does not abandon a powerful
political engine without good reason. He ought to
have known that the sudden furling of our sails was
a proof that we felt the approach of a storm.

Senior.—Guizot thinks that on the 24th of February the King lost his head.

Barrot.—It is true. A man who has lived for
years in a dark room, who has systematically prevented any light from penetrating to him, is dazzled
as soon as his shutters are broken open. He chose
to say that his '*Pays légal* was France.' He allowed
no one to suggest to him any doubts as to the safety
of a system which consisted in the purchase by the
deputies of a majority of the electors, and in the
purchase by the King of a majority of the deputies.
When that system broke in his hands he was a
magician deprived of his wand.

Monday, September 24th.—This was our last morn-

ing at Héry.   Changarnier seldom appears early; the
rest of the party met in Duvergier's study before
breakfast.

Target read to us a letter from Paris.   As it came
by the post, I was struck with its freedom.   Louis
Napoleon was called Jupiter Scapin, and his answer
to Farini and Cialdini at Chambèry, ' *Faites, et faites
vite*,' was repeated.

Duvergier read to us one from M. Merikof, the
great banker in Naples.   Before the disturbances, he
had sent his children for safety to Switzerland; he
was now in Switzerland to bring them back to
Naples.

I asked Duvergier what rank among generals
public opinion gave to Changarnier.

Duvergier.—The very highest.   Bugeaud hated
him, but when military merits were discussed he
always put Changarnier next to himself, far above
Pellissier, Canrobert, and even Lamoricière.   He has
sacrificed to the constitution rank, power, wealth,
and even fame.   If Bugeaud had been in his place
on the 29th of January, 1849, he would have made
the *coup d'état* for Louis Napoleon.

Senior.—Why did he refuse the command in the
Crimea ?

Duvergier.—He did not refuse, for it was not
offered to him.

Senior.—Not directly; but was he not told that
he might have it ?

Duvergier.—Never.   Louis Napoleon would not

have put an army into the hands of a man who treated him as an usurper, and Changarnier would not have taken one, either with the design of being a faithful servant of the existing Government or with the *arrière pensée* of overthrowing it. His greatest victory was a bloodless one. It was on the 16th of April, 1848. The extreme Republicans had organized a Rouge Revolution. Changarnier had no military command. He was to be our minister at Berlin, and went to the *Affaires Etrangères* to take his last instructions. He was told that Lamartine was at the Hôtel de Ville, went thither, and found him, with those among his colleagues who were not in the conspiracy, sitting in helpless fear. They expected an attack from 30,000 insurgents. Changarnier offered to take the command of the National Guard; he was allowed to do so. He collected in the course of an hour or two thirty or forty thousand men, on the left bank of the Seine. He stationed half of them on the Quai d'Orsay, near the Pont de la Concorde, and the rest on the Isle du Palais, near the Pont d'Arcole. He let the insurrectionary column pass along the Quai des Tuileries and the Quai du Louvre, and then crossed the Pont de la Concorde and formed behind them. At the same time, his men from the Isle crossed the Pont d'Arcole, and established themselves on the Quai Pelletier, and the Place Châtelet before them. They felt that they were in a trap, and disbanded among the narrow streets of the Halles. This was the foundation of his Parisian fame. He

now lives, on a narrow income, modestly and re-
tiredly, in a small apartment in the Rue Corcelle.

Immediately after breakfast we left Héry for
Paris. Ou our road we spent a couple of hours at
Bourges.

It is difficult to say whether the Cathedral of
Chartres or that of Bourges be the finer. Chartres is
longer, Bourges is loftier and wider, the widest,
indeed, that I know, being 131 feet. The architecture of each is of the thirteenth century, simple
and grand, but less massive than the earlier Norman.

Bourges has no transept. This I think a defect ;
but the four aisles, two on each side, of gradually
increasing height, and the chapels surrounding the
choir, built out—as is the custom in the French
cathedrals—so as not to interfere with the Chevet,
give the intricacy and variety which are the objects
of a transept. The painted glass is fine. It formerly
filled all the windows, but a hundred years ago the
chapter thought the church too dark, and removed
it from the lower windows of the clerestory of the
choir. In the crypt is a remarkable Entombment, in
painted stone. The Christ is good, particularly the
head.

Jacques Cœur's house is interesting. He was far
better lodged than Mary, Queen of Scots, a hundred
years later. It is now the Hôtel de Ville, deformed
by modern rooms and furniture, but has been bought
by the Government, and is to be restored.

September 25th.   Paris.—The first person that I saw to-day was General de Fénélon.   He is an old African friend.   When I knew him at Algiers he was colonel of a regiment of Chasseurs d'Afrique.   He married a daughter of Marshal Randon, was made general after the battle of Solferino, and now commands a brigade in Paris.   He asked me what were Changarnier's criticisms on Lamoricière's defeat.

Senior.—He says that it is difficult to form an opinion at this distance, but that Lamoricière appears to him to have too much scattered his troops.

Fénélon.—That they were too much scattered is evident, but Lamoricière is so admirable a tactician that I cannot easily impute to him an obvious error. I believe that his dispositions were made for the mere purpose of repelling Garibaldi, and that the invasion by the Piedmontese, with whom Rome was at peace, took him, and had a right to take him, by surprise.

We ought to know before we judge him what sort of an army he had.   Men raised from different countries, with no mutual confidence, no patriotism, or feeling of national honour, mere mercenaries, are seldom good troops.   Probably, however, they were better than the Piedmontese.

Senior.—Where do you put the Piedmontese?

Fénélon.— The original Piedmontese army, that which fought by our side in the Italian campaign, was not a bad one, but could scarcely be called a good one.   It was not first-rate, not good second-rate; it was good third-rate.   The present Piedmontese army, having lost its best portion, the Savoy brigade, and having gained an undisciplined rabble from the least military countries in Italy, must be positively bad. Sixty thousand Austrians could drive them into the sea.

Ten thousand Tuscans were encamped near us in Lombardy. Two or three horses broke loose,—the Tuscan force was terrified. They thought that they were attacked by the Austrians, and their behaviour under that fear indicated slightly what they would have done if they had been seriously attacked.

The Austrians are really good troops,—the best I have seen after yours and ours. They are well disciplined, they fight well, they retreat calmly and silently. We beat them ; but the victory was hardly earned and not decisive.

I put to him a question which has often been put to me : ' What is the rainy season in Algiers ?'

Fénélon.—November and December, and March and April. January and February are fine.

From Fénélon I went to Mérimée.*

---

* The well-known author of *Colomba*, *La Chronique de Charles IX.*, &c., and of many short stories of exquisite finish. He was born in 1803, the son of a painter, whose artistic talent he inherited, for painting — sketching from nature, taking small copies in oil of the great pictures in the galleries he visited — was one of his principal recreations. He studied law, and was called to the bar, but never exercised his profession. After 1830 he became successively Secretary to the Cabinet of M. D'Argout,

Mérimée.—My belief is that, in a short time, the only fruit that will remain of the Italian campaign will be our acquisition of Savoy and Nice.

Garibaldi is intoxicated, and he has about him men more mad than himself.

Mazzini is in Naples. Sicily is in the hands of men the best of whom are rogues and the worst are murderers.

They will attack Venice; they will be beaten disgracefully. Austria will restore the expelled families, and '*revendiquer*,' as is now the term, Lombardy.

Senior.—Will the Emperor suffer this?

Mérimée.—Why not? He had rather see it than

---

to the Board of Trade, Clerk to the Admiralty, and Inspector of the Ancient and Historical Monuments. In 1844 his writings obtained for him a place in the *Académie Française.*

Prosper Mérimée was a great friend of Madame de Montijo, the Empress's mother; he had been very kind to the little Eugénie, and after her marriage was appointed a Senator, for which he was coldly looked on by many of his old friends. He was an excellent and voluminous letter-writer, and his published *Lettres à une inconnue*, excited much attention at home and abroad. His conversation was full of wit and epigram, with an affectation of caustic indifference which formed a piquant contrast with his real qualities of head and heart. Although he often laughs at the English in his writings, he had a great many English friends, and he liked to be told that he had *l'air anglais.* He had a fine tall figure, an interesting and expressive, though not a handsome face, and a studiously quiet manner. He died in 1870.—ED.

an united Italy at his gates. France cares nothing about Italy. She has got all that she wanted,—a good military frontier, while Piedmont has none.

Senior.—France may care nothing about Italy, but does the Emperor care nothing?

Mérimée.—Very little.

Senior.—Will not his vanity be hurt by such a result of his promise to free Italy to the Adriatic?

Mérimée.—That promise was a silly one ; but by this time it is forgotten. And as to his vanity, nothing can hurt that more than the conduct of Piedmont does. Piedmont breaks his treaties, despises his advice, attacks his friends, and creates herself into a first-rate power in defiance of him.

Senior.—Do you not believe that Piedmont is now his instrument? that he said to her, '*Faites, et faites vite?*'

Mérimée.—I do *not* believe it. I admit that the course taken by Piedmont was the proper one, that it was the only means by which the Roman States could be saved from a violent revolution. I admit, too, that in endeavouring to restrain Garibaldi, Cavour opposes the most dangerous and the most insolent enemy whom Louis Napoleon has ever encountered.

Still, the invasion of the territories of a sovereign, not merely neutral, but friendly, on the pretext that he has raised a mercenary army, is so anomalous, so opposed to all the diplomatic traditions which constitute what we choose to call the law of nations, that

I cannot think that he has ventured to advise it. He
may wish Piedmont to do, and to do quickly, but he
has not said so.

You must recollect, too, that Austria is to be
stopped only at the expense of a general war. The
German spirit is up. If Austria be wantonly attacked
—as she will be—by Piedmont, under the name of
Garibaldi ; if she defeats—as she will do—the revolutionary army, and follows it—as she will do—into
the countries whence it came, and the Emperor
comes to the rescue, will Germany, scarcely restrained
when Austria was apparently the aggressor, keep
quiet when Austria has all justice and all international law on her side?

If we make another war on Italy, it will most
assuredly be followed by a war on the Rhine.

Louis Napoleon is quite '*désillusionné*' as to
war.

What he saw at Magenta, followed by what he
saw at Solferino, astonished, and frightened, and
disgusted him. He says that it is not his '*métier.*'
He has commanded an army, he has won his spurs
—'*il a reçu le baptême du feu*'—he is satisfied, and
will not wantonly run such hazards again.

Senior.—You say that the French war in Italy
will bring on a war on the Rhine. Do you suppose
that the Germans will be mad enough to invade
France?

Mérimée.—Why not?

Senior.—Because they would be beaten.

Mérimée.—So *I* think ; but they do not. They think that they might get Alsace.

Senior.—I give them credit for more sense.

Mérimée.—I never give credit to a nation for any sense. Look at the conduct of Prussia towards Austria. Austria is her rival,—almost her enemy.

The countries differ in religion, in government, in education, in feelings, and in interests. If Austria falls to pieces, Prussia will be her heir,—both in territory and in influence. Yet Prussia, merely from a sentimental German feeling, is eager to fly to her assistance. As a general rule, nations are fools.

Senior.—What will you do if the Pope leaves Rome ?

Mérimée.—Leave it ourselves. We have no motive for staying there.

Senior.—Not the motive of excluding Austria?

Mérimée.—No. I repeat that we care little about Austria or Italy. Austria is no longer formidable. The farther she spreads, the less coherent she becomes. We have got all that we want. If we keep quiet, no one will attack us. What I wish is that the Pope should go to Spain. What I expect is, that he will go to Austria. This will put an end to his influence in Italy. He has less there now than he has in any other country that calls itself Catholic.

25th September.—We breakfasted at A—— to-day, but found there only Madame A. B. C. A. B. C.

had been suddenly called to Paris, and crossed us on our way. We talked of English and French children. Madame A. B. C. praised the *physique* of the English; we the *morale* of the French. These differences are accounted for by differences in the modes of education. French children are seldom sent to school. In every house that we have visited, except Guizot's, there was a tutor.

There seems to be no nursery in a French house. The children live with their parents, always breakfast and dine with them, however large the party, and keep their hours. I have pitied poor little things of four or five years old dying from sleepiness, but kept up till nine. They are certainly, as Madame A. B. C. lamented, less strong, less rosy, and less healthy, than ours. Ou the other hand, they are far better behaved. English children are always trying to attract attention, always obtruding their own wants, and opinions, and likes and dislikes. French children are quiet and silent. They are instantly checked if they give any audible signs of their presence. They are neither shy nor vain.

September 26th.—We dined with Marshal Randon, the Minister of War, and met the Fénélons and M. Périer, brother of Casimir Périer. We talked of the new weapons.

Randon.—As respects fortresses, they are more favourable to the attack than to the defence. The attacker can choose his distance. Mayence, till now, one of the strongest places in Europe, is found to require advanced outworks, and a larger garrison.

Senior.—Does Verona deserve its reputation?

Fénélon.—Its strength depends on its position. Close to the mountains, and on the rapid river which runs through it, it can neither be turned nor invested. It is rather an entrenched camp than a fortress. It requires an army to defend it ; but that army could resist one of double its own numbers. It is a Sebastopol, but better fortified. In Sebastopol the garrison was ill protected. The loss of the Russians at one time was from 1500 to 2000 a-day.

Senior.—What do you suppose to have been the whole loss during that war?

Randon.—We lost about 90,000 men ; you lost 25,000 ; the Turks at least 85,000 ; the Piedmontese none.

The Russians admit a loss of 650,000. But the Russian army is subject to an organised system of robbery. The colonels draw pay and rations for the number of men whom they return as present under arms ; they habitually overstate that number. The 650,000 include many of these men of straw. Still their real loss cannot have been less than 500,000. As there has been no recruitment since the peace, the Russian army must be comparatively small—quite unfit for operations beyond the frontier.

Senior.—What was your loss in the Italian campaign?

Randon.—In men actually killed in battle, in

round numbers, 7000. You may add 3000 more
for those who died of their wounds or of sickness.
The sickness was small, as the campaign was short,
and in fine weather.

Senior.—I supposed the loss to have been much
greater. We are told that the battle of Solferino was
very sanguinary, so sanguinary that the sight of the
field gave Louis Napoleon a horror of war.

Randon.—It *was* very sanguinary. We lost
15,000 men, *hors du combat;* the Piedmontese, 7000;
the Austrians, about 38,000. That makes 50,000
killed and wounded.

Senior.—The Austrian and Piedmontese loss
bears no proportion to yours.

Randon.—Because they were beaten. The Piedmontese were opposed to the best of Austrian
generals, Benedec. They were ill disposed, ill commanded, and fought ill. Their loss would have been
much greater if Benedec had not been recalled, by
the defeat of the centre. The Austrians fought well,
but, as I said before, they were beaten; and, as is
always the case, their principal loss was after they
had given way.

Fénélon.—I do not believe that the Emperor was
much shocked by what he saw on the field of battle.
Such a scene is not so frightful as perhaps you
suppose. The killed and wounded are dispersed over
a very large extent of ground. The wounded are
still excited by the contest. You hear men unable
to rise crying, *'En avant!' 'En avant!'* I gave some

water at Solferino to a young *tirailleur*. His leg was broken, and his arm stripped of its muscles by a shell. '*J'espère*,' he said, '*que j'ai joliment fait mon devoir*.' What is really depressing—almost overpowering—is to go into the ambulances after a battle. The excitement is then over; the wounded are depressed by suffering and loss of blood. Some are undergoing painful operations, some are in dread of them. This is a scene that may well have shaken Louis Napoleon's nerves.

Senior.—Homer's battles are full of

$$\text{' οιμωγη και ευχωλη}$$
$$\text{ολλυντων τε και ολλυμεχων.'}$$

Fénélon.—There is nothing of that in a modern battle; men do not scream when they are hit.

I should be amused if it were not mischievous at the Gallophobia of Europe.

Senior.—It is not wonderful, when you make wars for ideas.

Fénélon.—But we have no ideas now to fight for.

Senior.—Not the Rhine?

Fénélon.—Certainly not. What should we gain by adding to France Rhenish Prussia and Rhenish Bavaria—strangers to us in blood, in language, and in interests? Our strength consists in our homogeneity, in our having no Ireland, no Venetia to keep down. Those provinces would cost far more than they are worth, and would revolt on our first disaster. As to Belgium, we ought perhaps to have taken it in 1830, when it had broken from Holland, and wished to belong to us. `But now it has gained a national feeling; it has an excellent king; it is the freest, richest, and most prosperous part of the Continent. It would be a disaffected province, and a mischievous neighbour to our manufactures. The Belgians say, I believe with truth, that Verviers would ruin Sedan in three years.

Senior.—If Austria is attacked, and beats Piedmont, will France remain quiet?

Fénélon.—Why not? We owe nothing to Piedmont.

Randon.—I am not sure that we should suffer Austria to retake Lombardy; but we should be delighted to see her restore the Dukes and the Pope.

Fénélon.—The disappearance of Austria would be a European calamity. Hungary would fall to Prussia; perhaps also the Danubian provinces; perhaps even Constantinople. Austria is necessary to the balance of power. I believe that the Emperor feels this, and that he would be very sorry to be the accomplice of Garibaldi. He readily gave Lamoricière permission to serve the Pope.

Senior.—Corcelle assured me that Lamoricière did not ask his permission.

Fénélon.—I myself saw the letter to M. Delangle. Corcelle must have supposed that as Lamoricière did not ask the permission of the Emperor or of the Minister of War, he asked *none.* But if he had entered a foreign service without a permission regularly granted by the *Garde des Sceaux* he would have ceased to be a Frenchman. Lamoricière probably values little the favour of the Emperor, but he is not fool enough to sacrifice to a punctilio his rights as a French citizen.

September 27th.—I called this morning on Cousin.* He is excited and unhappy.

* Victor Cousin, the well-known philosopher, author of *Du bien, du vrai et du beau,* of many biographies and studies of the ladies and society of the seventeenth century, &c. He was the son of a watchmaker, born 1792. He was educated at the *Lycée Charlemagne,* and carried off the first prize for rhetoric. He next entered *l'Ecole Normale,* where the teaching of Royer-Collard and others induced him, though passionately devoted to art, to turn his attention to philosophy. He became Professor of Greek in 1812, and in 1814 Senior Lecturer on Philosophy; at the same time he gave Lectures in the *Lycée Napoléon.* During the *Cent jours* he enlisted in the Royal Volunteers, and in 1815 he followed M. Royer-Collard as Professor at the Sorbonne; where he taught the Scotch philosophy. In 1817, he travelled in Germany, and adopted the philosophy of Kant, Fichte, Shelling, and Hegel, whose doctrines he taught in his Lectures delivered in 1819–21. This drew upon him his first persecution; he was deprived of his professorship. Whilst a private tutor, he brought out editions of the works of Proclus, Plato, and Descartes. During a second visit to Germany in 1824, Cousin was accused of Carbonarism, and imprisoned for six months. On his return to France, he threw himself into the party of the Opposition, which, on coming into power, restored to him his Professorship at the Sorbonne, where he shared the glory of Messrs. Guizot and Villemain. Under Louis Philippe, Cousin was made a Counsellor of State, a Member of the Board of Public Instruction, a Member of the Academy of Moral

Cousin.—Everything that is going on in England, in France, in Italy, and in Germany, gives me pain. In England, you are doing all that you can to ruin Parliamentary Government. You are worse than Louis Napoleon. He merely killed it, or suspended it, in one country, and the contrast between his reign and that of our constitutional kings is favourable to it. You are discrediting it. There is no honour, or truth, or patriotism, in your debates. It is a mere struggle for place, or for notoriety. As for the States of the Church, the total want of administrative knowledge or experience in ecclesiastics has made the papal rule, however good the intentions of the Pope or of the Cardinals may be, so vexatious, mischievous, and oppressive, that the most active and energetic Romans, confounding, as indeed the Pope himself does, religion and government, are opposed to both ; are atheists, as well as revolutionists. There cannot

---

and Political Science, an officer of the *Légion d'Honneur*, and a Peer of France. In 1840, he formed part of the Cabinet of M. Thiers. He favoured the Revolution of 1848, and contributed to its success, by publishing, with a Republican Preface, a popular edition of the *Profession de foi d'un Maire Savoyard*. After 1849, he ceased to take a part in public affairs and devoted himself to literature. He translated Plato, and was one of the greatest philosophical writers of France. His great delight, however, was in everything connected with the seventeenth century, and his passion for Madame de Longueville caused no little amusement to his friends. He had extraordinary wit, spirits, and vivacity, and his conversation was delightful. He died in 1867.—ED.

be a worse combination. It releases men from every
obligation, even from every scruple. You Protestants are mistaken, if you think that the destruction
of Roman Catholicism will produce a purer or a more
rational Christianity. The religion of the people of
the South, of the French, of the Italians, and of the
Spaniards, is based, not on reason, but on tradition.
The higher classes are philosophers, the lower classes
believe or disbelieve from habit. In Italy the habit
now is to disbelieve. In France it is to believe. But
that habit might be rapidly altered. At the accession
of Louis XVI. the French were enthusiastically loyal
and monarchical. Not twenty years after, they had
killed the King and the Queen, and had abolished
royalty.

If the Pope leaves Rome, if he becomes an
Austrian or a Spanish subject, all confidence in him,
all respect for him will be gone. We shall tear to
pieces our Concordat. I was once *Ministre des
Cultes*, and I know from experience the value of the
Concordat. The Pope's power of rejection has prevented the proposal to him of improper persons as
bishops, and has prevented their actual appointment
if proposed. Do you suppose that we shall degrade
ourselves by submitting our choice to the confirmation
or rejection of an Austrian subject, or even of a
refugee in Austria ? We shall shake off the Pope,
and with the Pope we shall shake off religion. And
then what will restrain us, except mere legal or
military force ?

I believe that all this enters into Louis Napoleon's plans. He is at heart an Atheistic Jacobin. His wish is to be an imperial Robespierre, but with no more actual bloodshed than he thinks absolutely necessary. He does not refuse to shed blood, he massacred thousands on the 5th of December, but he prefers inflicting slow, distant, unrecorded death. Lambressa and Cayenne are his guillotines, and they have destroyed many more than those who died under the Revolutionary Tribunal. The clergy is the only body in France that makes any show of resistance. Whatever strength and whatever independence they have, is derived from the Pope. His object is to destroy the Papacy, in order to subjugate the clergy. And the first step towards the destruction of the Papacy is to drive the Pope from Rome.

The only event which I see with pleasure is the acquisition of Savoy. Partly for our own sake, as it gives us the frontier which we wanted; but more, for the sake of the Savoyards themselves. They are a brave, good people. I lived two autumns with them, and I love them. Wherever I went the people asked me,—' When will you deliver us from these Piedmontese? They grind us down with taxes, they involve us in wars in which we have no interest, they oppress our clergy, they insult the Pope. Our deputies are not listened to in the Assembly, our produce has to cross the Alps to find a market. Nature, habits, language, and interests, make us French. When will you come and take us?'

September 28th.—We dined at Château d'Issy, now occupied by M. and Madame Chevreux. He is a brother of the late Madame Say. We found there Ampère,* who is domesticated with the Chevreux, the Léon Says, and the Abbé Gratry,† an Oratorian, the first priest that I have met in society. He is a very gentlemanlike man, and talked well on political economy.

Ampère, who has spent two or three of the last winters in Rome, says that the anti-papal feeling of the Romans has extended itself to the French garrison. They feel ashamed and degraded at being the supports of a government which the Romans execrate, and of a religion which they disbelieve.

---

* Jean Jacques Ampère, who was born in 1800, and who died in 1866, was the son of the celebrated mathematician, André Ampère. His tastes, unlike those of his father, were not scientific but literary. He was professor successively at the Athénée of Marseilles, at the Sorbonne, and at the Collége de France. His Lectures were published, and, together with his articles and travels, form several volumes. But he was far more eminent as a talker than as a writer. His early days were spent in the society of Madame Récamier and Chateaubriand, and he possessed, as his friend Tocqueville said of him, the real old French *esprit*. He was very animated and full of action. He read aloud admirably, and was a most delightful companion and friend. The lives of the two Ampères, written by Madame Chevreux, were reviewed in a charming article in the *Edinburgh*.—Ed.

* The Abbé Gratry was a great preacher, and a liberal and distinguished ecclesiastic. He wrote several theological and devotional books.—Ed.

Ampère.—I believe that Louis Napoleon's real
wish is, that the Pope should leave Rome, though
he and the Duc de Grammont, and General Guyon,
are forced to perform the farce of urging him to
remain. Louis Napoleon cannot break with Mazzini.
He cannot break with the revolutionary party in
Italy or in France. He hates Mazzini and Garibaldi
as rivals, but he dreads them. Garibaldi gave him a
significant hint when he took into his service a
brother of Orsini.

Louis Napoleon has played several parts with
more or less success. In England he was a Conservative. So he professed to be as candidate for the
Presidency, so he professed to be in 1851. He made
the *coup d'état* in the name of order and peace. He
raised the salaries of the priests, he begged the Pope
to crown him. The aristocracy were irreconcilable,
and he resumed the Socialism of his youth. He
artificially lowered the price of bread, he undertook
great works in order to give employment, he made
loans at absurdly low prices, and distributed them in
small portions among the people. Finding that little
was to be done by such means, he is now courting
the Revolutionists. They are a minority among
Frenchmen, but they are a majority among French
politicians. The bulk of the people care nothing
about politics, except in times of excitement, and
then they fall into the hands of the revolutionary
party. Louis Napoleon sympathises with this party.
They both hate liberty; they both hate aristocracy.

They both wish for a despot and all flat below him. Jacobinism is his last card, and he will play it.

The Château is a palace built by Mansard for a Prince de Conti.

The reception-rooms are magnificent. Our dining-room was above sixty feet long, forty wide, and twenty-five high. The park is large, and well wooded. But it is in a disagreeable neighbourhood, about a mile from the Barrière d'Issy, one of the worst parts of France, and adjoins a most squalid suburban town.

It has been bought by a Company for 80,000*l.* They intend to pull down the Château, and sell the park in lots for building.

The Chevreux are temporary tenants.

September 29th.—We breakfasted with Madame Mohl. She returned yesterday from a tour in Germany and Hungary. Her first stage was Oberammergau in Bavaria. She spent some days there to see the Mystery of the Passion, which has been performed there every ten years, ever since the eleventh century.

The theatre is a gently sloping valley, in which thousands can sit and hear. The scene consists of houses, which represent indifferently a street in Jerusalem, the Garden of Gethsemane, Pilate's Judgment Hall, and Calvary. The play begins at eight in the morning, and lasts till four in the evening.

Between the acts, tableaux viyans represent some of the typical events of the Old Testament, such as the sacrifice of Isaac, the brazen serpent—a chorus of angels on the proscenium explaining them. The mystery opens by the entry of Christ into Jerusalem on Palm Sunday, then follow all the events of the week, ending with the resurrection.

Madame Mohl.—The acting was exceedingly fine, the *poses* magnificent, and the words simple and affecting. I was there for eight hours, and never felt tired, and what on reflection surprised me, never felt that there was the least profanation. It was a realisation of the greatest event in history. The people about me were deeply affected, weeping, sobbing, almost fainting, with emotion. The actors and actresses probably followed a tradition of gestures and tones which had been elaborated during 800 years ; add to which, the inhabitants of this part of Bavaria, near the mountains of the Tyrol, inherit art. They live chiefly by a miniature sculpture in wood, which is the best in the world, far better than that of Switzerland.

I asked what were her impressions as to Hungary.

Madame Mohl.—That the people are good, but that they are oppressed by a contemptible aristocracy. From the time that the Hungarians committed the folly of electing as their constitutional king the sovereign of countries more powerful in the aggregate than Hungary is, they felt their constitution to be in

danger, and tried to retain it by refusing to allow
any change whatever. They thought that if they
permitted any part to be touched, all would come
down, so that 1848 found the present generation in
the feudal state of the middle ages—a subservient
peasantry, tyrannised over by a high-spirited, gentlemanlike, ignorant, oppressive, and dissolute nobility.

We lived with my nephew-in-law, who is judge
and sous-préfet of the· district of Koloska, which
contains the estates of the Archbishop of Koloska.
Though the see has possessed them for years, it has
done nothing for them; there are no roads, no
schools, no drainage, no embankment against the
floods. None of the duties of property have been
performed, while all its rights have been fully
exercised. A fine soil, a fine climate, and a fine
people, are all misused and neglected.

We went from time to time to balls given by the
nobles. The company consisted of nobles, that is,
by birth, but, in fact, men working for their bread—
lawyers, notaries, medical men, and government employés. It was the society of a country town, but I
never saw such grace of manner, not even in Paris.
As they talked only Hungarian I could not follow
them, but I fancy that I lost nothing, that their
conversation was as empty, silly, and low-minded as
their manners were good.

Sometimes people visited us who talked French.
Once the Rhine was mentioned; somebody asked,
'What is the Rhine?' 'Oh,' said the most intel-

ligent man present, 'it is a river somewhere in Germany.'

One young lady, after her first visit, told us all her history. How she was in love with a young man, how he was very handsome, how he was a Protestant, how the archbishop's doctor out of jealousy told it at the palace, and how the archbishop told her father and her uncle that if she married a Protestant, they would be turned out of office. 'So,' she said, 'I was forced to give him up, which was a great shame ; but the doctor shall get nothing by it. I won't marry *him*, he does not come up to my chin.'

Another lady, also on her first visit, told us that her husband had a mistress, and that she was advised to divorce him, but that there would be great trouble in dividing all the furniture, and sheets, and towels.

A German employé said to me, 'I like the Hungarians ; they are so good-natured and agreeable.' 'Are they honest ?' 'Oh, no,' he answered ; 'they do not know what honesty means.' 'Are they just ?' 'Oh, no; they do not know what justice means. But they are so patriotic. We Germans have nothing like their patriotism.' 'It shows itself,' I said, 'I suppose, in caring for the welfare of their people.' 'Not in the least,' he answered ; 'it shows itself in wearing the Hungarian dress, in talking the Hungarian language, and in lamenting the loss of their privileges, above all, that of immunity from taxation.' He showed me an order which he had just received from Vienna. It was to inquire whether it were true that boys were flying kites, painted black and gold, in which case the kites were to be confiscated and the boys punished.

In short, to visit Hungary is to walk into the fourteenth century. It is more like Spain than any other European country. In grace, and in utter absence of education, the ladies put me in mind of the Spanish women.

Senior.—What is the character of the priests?

Madame Mohl.—In the Koloska district, which is Catholic, very bad; they almost all have children by their housekeepers. The peasants, as far as I could hear, are loyal to Austria. The Emperor and the Imperial bureaucracy are their shield against the feudal tyranny of the landlords.

Senior.—What did you find the feeling in Vienna respecting the Emperor?

Madame Mohl.—I had no good means of information. We had letters for many of the best people, but we found that M. Mohl had been denounced as an emissary of Louis Napoleon with a revolutionary mission; we were afraid of compromising our ac· quaintances and did not deliver them.

I had heard that she was writing a book and asked about it.

Madame Mohl.—Its peg will be Madame Récamier, its substance will be a comparison of French and English manners. I shall be forced, however, to suppress much, for fear of offending relations.

Senior.—What is the story of Madame de Staël's liaison with Auguste Schlegel?

Madame Mohl.—It was not a liaison; for a liaison there must be two parties. He was in love with her, but she was not in love with him. Schlegel lived with her as her son's tutor. He rather '*affichéed*' his admiration for the mother as an excuse for performing such an office for the son. Barante, also, was very much in love with her. Once when he was leaving the house she wished for a parting interview, but Schlegel was always in the way, so she begged Madame Rècamier to take possession of Schlegel for a couple of hours. When the parting was over, Madame Rècamier asked Madame de Staël how it had gone off. '*À ravir,*' said Madame de Staël, '*nous étions tous les deux au désespoir.*'

Here M. de Lomènie * joined us, and the conversation turned on the Revolution of 1848.

---

* Louis de Loménie belonged to an ancient family, and was born in 1818. He devoted himself from an early age to literature, and published some biographical essays in 1840 in the *Galérie des Contemporains illustres*, which made his reputation. He wrote frequently in the *Revue des Deux Mondes*. His articles on Beaumarchais were afterwards published as a book. He was successively a Professor of Literature in the Collège du France and in the Ecole Polytechnique. He was a stanch Orleanist, and would accept of no appointment under the Empire. His conversation was as full of grace and vivacity as his writings. He was elected a member of the Académie Française in 1871. He died in 1878.—ED.

Loménie.—On the 24th of February, partly from curiosity and partly in the hope of doing some good, I accompanied the mob in their march on the Tuileries. They were armed, some with guns and swords which they had wrested from the soldiers, and some with arms which they had seized in the *repertoires* of melo-dramatic theatres. By my side was a man armed to the teeth, with helmet, sword, and pistols, plundered from the Gymnase. Before us was a battalion of National Guards. The commandant was a man of few words, and with little variety of sentiment or ex-pression.

From time to time, news was brought from the Tuileries. He always halted his battalion to hear it.

First, it was said that Thiers was no longer minister. ' *C'est une opinion individuelle,*' he an-swered, ' *au pas ordinaire,—Marche!*'

Then, that the King had abdicated. '*C'est une opinion individuelle, au pas ordinaire,—Marche!*'

Then, that the Duchess of Orleans was Regent. '*C'est une opinion individuelle, au pas ordinaire,— Marche!*'

At last we got to the Carousel, found that the troops were leaving it, and the battalion and its single-speech commander followed them.

My heavily armed companion and I were carried into the château and up the staircase, by the crowd behind and round us.

' *Je crains,*' he said to me, ' *que tout ceci ne tourne pas bien.*'

I sympathised.

'*Je crains,*' he added, '*que ceci ne fasse pas aller le commerce.*'

I also assented.

'*Tel que vous me voyez,*' he continued, '*je suis garçon de café. Je voudrais bien être chez moi.*'

We lost one another in the crowd at the top of the staircase. Some were striving to get out, some to come in. We were wedged in a mass. I was pressed against a man with a long sword, which he held before him.

'Take care,' I said to him, 'or you will poke my eye out with that sword.'

'I am afraid,' he answered very piteously, 'that I shall poke out my own. I know that swords are very dangerous things, and as I had no sheath, I stuck the point of mine into a bottle-cork, but the cork has tumbled off. I cannot pick it up, and I am in constant fear that my sword will prick me or somebody else.'

During all this time I heard nothing of the Republic. The only cry was '*La Réforme!*' The cry of '*La République!*' had not been heard during the century.

Senior.—Not in 1830?

Loménie.—If at all, only for an hour or two. It was instantly stifled in the cry of '*La Charte!*'

An odd attempt was made to familiarise the people with the word. All Paris was informed on the 25th of February, that the slain of the previous

day were to be seen in the great salon of the Hôtel
de Ville. I went with the rest to see them. Sentinels
were at the door, who let us in three by three. There
we found five or six hundred bodies, naked, lying in
rows on the long table on which Robespierre lay
wounded on the 9th Thermidor.

A man at the door addressed each party of three
as it came in, in the following words :—

'*Ce n'est pas pour "La Réforme" que nous avons
combattu. C'est pour "La République." J'en atteste
ces cadavres. Citoyens, criez, "Vive la République."*'

My two companions, honest charbonniers, as black
as their own charcoal, who had been crying '*Vive la
Réforme!*' for three days, and perhaps were not quite
sober, did not pay much attention, and mechanically
called '*Vive la Réforme!*'

'*Vive la République!*' cried the man.

'*Oui, oui,*' they repeated, '*Vive la Réforme.*' So
they were hustled out as quickly as possible lest their
bad example should be contagious.

When we had got out of the Hôtel de Ville into the
Place, we found a circle, whom a man was haranguing
against the Provisional Government, then sitting
within.

'What does a great enlightened nation like this,'
he said, 'want with a government? Why cannot we
govern ourselves? Why should we take half-a-dozen
talkers out of the street, or out of the Assembly, and
submit to them? I am for turning them out and
doing without a government.'

When he had done, I addressed them. I was taken for an *Écolier*, for I wore a little grey capote, the costume of the old *Écoliers* who cannot pass their examinations and get their degrees by mere time. The *Écoliers* were popular in that quarter, so they listened to me.

'I utterly differ from the honourable citizen,' I said ; 'I wish for a government. I wish for one so much, that rather than not have one, I would even take the honourable citizen himself for my governor.'

'*Et pourquoi pas moi*,' he replied, '*aussi bien qu'un autre ?*'

There was a laugh, and the circle broke up.

September 29th.—We spent the day at A——.

A. B. C.—Louis Napoleon's policy is adventurous without having been premeditated, and tortuous without being prudent. He is like a bad billiard-player, who, without any definite object, makes a violent stroke, in the hope that if the balls are all set running about the table, one of them may fall into a pocket. The result is, that he has so '*embrouillées les choses*,' that the next act in this tragedy, whatever be its nature, must be one full of danger. He may get through these dangers, but he will have to run them.

I think that his wisest plan would be to protect Rome and the person of the Pope, but for the present not to interfere further. Garibaldi and Piedmont will attack Austria ; they will be beaten. Austria will be able and willing to execute the Treaty of Zurich ; to restore the sovereigns of Parma, Modena, and Tuscany ; to give back the estates of the Church to the Pope, and Naples to its King. All this, or nearly all this, he ought to allow ; only requiring from the restored sovereigns some necessary reforms. Austria will also be able to retake Lombardy. This I think that he ought not to suffer,—at least he ought not to allow her to retake it for herself. He ought to require Austria to unite Lombardy and Venetia into an independent principality, under the Archduke Maximilian, if it is thought best, to serve as a counterpoise to Piedmont.

Perhaps to make this more palatable to Piedmont, he may require that she be allowed to keep Parma and Modena. Piedmont, the new Principality, Tuscany, the Pope, and Naples, might then form a confederacy—a bund—the only union of which I believe them to be capable. We should keep Savoy and Nice, and we should have—what we ought to have on our south-eastern frontier — weak, divided neighbours, instead of one formidable King of Italy.

This, I think, would be his wisest conduct. But it is subject to two great objections. One of them is, that Italy would be replaced under the Austrian yoke : Austria would have in the Confederacy four votes out of five. She would have far more than her former influence, for she would have it legally. This would be a melancholy contrast to the programme of 1859.

The other objection is personal.   It is the danger
to Louis Napoleon from the Italian daggers.   The
feelings which drove Orsini against him in 1858,
would be fiercer than ever.   There would be more
attentats, and one of them might succeed.   His escape
from Orsini was almost miraculous.

Still I think that this is the least dangerous exit
from the position into which his folly has led us.
For that very reason I think that it is the least probable one.

I believe that he will assist Piedmont against
Austria, in which case a general war, in which you
will have to take part, seems to me inevitable.

I think that such a war will begin early, for I do
not think that Germany will allow Austria to be
beaten before she engages herself.   But if she do, the
next step will be to place Murat on the Neapolitan
throne.   The papers on that subject reveal the whole
plot.

First, Murat says that he does not wish for the
throne ; but that if it is offered to him, his sense of
duty will prevent his refusing it.

Then the Garibaldi party proclaim that the Emperor cannot permit so flagrant a violation of the law
of nations.

Then the *Moniteur* answers that so unlimited is
the Emperor's devotion to universal suffrage, that he
cannot refuse to acknowledge its validity, even
though it should be used to give a throne to his
cousin.

Will Europe submit to this? Will she be complaisant enough to let Murat also have Sicily ?

If all this be submitted to, will she see us take the Rhine?

At whatever step the forbearance of Europe is exhausted—and exhausted it will be—the general war begins.

I do not attach much importance to the reinforcements sent to Guyon.

We cannot leave Rome while the Pope remains there ; and our force ought to be sufficient, not only to keep off the Piedmontese, but to oblige them, if it be necessary, to obey our orders.

Nor do I attach much to Louis Napoleon's advice to Farini and Cialdini,—to do their work quickly. It was necessary to stop Garibaldi. Cavour may perhaps not be the tool that I suspect him to be, but he has common sense—he is manageable. Garibaldi is a fool, and one of those dangerous fools who do not suspect their own ignorance. But I do attach importance to the presence in the revolutionary armies of not less than six of Louis Napoleon's cousins. I attach importance to his protestations against the aggressions of Piedmont, and to his asseverations that if she attack Austria, and is beaten, he will leave her to her fate. His words are like witches' prayers, they are always to be read backwards. Above all, I found my conjectures on my intimate knowledge of his character, of his restless, irrational reveries, of his hunger for change and excitement.

In the spring he amused himself with the annexation of Savoy, then with intrigues in Germany, then
with a tour of triumphal arches, addresses, and deifi-
cations.   In October and November there will be reaction, the excitement will be followed by depression.
He will smoke and scheme, publish some absurd
pamphlet in December, and commit some extravagance on the first of January.

September 30*th.*—We left Paris.

[Soon after Mr. Senior left France in the preceding year, the Sardinian troops, under Victor Emmanuel, entered the kingdom of Naples (October 15th, 1860).

But while Rome and Venice were still severed from the rest of Italy, Garibaldi did not consider his work as accomplished, and it was with great mortification that he found himself obliged to yield to men of more moderate views, bid farewell to his army, and retire to his home in the island of Caprera. The first Italian Parliament assembled at Turin in the following February.

Extreme distress was at this time prevalent in the manufacturing districts of England, on account of the American war, which stopped the supply of cotton. There had long been a growing hostility between the Northern and Southern States. The North was far more prosperous and populous than the South, and the principles adopted by its candidates for the Presidency were diametrically opposed to those put forward by the South, which advocated the institution of slavery and free trade, while the North was for limiting the area of slavery and for a highly protective tariff. At length, on the election of the Northern or Republican candidate, President Lincoln, in 1860, seven of the Southern States determined on secession, and elected Mr. Jefferson Davis as the President in the following February. Ou the 12th of April, the Southern forces attacked and carried Fort Sumter, four other States joined the Southern Confederates, and civil war began.

On the 4th of February, the Emperor delivered a remarkable speech to the French Chambers. He said : ' I have decided that every year a general statement of the situation of the Empire should be placed before you, and that the more important diplomatic des- patches should be laid before your bureaux. You can also, in your Address, express your opinions on the facts of the day ; not, as formerly, by a simple paraphrase of the Speech from the Throne, but by the free and loyal expression of your opinion. . . . . . Exhaust, gentlemen, during the vote on the Address, all points of discussion according to the proportion of their importance, that you may have the power afterwards to devote yourselves entirely to the affairs of the country ; for if these points demand a profound and conscientious examination, the other interests in their turn impatiently expect prompt decisions.'

This approach to freedom of debate was hailed with great satisfaction by all parties.

On the 1st of March, Prince Napoleon made a

very fine speech defending the Imperial policy, and about a fortnight afterwards an answer was published to it by the Duc d'Aumale, in the form of a letter to the Emperor, so strongly expressed that it almost amounted to a challenge.—ED.]

Hôtel Bedford, Paris. Thursday, March 28.— We slept at Amiens on Tuesday, and reached Paris by two o'clock on Wednesday. The only thing worth recording on the journey was a conversation between two elderly Frenchmen.

'I think,' said one, 'we shall have war with Russia. Poland will rise, and we must help her.'

'I hope not,' said the other. 'I should not dislike a war, but I had rather it be *là bas. Les Russes sont de braves gens, les Anglais sont une Canaille. Ils nous ont horriblement dupé. Mais Napoléon le sait. Il en finira avec eux, aussitôt qu'il est prêt, il les enfoncera joliment. Il les coupera en deux.*'

Ou my arrival I went to Guizot's. Only Monsieur and Madame de Witt* were at home.

De Witt.—You will find Paris more animated than it has been for years. We are enjoying this shadow of parliamentary life as the Roman slaves did their saturnalia.

---

* M. Guizot's son-in-law and daughter.—ED.

Senior.—I hope that it will last longer.

De Witt.—I think that it will. As yet, however, it interests only the higher classes, and of them, only the politicians. Odillon Barrot and Thiers are to be candidates at the next election. The people take no part in it, and until they have done so Louis Napoleon may revoke the liberty which was *given* by him, not *extorted;* but I do not think that at present he is dissatisfied. The clerical party and the Rouges have shown their colours, and disgusted all sensible people. Prince Napoleon's speech created a scission even among the Bonapartists. The old '*parti de l'ordre,*' which prizes tranquillity above all things, which would not buy liberty, or even glory, at the expense of a new revolution, is being re-created. That speech drew up a veil. It told the Rouges what they had to hope, it told the Moderates what they had to fear.

Senior.—Was Keller's speech very good ?

De Witt.—Admirable. It was so skilful, that its tendency was not at first perceived. An Imperialist deputy, a friend of mine, said to his neighbour, 'It is a pity that so good a speaker should be opposed to us.' 'Is he,' said the other, 'opposed to us ? I don't think so.' It was not until Billault complained of the bitterness of the attack that the greater part of the Chamber saw there had been an attack.

Another advantage which Louis Napoleon has obtained is, that he has ascertained that France is as much opposed to Italian unity as he is, though, perhaps, on different grounds. We are opposed to it because we do not wish for a powerful neighbour.

Senior.—That neighbour would be under your influence.

De Witt.—Only as long as she fears Austria, which will be only as long as Austria fears her. Let Venetia be once sold or ceded or become independent, and Austria and Piedmont having nothing to fight about will be united by their common dread of France. These, however, are not Louis Napoleon's motives ; he cares for nothing but himself and his family. He admitted to a friend of mine that he would have stopped the Piedmontese if he had dared, but he said, '*J'aurais été renversé, vous ne savez pas ce que ce sont que les sociétés secrètes.*' By '*renversé*' he meant assassinated, for there is no political power that can overturn him. Without doubt he is brave, but as other brave men, Cromwell, for instance, have done, he fears assassination. It was not so in the beginning ; as President, and even as Emperor, he defied the Carbonari daggers, but Orsini's bombs demoralised him. He broke out into the extravagant complaints of England, which first opened your eyes. He ordered Persigny to terrify you into passing an alien act. He coquetted with Orsini, and tried to pardon him. He made the infamous '*Loi de sureté pvblique,*' and sent thousands of innocent men to die in Cayenne and Lambressa. He fears their relations and friends, and, above all, he fears the Carbonari, for he has been one. He wants, too, his portion of Italy.

Senior.—Genoa ?

De Witt.—No ; Naples for the Murats.

Senior.—I thought that Murat was an unproducible candidate.

De Witt.—Achille Murat, but not his son, who is a charming young man—intelligent, amiable, and with excellent manners. The Bonapartes have left good recollections in Naples. Joseph was far above the average of kings in talents, and knowledge, and good intentions ; and King Joachim, though a bad politician, was kind and popular, and had the dash, the '*élan*,' which delights a southern people. Then the Neapolitans hate the Piedmontese as cold, harsh, and overbearing. The people care nothing for liberty or for Italy ; the higher nobility are Bourbonists : they prefer a Murat to a Piedmontese, because, like all bad politicians, they are governed by precedent. They expect the Bonapartes to fall in France, and then to fall everywhere else, as they did in 1815, and fancy that Naples left vacant will be restored to the Bourbons, which it could not be if a part of the kingdom of Italy. If Piedmont were to resist, nothing would be more popular than a war against her. France hates her for her selfish ingratitude, for her claims to share our military glories. '*Nos soldats ne prennent pas l'armée Piedmontaise au sérieux.*' They say that it did nothing in the Crimea, and worse than nothing in Italy.   A General Valency, whom I know, is aide-de-camp to Baraguay d'Hilliers. When the battle of Solferino was clearly won, Baraguay resolved to pursue the enemy.   He sent Valency to La Marmora; '*Faites lui,*' he said, '*mon compliment,* and say that I intend to advance.'   So Valency galloped off and delivered his message.   '*Il n'y a pas de quoi complimenter,*' said La Marmora.

Guizot now came in.   He asked about English news, and especially about Mrs. Austin,* from whom

---

* Mr. and Mrs. John Austin were amongst the oldest and most intimate friends of Mr. Senior.

John Austin, born in 1790, was the eldest son of Mr. Jonathan Austin of Creeting in Suffolk.   His younger brother, Charles, was more conspicuous than himself for brilliant success at the bar; but in learning and power of intellect John had no rival.   He entered the army in early life, and served under Lord William Bentinck with the British troops in Sicily: something of military precision hung about him through life.   But on returning to England he retired from the army and read for the bar.   As a practising advocate he had no success.   But he devoted himself the more earnestly to the study of the philosophy of jurisprudence, and in this branch of his profession he attained to eminence. Living in Westminster, next door to Mr. Bentham, he formed a close intimacy with the Radical lawyer and politician of the Westminster school, whose opinions he shared.   Upon the foundation of the London University he was elected to the Professorship of Jurisprudence there; and he repaired to Germany to prepare the course of lectures which he subsequently delivered.   These lectures formed the basis of his work, entitled

he had just received the new edition of Austin's *Jurisprudence*.

---

the *Province of Jurisprudence*, which was completed 'from his notes by his wife after his death.

He held at one time the office of a Commissioner to digest the Criminal Law, and in 1836 he was sent to Malta, with Mr. Cornwall Lewis, to report on the affairs of that island. But his previous health, and a certain morbid tendency of mind, disqualified him from taking a sustained and successful part in public affairs. His later years were spent in Dresden, in Paris, and at Weybridge, where he died. His reputation as a powerful thinker, writer, and jurist, has increased since his death. In conversation few men could surpass the energy, variety, and perspicuity of his language; and it was a constant subject of regret to his friends, that with such talents and such acquirements, the result was comparatively small.

In 1819 John Austin married Sarah, youngest daughter of Mr. John Taylor of Norwich, a woman remarkable alike for the graces of her person, the cultivation of her intellect, and the buoyancy of her character. She took her place at once in the brilliant, though somewhat dogmatical society of Queen's Square; and although the means at her disposal were always very limited, she contrived through life to make her drawing-room the resort of all that was most distinguished and attractive in the society of her time, both in this country and abroad. The Grotes, the Mills, Lord Lansdowne, the Romillys, Sidney Smith, Hallam and Senior, were her most intimate friends; and in Germany and France she was equally popular.

Her literary works were chiefly confined to translations from the French and German, on which she was incessantly employed. But her admirable English style imparted to her translations the value of originals; and in Ranke's *History of the Popes*, she gave to English literature a work of the highest order and merit. She survived her husband some years, dying in 1867, and devoted

Guizot.—I have not read it, but I expect much instruction from it. Austin had one of the most comprehensive, the most accurate, and the most original minds that I have ever come in contact with. I do not know a more masterly state paper than his last work, *A Plea for the Constitution.*

What do you hear from America ? I suppose that in England you are delighted with the separation.

Senior.—If the separation can be peaceable, if the two, or perhaps the more numerous confederacies can live together in peace, we shall not regret it. They will keep one another in order. The old union was showing the vices of an unchecked democracy ; it was insolent, aggressive, and selfish. It has broken up through its own vices, because the South wished to sacrifice everything to slavery, and the North everything to protection.

Guizot.—We regret the separation. The insolence and aggressiveness of the Old Union was excited only against its neighbours, you, Mexico, and Spain. Its protective tariff did not affect France, whose peculiar exports America cannot rival, and as a formidable

---

herself with success to the arrangement and publication of his unfinished papers.

Lucy, the only child of John and Sarah Austin, married to Sir Alexander Duff Gordon in 1840, also left a name in literature and society, for she inherited much of the talent and the style of her accomplished parents.—Ed.

naval power she kept you in check. *Now* you will
have your own way with the Southern Confederacy.
You will be their greatest customers. They have
already abolished their navigation laws, which will
give you the monopoly of their carrying trade. They
will have neither a mercantile nor a military navy.
The North must reduce hers. You will be masters
in America, and you cannot expect us to like that.

Are you still as Italian as ever ?

Senior.—Quite ; partly, perhaps, because though
you are Unionists in America you are anti-Unionists
in Italy.

Guizot.—I own that I neither wish for Italian
unity, nor expect it. The only real Italian Unionists
are Piedmont, Tuscany, Modena, Parma, and the Romagna. I doubt whether Lombardy wishes for union,
I know that Naples does not. We shall perhaps see
the *dénouement* in a year. Piedmont will attack
Venetia and be beaten ; we shall save her, and shall
ask for Naples as our pay. You and Holland, and
Norway and Sweden, are the only tranquil parts of
Europe. Belgium knows that she exists only by suf-
france, Denmark expects both foreign and civil war,
Turkey is dying, Poland is demanding something
resembling free institutions, and will extort it ; Russia
will claim from her emperor whatever is given to
Poland. The old reverence for the Czar is gone ; the
government has deprived the nobles of many of their
privileges and much of their property. Prussia is
intriguing against Austria and aiming at the leader-

ship of Germany, the Austrian government is hated by all its neighbours, and by almost all its subjects. Spain is perhaps the only really loyal country on the Continent.

Senior.—Is Spain loyal to such a queen ?

Guizot.—The great use of a constitution is to make good sovereigns out of bad men and women.

Senior.—Still, it cannot efface the difference. Where should we now be if for the last twenty-four years we had been governed by a Stuart ?

Guizot.—Queen Victoria is an exception to all rulers, and so were the two last Stuarts. Between the best possible sovereigns and the worst the difference is certainly enormous. But Queen Isabella is far from being one of the worst. Her morals are not pure, nor were those of the Empress Catharine ; but after her own fashion she is religious and constitutional, and does not suit the Spaniards ill.

I drank tea with Madame de Circourt. We talked first of the memoir and letters of Tocqueville.

Circourt.—We are very anxious to see what Mrs. Grote and Mr. Reeve, who knew him so well and valued him so highly, will say about him. Portraits of Frenchmen by Englishmen are always valuable. They see everything from a different point of view.

Madame de Circourt praised Beaumont's memoir. I said that I thought the spirit of it charming. I complained of his ultra-discretion.

Circourt.—Can a contemporary biographer be too discreet ?

Senior.—I will give you an instance. In a letter in the autumn of 1858 there are two lines of asterisks. I have seen the original; the sentence left out is, 'Milnes is with us, and has brought with him Arthur Russell; he is a very pleasing and intelligent young man.'

We soon went to politics.

Madame de Circourt.—Is your volunteer mania as fierce as ever ?

Senior.—Certainly, and I hope that it will increase. We have 150,000 volunteers now; next year we shall have 200,000, and in case of invasion 500,000.

Madame de Circourt.—You yourself do not participate in the fears, which I will venture to call absurd, of invasion.

Senior.—My fears depend on the adequacy of our preparations to resist one. If we render its success impossible, there will be none; if it appear to you to be practicable, I believe that the attempt will be made.

Madame de Circourt.—What are your grounds of belief ? The French are not robbers or pirates. M. de Boissy does not represent us.* Our wish

---

* This refers to an absurd speech insulting England. The Marquis de Boissy was the second husband of the celebrated Countess Guiccioli, Byron's friend.—ED.

is to be on good terms with you, if you will allow us.

Senior.—I am not thinking about the French; the will of the French has nothing to do with the matter, or rather you have no will of your own. You have absolutely surrendered yourselves, and all your will, and almost all your opinions, and all your conduct, into the hands of one man, not a Frenchman by race or by education or by feelings,—an Italian conspirator, with a wild imagination, extravagant wishes and plans, and an unsound judgment. Nothing would gratify his vanity so much as to issue a bulletin from London.

Madame de Circourt.—It is true that you have given him sufficient provocation. You have opposed all his plans of aggrandisement ; you are avowedly arming for a war with him.

Senior.—Of course we are, because we know that he is arming and for what purpose. We are in the state of a man who knows that his opposite neighbour is collecting materials and hiring ruffians for the purpose of burning down his house, pillaging his property, and murdering his children. We shall owe to him, I hope, that we again become a military nation.

Circourt.—Well, I hate him as much as you do, and with more reason, for he is only alarming you, while he is degrading and demoralising us. But I think that you do him injustice in one respect; I believe that he is friendly to you.

Senior.—You put me in mind of the answer of a New Zealand chief to the question how he liked the English Governor : ' Him like him very much ; if him catch him, him eat him.'

Madame de Circourt.—And are you as Italian as ever ?

Senior.—Quite.

Madame de Circourt.—In order to give us another enemy ?

Senior.—I believe that our sympathy with the Italians is really unselfish, but we shall not be sorry to see the Great Powers increased from five to six.

Circourt.—My suspicion is, that Louis Napoleon's preparations are directed not so much against you as against Naples. Copying, as he always tries to do, his uncle, he intends to put young Murat there. The first obstacle was the king. He sent Garibaldi to revolutionise Sicily, to drive him from his capital, and to excite a civil war which should give an opportunity of occasioning a Muratist demonstration, and enable a French fleet to carry Murat to Naples as the '*élu du peuple*.' Garibaldi and Cialdini were too quick for him, though he prolonged the resistance of Gaeta until he was forced to yield to general disapprobation, and perhaps to the fear of the Carbonaro dagger.

But though foiled for the present, he has not given up his scheme. His agents are actively exciting discontent and insurrection in the Neapolitan dominions. He will not quit Rome, and still less Civita Vecchia; his army and fleet are there, ready for a *coup de main*. They can lie in the Bay of Naples, for the purpose of preserving order and protecting French subjects and French property, within twenty-four hours after the Lazzaroni have been hired to proclaim Joachim II. King of Naples. Victor Emmanuel has set the example. He invaded a friendly country and dethroned a friendly sovereign, in obedience to what he called the will of the Neapolitan people. Louis Napoleon will say that the Neapolitan people have changed their minds, and that, as the Piedmontese army entered Naples in order to give effect to their *former* wishes, so the French army enters Naples merely to give effect to their *present* wishes.

Senior.—Will the Pope leave Rome?

Circourt.—That depends on Corcelle. Corcelle's high character and sincere affection for the Pope and for the papacy give him unlimited ascendancy. I doubt Corcelle's advising the Pope to take an irrevocable step. Victor Emmanuel, too, ought perhaps to try to keep the Pope. As long as he is in Rome the Romans will wish for the Piedmontese. If he should go they will hate their new fellow-subjects and their new masters, and regret that Rome is no longer the centre of Christendom.

March 29th.—I drank tea with M. de Lamartine. The other persons present were two gentlemen, one of them a M. Pelletan,* and three ladies. Madame. de Lamartine was in bed.

A hall has been opened for the delivery of lectures on Social Science. There is no discussion, that being illegal. The lecturer sits on a platform and speaks. Ou Monday, M. Pelletan lectured on *la propriété*. Lamartine praised the ability of the lecturer and the attention of the audience.

Pelletan.—They were of many different *nuances*. Some Orleanists, such as d'Haussonville, some Legitimists, many students from the École Polytechnique ; but the bulk consisted of those who were the Republicans and Rouges of 1848. Almost all the leaders of 1848, who are not dead or in exile, were present. They are now altered men. When the next revolution comes, you will find them firm but moderate Republicans.

---

* Born in 1813, the son of a notary, M. Pelletan began life as a law student. In 1837, he wrote his first articles and criticisms for *La France littéraire*, and, in 1839, began his long and important contributions to the *Presse*, which, however, he often interrupted, and changed from one paper to another, in order that he might write for the publication which, at the time, advocated the most strongly the cause of liberty. In 1863 he entered upon a parliamentary career, was elected deputy, joined the Republican opposition, and made several brilliant speeches. He was the chief editor of the *Tribune*. In 1870 he was a member of the Government for the 'National defence,' and employed himself usefully during the siege. In 1871 he joined M. Jules Simon in attempting to reconcile the views of the Provinces with those of Paris, and has continued to belong to the Left in the National Assembly.—ED.

When you, M. de Lamartine, had left the hall, they stood round me, talking of you, and of 1848, and of the scene before the Hôtel de Ville. 'We came,' they said, 'determined to overthrow the Provisional Government, and Lamartine as its head. But we were children in his hands. We were cowed when he reproved us, proud when he praised us, and obedient when he commanded us.'

Lamartine.—I have addressed different audiences, but the only one worth talking to *c'est la foule.* In an assembly your friends, or rather your party, treat the debate as a game, yourself as a piece, or as a pawn, and your speech as a move ; your adversaries think of you only as an enemy, and of your speech only as a thing to be refuted. The rest, the impartial part of the audience, go to the debate as they go to an opera, consider your speech as a work of art offered to them as a subject for criticism, and praise you or blame you as they have been bored or amused. No one changes his opinion ; no one is convinced ; no one is even moved. The best speech does not alter a vote. It merely renders the vote, which every hearer had premeditated to give, more or less pleasant to him. No one cares whether the speaker is or is not sincere. It is well known, indeed, that he must often be insincere, since he speaks, not his own opinions, but those of his party, or rather those which it suits his party to profess for the time being. No one cares for their truth. What is wanted is that they be plausible, and afford a good excuse for the vote.

La foule is sincere. It comes to you for information and counsel. The first, almost the only quality which it demands from you, is sincerity. You may reproach it, you may laugh at it, you may run counter to its prejudices — it will bear anything from you while it believes you to be honestly anxious to give it good advice. But beware how you are found out in flattering it. Beware how you are found out in saying anything which it believes to be insincere. That instant your influence is gone. Inferior men may be powerful mob-orators, if they have the same prejudices and feelings as their hearers. They reveal to every man that he is sympathised with by them, and sympathised with by his neighbours. They render every folly contagious. They strengthen wrong opinions, and excite passions already too violent.

The real triumph and the real usefulness is not to stimulate, but to moderate, to control, to alter, and often to reverse. So far as I effected these things, or any of these things, before the Hôtel de Ville, I was useful.

It is remarkable that there is a sort of dualism in a speaker's mind. However eager, however impassioned you may be, you hear from behind you a quiet, impartial voice, judging, censuring, and advising ; whispering to you an impartial commentary, generally of blame or of warning. 'That argument,' it says, 'is false ; that fact is exaggerated, you do not believe what you are saying, and they will find it out ; you have said enough on this subject,—keep away from that subject.' The voice never comes from before you ; the whisperer seems to be perched on your shoulder, with his mouth close to your ear. He never leaves you. In your fiercest emotion, ' *dans tout l'abandon et toutes les témérités de votre éloquence*,' whether you are bursting with anger and indignation or intoxicated by the sympathy and cheers of your audience, the cold, equable voice pursues you, and directs and restrains without interrupting you. There is, as I said before, a dualism in your mind. You are at the same instant the fervid, impetuous orator and the calm, unexcited critic.

Senior.—The debate on the Address shows that your speakers have not degenerated.

Lamartine.—Kolb and Billault were good, and Keller was admirable. He is a young Alsatian, scarcely thirty years old, of good family and fortune. He went from the École Polytechnique to the army, and was a *sous-lieutenant* when he fell in love with his present wife. Her father, a man of high station in Alsace, could make only one objection to the match. He did not wish his daughter to be the wife of a *sous-officier*, and asked Keller to make the sacrifice of his epaulette. Keller, though fond of his profession, consented, married, and took to the life of a country gentleman.

He is very religious,—was deceived by Louis Napoleon's early professions of attachment to the Church, and became an Imperialist. In this character he was brought forward by the Government at the last election for the Corps Législatif, and came in triumphantly. He prepared his speech carefully, wrote it out and gave it to a friend who was to be near and prompt him. But as he went on, his views altered. He changed the order, the language, and even the substance of his speech. From a recitation it became an improvisation. The allusion to Orsini was a '*coup de théâtre.*' The letter,* so celebrated three years ago, had been forgotten; and when, after reading it, he named the writer, the whole chamber, Imperialists and all, were electrified, and yet in the written speech it was introduced in a different way. A man who can do such things has a great political *avenir.*

Senior.—Was Jules Favre good?

Lamartine.—Not for him. He was timid, did not venture to let out his whole mind, and was cowed by the hostility of the Chamber. He does not belong to any of the parties. He is neither Popish, Catholic, Orleanist, Legitimist, nor Bonapartist. He is one of the small knot of Republicans.

Senior.—Will this freedom of speech last?

Lamartine.—Impossible. France has spoken out. She has told Paris that she disapproves *Celui-ci's*† policy, and Paris will tell the story to the provinces. A sovereign so slightly rooted, stained in 1851, in

---

* The letter was from Orsini to Louis Napoleon.—ED.

† Louis Napoleon.—ED.

1852, and in 1858, by such cruelties, disgraced by the *friponnerie* of the court, hated and denounced by the Church, ridiculed by the chiefs of the army, and served by ministers whom neither he nor the nation trusts, cannot endure public discussion. The publication of the debates will be prohibited. The Corps Législatif will become hostile, it will be dissolved.

Senior.—I hear that Thiers and Odillon Barrot will be candidates at the next election. Will you be one?

Lamartine.—It is out of the question. My political life is ended. I am henceforth a mere *littérateur;* earning my bread painfully and diligently, and I hope usefully, by my pen. I have not taken the oath, and I never will take it.

Well, to continue my prophecy, the next Assembly will be more hostile than this has been. When this Chamber was elected, the Church supported him, now it execrates him : by that time it will have excommunicated him. Those who think that France is irreligious are mistaken. The towns are irreligious, especially Paris ; that is to say, the men are irreligious, the women are not ; and there is no country in which they have such influence. The irreligion of even the men is principally a dislike of the troublesome observances of Catholicism. They hate confession, penance, and fasting. But they respect Christianity. No respectable man would take an unbelieving wife. And they value the Papacy. They think that the spiritual power of the Pope is a moderator of the temporal despotism, to bend under which seems to be our normal condition. The Emperor cannot again dissolve ; it would be useless. He must abolish. There will be another *coup d'état*. He will deprive us of even this shadow of parliamentary government. By that time, or perhaps six months after, he will be again at war, and his war will be revolutionary, for the general and growing distrust will unite all sovereigns against him. We shall find ourselves again where we were in 1793, opposed to all Europe. *Mais c'est impossible d'avoir un Quatre-vingt-treize au dehors sans avoir un Quatre-vingt-treize au-dedans.* You and he are trampling on all treaties, on all established rights, on all the traditional maxims, which form what is called ' the law of nations.' You are breaking with the past. *You*, perhaps, can afford to be revolutionary abroad and conservative at home. Such seems to be the opinion of your statesmen. But *he* cannot. He must throw himself into the hands of the Rouges. We shall have a far more frightful revolution than that of 1848. We shall have such a revolution as that of 1848 would have been if the Rouges had—as they were more than once on the point of doing—overthrown the Conservative Republicans.

Senior.—I admit that in giving our moral support to the union of Italy, we have sanctioned the violation of treaties, of rights, and of international law. I regret that such great sacrifices should have been necessary. But the object was also a great one.

Lamartine.—Not *au point de vue Français.* You

cannot expect a Frenchman to see with pleasure a great power rising on our south-eastern frontier.

Senior.—I was thinking of the interests of Italy, not of ours, or of yours. But I believe that it would be good for even your own selfish interests to have a powerful neighbour. With your aggressive propensities, you are much too strong even for your own welfare. Absolute power, or greatly preponderant power, is dangerous to everybody, and most of all to its possessor. You have more than once sacrificed your liberty to the means of gaining it, or of retaining it.

Saturday, March 30th.—Madame Mohl and I went this morning to see the Emperor's model of a Roman trireme. If constructed, as I suppose it is, according to our best information, it shows that the Roman trireme was a considerable vessel. It is forty *mètres*, or about 250 feet long, and five *mètres*, or about thirty-one feet broad. There are two decks, the lower about three feet below the main-deck, just high enough to allow the men to sit and row. Two ranks of men placed thus * * * * * * * *, sit on the lower deck, and one rank on the higher. The fighting men stand on a ledge about six feet wide, raised four feet above the higher deck, running along each side of the vessel, protected by a bulwark about four feet high. Each of the ranks of rowers contains twenty-three men, so that there are 126 oars in all. In the centre is a single small mast, capable of carrying one large sail. I could not learn the rate at which 126 men could force such a mass through the still water; I doubt whether they could drive her through the tideless Mediterranean at the rate of more than four miles an hour.

It is an interesting model, and explains well what a trireme may have been, but leaves unexplained the structure of a pentecontor.

Duvergier called on us, and was soon followed by General Changarnier. We talked, as every one does, of the debate.

Duvergier.—It has been mischievous to Louis Napoleon. It has shown the incompetence of his ministers, it has shown the power of the religious party, it has forced the Government to end by giving promises which it began by refusing. And what was the consequence? As soon as Louis Napoleon had given to France a pledge that he would continue to hold Rome for the Pope, the Turin parliament declared Rome to be their capital. If this was done, as everybody believes, with Louis Napoleon's consent, what treachery on his part; if it was done without his consent, what a defiance on their part; and whether done with or without his consent, what an insult. Everybody feels that he is degrading himself before the priests in France, and before the Carbonari in Italy. Keller's speech was a wound which will be long before it heals, and will remain a brand when it has healed. His prestige is going, or rather, the talent, and far-sightedness, and decision which he appeared to show from 1849 to 1854 are discovered to have been a mere prestige. They were inspired by bolder, more sagacious, and resolute men. Since he lost Drouyn de Lhuys he has struggled and foundered from blunder to blunder. He has managed to incur, and to appear to deserve, the most inconsistent reproaches. You hate him because you think that he has threatened and deceived you ; we think that he has been meanly subservient to you. The Church denounces him as Pontius Pilate, the Carbonari propose to murder him as the friend of the Pope.

Senior.—What will be the next subject of debate ?

Changarnier.—The budget. There is much that can be said on it, and that, I trust, will be said. The 1,950,000,000 (78,000,000*l.* sterling) that appear in it do not represent the whole income. You must add the *cautionnements*, and you must add the 40,000,000 received every year from the 20,000 conscripts who pay instead of serving.

Senior.—You must deduct the expense of finding *remplaçants.*

Changarnier.—The Government buys its *remplaçants* cheap. It takes idlers and *vauriens*, men who want the diligence, or the character, or the intelligence, which are necessary to earn their bread as working men. They are the pests of the army ; they suffer ten times as many punishments as are inflicted on the conscripts, and degrade the service. The

conscript who serves unwillingly, who parts in tears
from his family, from his *curé*, and from his *fiancée*,
who hates garrison life, and counts every day till his
return, makes by far the best soldier. He carries his
virtues into the service, feels that he is paying his
debt to his country, is proud to think that he is
paying it faithfully, and despises his comrade, the
remplaçant, as a mercenary. France is rather *guer-
rière* than *militaire*. We like war, as a means of
satisfying our vanity and our ambition, as giving us
glory, and power, and influence, but it is a small
minority, and that the worst minority, of our *pro-
letaires* that wishes to serve. We could not, as you
can do, raise an army by voluntary enlistment, and
if we could do so it would not be, as yours is, a
good one. You see in Lamoricière's fate what sort
of an army is raised on the Continent by enlistment.

Senior.—Is not the badness of Lamoricière's army
to be accounted for partly by the unpopularity of
their cause ?

Changarnier.—Not in the least. In the rural
districts in which that army was raised, Umbria and
the provinces to the south and west, the Papal power
is popular. They are free from conscription, the tax
that falls most heavily on the rest of the Continent.
The peasants are devout, unintelligent, and uncom-
mercial. They do not want roads, or manufactories,
or books, still less what you want to give them—
Bibles.

The Romagna threw off the Pope as soon as his

troops had left it, but Umbria and the sea-board, though held by not 3000 Pontifical troops, remained perfectly quiet. It is only in the towns that there is disaffection. Lamoricière tells me that nothing but the devoted zeal and assistance of the peasants would have enabled him and his 200 companions to get from the battle into Ancona.

Senior.—Will Rome accept Victor Emmanuel ?

Duvergier.—Rome may, if it is to be his capital ; but Naples, though she has accepted him, will not keep him.

Senior.—Will you let her do so ?

Duvergier.—Certainly not. France will not tolerate an united Italy, and Louis Napoleon wants Naples for a cousin.

Senior.—Which cousin ?

Duvergier.—I suspect that he would prefer Prince Napoleon. That is the opinion of the Murats. They complain that they are sacrificed ; but I doubt the Prince's wish for a throne. He has talents and courage, at least civil courage, but he has a fatal defect. *Il ne peut pas se gêner.* He cannot submit to the trouble, to the restraints of sovereignty.

Senior.—Sicily will scarcely form a part of your southern kingdom.

Duvergier.—You want it to be under your thumb.

Senior.—We want nothing from it but oranges, sulphur, and sumach. What possible result could we get from the possession of Sicily except the expense of defending it ?

Duvergier.—I do not suppose that you wish to possess it, but you would like to have it under your influence, to make a Portugal of it.

Senior.—And what should we get from that? What do we get from Portugal? Except as allies in war, which Sicily cannot be, the only use that we can make of foreign countries, or indeed of our own dependencies, is to trade with them. Now what is our trade with Portugal? About 1,700,000*l.* a-year, not one third of our trade with Holland, over which we have no influence; not one fifth of our trade with the Hanse towns. Trade may give influence, but influence never gives trade.

I spent the evening at Drouyn de Lhuys. People were talking when I went in of the violent article in the *Patrie,* against the presence of the Orleans princes at the funeral of the Duchess of Kent.

Drouyn de Lhuys.—They forget that the Orleans family are connected with the Coburgs. It would have been impossible to avoid inviting them, even if it had been desirable. The strange thing is, that between the funeral and the appearance of this anti-English tirade in a Government organ, there was a *Conseil des Ministres.* Such an article could scarcely have been published without the previous consent of the Government.

The Duke of Castel-Cicala, formerly Neapolitan Minister in London, and for the last seven or eight years Viceroy of Sicily, came in. We renewed our acquaintance. He deplored bitterly, as might be expected from an ex-Viceroy, the present wretchedness of Sicily.

Castel-Cicala.—It was perfectly tranquil during my government. There was no discontent, persons and property were safe; you might travel without an escort through every province. Population, production, and commerce were increasing, when France and England sent Garibaldi to destroy everything—safety, industry, and trade. The lands are uncultivated, the provinces are full of banditti, and men are murdered in the streets of Palermo at midday.

Senior.—What France may have done, I will not conjecture, but Garibaldi was not sent by *us*. We deplored his expedition, believing that it would end in the useless sacrifice of brave men, and the disturbance and misery of the country.

Castel-Cicala.—You may have regretted the expedition at that particular time, but your agents had long been preparing the success of such an invasion. I know that English influence, and English intrigue, and English gold, had been squandered for that purpose for years.

Senior.—I feel equally certain that your belief is founded on false information. No English gold could have been so employed, unless the English Foreign Minister took it out of his own pocket. Our secret-service money in time of peace is a mere trifle, and is spent in small pensions, given in return for old

services. And what were we to get by a Sicilian
revolution ? We hate revolutions, as all commercial
nations must do. We are glad, indeed, to see an
United Italy, but on no peculiar selfish grounds. It
will be useful to all Europe.

Castel-Cicala.—Enjoy it, then, while you can ;
your pleasure will not be long. Naples will soon be
Bonapartist, and Sicily will set up for herself. It
was not her dislike of the King that made her submit
to Garibaldi, but her dislike of Naples. Self-government will be ruinous to her, but she will try it.

Sunday, March 31st.—I called on Marquis Jules
de Lasteyrie,* brother of Madame de Corcelle and
of Madame de Rémusat.

---

* Marquis Jules de Lasteyrie, grandson to La Fayette, and
brother-in-law to M. de Rémusat, was born in 1810. He entered
the service of Don Pedro, and joined the expedition, which, in
1832, drove Don Miguel out of Portugal. In 1842, he was deputy
for La Flèche, and voted with the Left Centre. In 1848, he
threw himself into the counter-revolutionary opposition, and, as
representative of Seine-et-Marne, he opposed both the Republic
and the President. In 1850, he was one of the seventeen
members chosen by the Ministry to prepare the electoral law
against universal suffrage. In the following session he proposed
the candidature of the Prince de Joinville, and protested against
the *coup d'état.* He was banished in 1852, but in the same year
he returned to France under favour of the Decree of Amnesty.
He has published articles on History and Political Economy in
the *Revue des Deux Mondes.* In 1869 he offered himself as a
Liberal candidate for the Corps Législatif, but was defeated by

Lasteyrie.—Corcelle is leaving Rome, and I am very glad that he does so. His presence there throws responsibility on him, but gives him no influence.

Senior.—I thought his influence irresistible.

Lasteyrie.—The Pope knows him to be a man of excellent sense, a good Catholic, and a devoted friend. If anybody had influence over him, it would be Corcelle, and the influence would be well directed ; for, as we all know, he is thoroughly liberal. But the Pope listens to nobody— indeed sees nobody. He shuts himself up, lets Antonelli and Mèrode do what they like, and contents himself with delivering from time to time an allocution, drawn up according to the precedents of the eighth century, and as unfit for modern times as a Chinese state paper—which Papal allocutions much resemble—is for European readers.

Senior.—He has thrown down the reins then.

Lasteyrie.—He has not thrown them down, for that implies volition. He has suffered them to fall.

Senior.—How has Louis Napoleon taken the slaps on the face, given to him by Cavour, and by the Parliament in Turin?

Lasteyrie.—He is delighted — at least so says Persigny, who is himself in the seventh heaven.

the Government candidate. In 1871 he was elected member of the National Assembly, where he sat in the Right Centre. —Ed.

They say that the slaps are given, not to him, but
to those whom they treat as enemies—the Chambers.
We are told that the decree annexing Rome to the
Kingdom of Italy was made by his order. I do not
believe that he actually ordered, or even advised it ;
but I feel certain that it was made with his con-
currence. His conduct is governed by his impulses
—not by his reason—and his strongest and oldest
passion is hatred of the Pope.

You find us more alive than usual. Between
the debate and M. Mirès we have something to talk
about.

Senior.—They are bad subjects for me. I have
not had time to read the debates, and we know
nothing about Mirès.

Lasteyrie.—I do, and I will tell you what I know.
In September, 1851, Péreire brought Mirès to me,
' *pour parler,*' as he said, ' *d'affaire.*' The affair was
this : Mirès had bought the *Pays*, and he came to
offer to my friends and me the complete direction and
use of the political portion of the paper, reserving to
himself the commercial part. We were to pay him
6000 francs a-year.

'You ought,' I said to him, ' to have known us
too well to suppose that we could accept the responsibility of editing a journal, any part of which was
out of our control.'

' I am sorry for it,' said Mirès ; ' I know nothing
about politics. I have bought the journal for my
own commercial purposes, and your names would

have given it currency. You are on the winning side.'

' Well,' I said, ' M. Mirès, in return for your good opinion, I will give you some advice. We are on the eve of a revolution. In less than three months there will be a fight between the President and the Assembly. If you wish to be on the winning side, do not adopt a flag too soon, or you may have to change it.'

Mirès followed my advice; kept the *Pays* at first neutral, and after the *coup d'état* tendered the management of its politics to the Government, who gave him Granier de Cassagnac for an editor. Soon afterwards he bought the *Constitutionnel*, and gave, or sold, its politics also to the Government.

Commanding the commercial portion of two great journals, he thought, with some truth, that he could puff every commercial scheme into temporary favour. Paris was then in a fever of speculation. We had no external politics; domestic ones were neither agreeable nor safe matters for discussion. Ambition was at an end. Court favour was despised, indeed rendered those who submitted to it despicable. Society was dull, and sometimes treacherous. Wealth became our only object, and its pursuit our only amusement.

Mirès established *la caisse des chemins de fer*, and raised by its shares a capital of fifty millions (two millions sterling), which was intended to be invested in railway shares, or lent at high interest

to railway companies. He followed the course of
Péreire, but with less skill. He dealt in shares, he
obtained concessions for railways at home and abroad;
and, above all, he bribed right and left. At last
his engagements amounted to above twenty millions
sterling. What may be the value of his assets time will
show. Much depended on the success of the Ottoman
loan. If it had succeeded, he might have floated a
little longer. It failed. Mirès was instantly a ruined
man, and the whole crowd of his creditors rushed on
him. So many great people were apparently in his
power, that he thought he could rely on being pulled
through by the Government. He wrote a letter to
the Emperor, three pages long, in which he attributed his ruin to the bribes which he had been
forced to give to the Emperor's friends, and he added
a list of the persons whom he could, and would,
expose, if he was not rescued. '*La chute*,' he said,
'*de la Maison Mirès pourrait entraîner une autre chute*.'
The Emperor was furious, and ordered him to be
immediately arrested and prosecuted.

Senior.—For what? What was there legally
criminal in his conduct?

Lasteyrie.—Offering a bribe to a person in authority
is an offence; but he was also accused of fraud. He
had taken large sums for the purpose of investing
them, and had misapplied them.

The affair has been put into the hands of M. de
Germigny, and has been carried on *administrativement*
—a term, happily, unknown to you. It is a criminal

proceeding, in which the forms of law are dispensed with. It resembles an inquiry by a Parliamentary Committee. Mirès remains at Mazas *au secret;* but great use has been made of his list. Between seven and eight millions (about 300,000*l.*) has been paid to his account by persons whom, he says, that he bribed, but who admit only that they had borrowed from him, and given no security. Young B—— is one of them. He is Conseiller d'Etat, and had received 100,000 francs—*pour faire,* according to Mirès — *un rapport favorable.* What adds to the scandal, he has since been sent out of the country on a mission, apparently in order to suppress his evidence. It appears also that he has bribed largely in Spain and in Rome. Queen Christina and Muñoz are among the *soi-disant* borrowers. All the money paid to Mirès by the shareholders on the new Roman lines has disappeared, and the railroads are scarcely, if at all, begun. It is obvious that the Government has not seen to the performance of the contracts. This is supposed to be explained by large sums debited in the books of M. Mirès to a brother of Cardinal Antonelli, who is a banker in Rome. In general, the Emperor has endeavoured to screen the delinquents, but his answer, as respects the Roman affairs, was, ' Spare nobody.'

April 1*st.*—I called on A. B. C. He asked what Corcelle was doing, and was glad to hear that he was returning from Rome.

A. B. C.—Even if he were listened to, he could give no useful advice, for no useful advice is to be given. I do not blame the Pope for shutting himself up in inactivity. How can he be usefully active? He can do no good by staying in Rome; he can do no good by quitting Rome. While he remains there he is degraded. As soon as he goes, he sows the seeds of the schisms which will destroy the unity of Catholicism; a unity which was its peculiar glory, and its great source of usefulness. We are now arrived at a turning-point in the history of mankind. An institution which has preserved religion and civilisation for 1500 years, which neither barbarians, nor tyrants, nor revolutions, nor wars, could permanently injure, will be destroyed by Garibaldi and Cavour— by a Nicene fisherman and a Piedmontese statesman.

Whatever be the place of refuge which the Pope selects, he will be virtually a subject there. Like every other guest he will be under the influence of his host. There will be no confidence in his impartiality. If he fixes himself in Austria and we are at war with her, shall we suffer our Church to be governed from Vienna? If he selects Seville, and we quarrel with Spain, shall we submit to be under the jurisdiction of a pope who has made himself a Spaniard?

We shall establish a Church of our own, that is to say, we shall make a schism. So will Spain and Austria, if the Pope reside in France. One schism will be followed by another, until Catholicism becomes a mere recollection.

Cavour's plan of the separation of Church and State may suit a small semi-republican country like Belgium, but it is inconsistent with all our habits and traditions. We have always thought the union of Church and State necessary, in order that each may control the other. If we cease to be Papal we shall not turn Independents. Our sovereign will become the head of our Church, and our priests will be Government officers ; spiritual gendarmes, without influence, scarcely even respected. I am grieved to the heart, both as a Catholic and as a Liberal.

Senior.—What has been the effect of the debate on Louis Napoleon's position ?

A. B. C.—Mischievous. Every one has long disapproved of his policy, but till now no one knew how widely that disapprobation extended. The debate has shown it to be universal, and the knowledge of that fact has made each man's private disapprobation more confident and more intense. The Chambers have told him that he has to choose between folly and treachery, to confess himself the dupe or thé accomplice of Cavour ; that if he does not see that Italian unity is an almost fatal blow to France, he is a fool ; that if, seeing it, he has sacrificed the interests of France to his hatred of the Pope, or to his fears of the Carbonari, he is a traitor. He has, in fact, left to himself, and to us, only two modes of escape. He must break the Italian unity by

seizing Naples, or he must restore the balance by
seizing the Rhine. And there is not a Frenchman
who would not, under the circumstances of the case,
endure a war of years for either of those purposes.

Senior.—Which of those attempts do you think
the more probable?

A. B. C.—The seizure of Belgium and the Rhine.
Europe is now like our earth, a crust under which
destructive gases are being generated and are accumulating. The first explosion will probably be on
the Danube. You may hear there the sounds of an
approaching earthquake. Hungary and Croatia will
rise, perhaps even Bohemia, for all the Sclavonic races
are disturbed.

Senior.—But how will that enable you to get the
Rhine?

A. B. C.—Everything is possible as soon as a war
breaks out. Prussia may assist Austria. Louis Napoleon may invade Prussia in defence of the principle of
non-intervention. Prussia may think that Austria is
breaking up, and may join her enemies in the hope of
getting some of her fragments. He may take part
with Austria and seize Rhenish Prussia as his frag-
ment; or he may join Prussia, take the Rhine, and
indemnify Prussia with Hanover and Saxony. Nothing, I repeat, is impossible when once the next war
has broken out. Which of the two courses of events
he would prefer, I doubt. There are strong reasons
for, and against each. The seizure of the Rhine
involves a war with you; a war which he always

contemplates, always prepares for, always perhaps intends, but yet dreads and defers. An Hungarian insurrection may force it on him. He cannot be a mere spectator of such an event; but if Hungary remains quiet he may prefer the easier seizure of Naples. But there, again, is a peculiar danger from which a German war is free, the Unionist dagger. As all his policy is . selfish and personal, he may rather encounter dangers to France than dangers to himself. He may rather expose us to ruin and dismemberment by an European coalition, than himself to a dagger or a bomb.

Senior.—What do you mean by the seizure of Naples? Is the Prince Imperial to be King of Naples, and Prince Napoleon the Viceroy?

A. B. C.—By no means, that would be too barefaced. It is not to be a conquest, but a restoration. A Murat is to go thither. And such has been the policy of all parties, that he will be able to say that he has right on his side.

The public law of Europe and America seems now to be that nations are mere voluntary partnerships, and that every individual, and every . aggregation of which they consist, has a right to dissolve partnership at pleasure; that there is no such thing as allegiance; that neither kings nor aristocracies have any rights against the people; that is to say, against the uneducated majority. Nothing will be easier than to induce, what he will call the Neapolitan people,—the Lazzaroni of the towns, and the peasants in the country,—to discard Victor Emmanuel, and demand Prince Napoleon or Joachim.

And who is to complain if we require that their will be obeyed ? Louis Napoleon has a right to say that the abolition of all rights of sovereignty and of aristocracy is not his doing. He carefully preserved them. He accepted Lombardy, not as the gift of the people, but of the sovereign. He reserved the rights of all the existing rulers, merely requiring their rule to be liberalised. He protected by French arms the two who alone remained at their post; he protested in favour of even those who had abandoned their thrones. The present state of Italy, he may well say, is not my doing. To England he has a right to say, '*Vous avez fait faire;*' to Piedmont, '*Vous avez fait;*' to the rest of Europe, '*Vous avez laissé faire.*'

So absurd and so mischievous has been the policy of all parties, that it is difficult to say which is most to blame. Louis Napoleon's wisdom left him as soon as he had made the peace of Villa Franca. It was the best arrangement for everybody. For us, to whom it left Italy in the state in which it is our business to keep her—a divided, and therefore an inoffensive neighbour. For Austria, whom it left safe in Venice, and unhumiliated in Florence. For the minor Italian powers, to whom it left the autonomy which they have enjoyed for fifteen centuries; and for Piedmont herself, whose wealth and power it doubled; and who, if she would have kept quiet, might have enjoyed an indefinite period of prosperous peace, protected by France, and friendly with her neighbours. But Piedmont listened only to her vanity and ambition. She resolved to play double or quits. Whether the Piedmontese people have gained by being absorbed into this new disjointed revolutionary kingdom of Italy, even if that kingdom continue to exist, remains to be seen. It was Louis Napoleon's business to restrain her. He pretended to do so, but secretly encouraged her. What he did secretly, you did openly. Such conduct was franker and bolder, but therefore only the more mischievous. The rest of Europe sulkily submitted. And see the result. Italy is in revolution, a disease from which it takes generations to recover; a disease which we have suffered eighty years, and from which we seem to be as far from recovery as we were in 1790. Piedmont has staked her liberty and her independence. France sees a new rival, probably a new enemy, start up on her very frontier, more formidable than any power on the Continent, more populous than Prussia; more homogeneous than Austria; more intelligent than Russia or Spain, and she will probably have to go through a war, or a series of wars, before she can either dismember this new giant, or obtain such an extension of territory as shall restore her just preponderance.

As for you, besides sanctioning the abolition throughout Europe of all public law, an abolition from which you will suffer severely, you will have

compelled us, either to absorb your dependency—
Belgium, and to break the force of your ally—Prussia,
or to extend our protectorate over all Southern Italy.

Senior.—As for Belgium and the Rhine, I admit
that we should feel their union to you a great evil;
an evil to be resisted even by war; and we shall
grieve if our hopes of an united Italy prove a dream.
But if there is to be a Neapolitan throne, I would as
soon see a Bonaparte on it as a Bourbon.

A. B. C.—But a Bonaparte dynasty would be
a really French dynasty; the Bourbons were only
nominally French.

Senior.—A Bonaparte dynasty would be French,
but would it be permanent? Would it outlast the
Bonapartes in France? And if it did outlast them,
would it be a friend to the dynasty of the next
restoration?

A. B. C.—You do not believe, then, in the Napoleonic dynasty?

Senior.—I find no one who does.

A. B. C.—To die, it must commit suicide; which,
I admit that it seems resolved to do. And whom
do you expect to succeed it?

Senior.—The House of Orleans.

A. B. C.—I am of your opinion. *Je crois que
les actions de la Maison d'Orléans sont en hausse et celle
de la Maison Bonaparte en baisse.*

Here we were interrupted by visitors.

April 2nd.—A. B. C. paid us a long visit this

morning. We returned to our conversation of yesterday, at about the point at which we had left off.

A. B. C.—You would tolerate a Muratist dynasty in Naples, if Naples is to have a separate government?

Senior.—Yes.

A. B. C.—But the Emperor's schemes are more extensive. He sends to Naples both the Murats; the father is to have Naples, the son is to have Sicily, with a separate administration, connected with Naples by a mere suzerainty, and the reunion of the two crowns is to be delayed until the father's death. Nor is this quite all. It is admitted that the Pope is a bad administrator; it is admitted that he cannot govern his own subjects, that he must always be maintained by foreign bayonets; it is admitted, too, that his temporal sovereignty interferes with his spiritual duties and with his spiritual influence. All this must be true, for all your public men, except a few Irish Ultramontane bigots, proclaim it. We bow to your authority. We propose, therefore, that he shall still have the military support which, you say, is necessary, and shall be relieved from the administration for which you say that he is unfit. We intend him to be the sovereign of the States of the Church, but not their administrator. He is to have *la nue propriété*. A Vicaire is to act under him and for him, and to be enabled to do so by receiving their revenues. Who can be so fit for this office as the King of Naples? Naples is already a

fief of the Church, the rest of the Roman territory is
to be so likewise. The Pope is to be the sovereign
of the whole, but on the same terms as to every
portion. Murat will give him a handsome civil list,
will acknowledge him as sovereign of Rome and of
the States of the Church, will surround him with
all the reverence which your East India Company
paid to the Great Mogul, and leave to him just as
much authority. If the people of the Romagna, or
of the Marches, or of Umbria, or of any other portion
of the Church, or the King of Northern Italy, object
to this arrangement, we have 25,000 men in Rome,
and 30,000 more within a day's steam who will prove
to them its perfect propriety.

The new King of Northern Italy will not be on
very good terms with the new King of Southern
Italy, but we shall keep the peace between them, and
the knowledge that we can use either to crush the
other will keep both of them our humble allies. All
the splendid ports of the Neapolitan dominions will
be open to us, and their marine will be virtually a
part of ours.

Such is our master's programme. There is some
violence and some perfidy in it, but those are defects
inherent to all large comprehensive schemes; they
are incidental to *la haute politique*.

It is subject, however, as I said yesterday, to one
real objection; it will drive the Carbonari mad. The
sentence against him as a false brother is now suspended; it will be so no longer. He will not be

safe in the streets, or in the Bois de Boulogne—scarcely in the Tuileries. Such dangers he once despised; he does so no longer. His nerves· have not recovered, probably will never recover, the shock of the *attentat*. Still, I believe that he will not abandon his scheme, but he will hesitate; he will procrastinate, perhaps, until he is engaged in his war on the Rhine, and then it may be too late. Italy may be consolidated, and we may have to content ourselves with getting in return the Rhine from Strasburg to Rotterdam. But it will be a bad compensation for the union of Italy. Ou the other hand, it is quite possible that our success on the Rhine may be so decisive and so rapid, that we may be able to carry into effect both schemes.

Austria may be paralysed by Hungary; Prussia may be wasting her forces in her absurd war with Denmark. You may find us a more dangerous enemy at sea than you suppose us to be. We have twice as much disposable revenue as you have, and for the first three months we shall have more sailors, and perhaps more and better ships. The war may not last three months, and then we turn south-wards.

One thing only pleases me in this vista of treachery, violence, and crime, that Nemesis will have her part in it, that *you* will be punished for your folly, Germany for her cowardice, and Piedmont for her wickedness. The next ten years will be a period of great moral revolution. Every nation will suffer, though not, perhaps, in proportion to its demerits.

Senior.—I own that this is no consolation to me. Crimes and follies are what I expect from nations. The object of punishment is prevention; there is no use in punishing nations, for they are incorrigible.

A. B. C.—I am not so philosophical; I wish to punish, whether I can correct or not. Nothing should tempt me to leave Piedmont unpunished. Her insolence, her impudence, her avidity, her falsehood, her treachery, form the most revolting picture of political wickedness that the world, ancient or modern, has ever seen. And you wish to reward her for all this by putting her at the head of a great nation, and to reward the author of it all, Cavour, by making him a great historical personage—an Italian Napoleon. I admire Cavour. He, Garibaldi, and the young King of Naples, are the only Italians for whom I care. Cavour has played his part with infinite boldness and skill. His conduct in the last debate was a masterpiece of both. He defied the French Chambers, but flattered the Emperor, and managed to throw on him the whole responsibility of keeping the King of Italy out of Rome. If we only admit that his end, Italian unity, is a good one, which I hope that he believes, and that the end sanctifies the means, which I fear he believes, he is a hero. I sympathize with him, and with Garibaldi. I should be sorry to see either of them hanged, though, if any political crimes deserve hanging, theirs do. But I have no sympathy with

Piedmont. She has been the unintelligent, unreluctant instrument of Cavour's ambition and of Garibaldi's fanaticism. My detestation of her crimes is not neutralised by any admiration.

Wednesday, April 3rd.—The Marquis de Chambrun* called on us. His family are Legitimists, with a large property in the Lozère. I asked him, as I ask everybody, what had been the effect of the discussion on Louis Napoleon's position.

Chambrun.—Very mischievous. People have communicated their opinions on the war and on its consequences, and every one finds that every one else utterly disapproves all that has been done. He is now as little trusted at home as he is abroad; all confidence, not only in his truth, but in his prudence, in his decision, and in his success, is gone. He has spent, they say, 50,000 men and 500,000,000fr. to make Piedmont a first-rate power.

There is a general feeling that he must be put under control, that he is not fit to manage our affairs, or even his own. All his wishes, too, are supposed

---

* The Marquis de Chambrun was at this time quite young. He had not long been married to M. de Corcelle's daughter, and Tocqueville, who thought highly of his intelligence, had done all he could to promote the match. Not many years after this period he lost his fortune, and although he could hardly speak a word of English, he emigrated to the United States, and has succeeded brilliantly at the American bar.—ED.

to be contrary to ours. He wants war, we want peace.

Senior.—Does the army want peace ?

Chambrun.—Not the soldiers, nor the officers under the rank of general. The soldiers who hate garrison life wish for war, *pour se désennuyer;* the officers want promotion, and confess that the great advantage which they hope from war will be the killing off their seniors. But the generals having acquired a high social position wish to enjoy it. They do not want to be killed off; they are as much opposed to war as we are. And yet all this may produce war. He may think it necessary *pour nous distraire*, and no distraction can be better than successful war. The war, to be sure, may be unsuccessful, and then he is lost, but he is accustomed to play for great stakes. Ou the whole, I am inclined to think that the chances are in favour of war.

Senior.—In what quarter ?

Chambrun.—Towards the Rhine and the Scheldt. It can be only for a maritime war that he is making these enormously expensive naval preparations, and we do not suppose that an Italian war would bring on an English one. I know that very large provisions of military stores are collected or are on their way to our northern frontier ; much larger than are necessary, or even useful, if the army is to be kept on our peace establishment, vast as that establishment is.

Senior.—You think that the distraction of

war would prevent an attempt to put him under control?

Chambrun.—Provided that we approved of the object of the war, and this we might do, though we might think that object not worth the risk or the cost. The peculiarity of the wars which he has made as yet was that we disliked the object as well as the means. We did not want to weaken Russia, still less to destroy her as a maritime power. We had no sympathy with Lombardy, and we hated Piedmont. But a successful war for the Rhine would be popular with everybody, and so would be a war to prevent Italian unity. We are a *nation routinière*, at least, as respects foreign politics.

The traditions of the empire attract us to the Rhine. The traditions of Richelieu tell us never to allow Italy, or indeed any of our neighbours, to be powerful. We require them to be small, weak, and divided. How much of the Rhine-land will you let us take?

Senior.—Not a village.

Chambrun.—And the same as to the Scheldt-land?

Senior.—Certainly. *You* are afraid of an Italy of 20,000,000; *you* are ready to lay waste the whole peninsula in order to prevent it. One of your most eminent statesmen told me the other day that he would die rather than see a United Italy or a United Germany. Are not we justified in taking every means to prevent a France of 50,000,000 from being created within twenty-four miles of us ? We cannot allow you to eat the artichoke leaf by leaf; we must make a stand somewhere, and that stand will be to prevent your extending yourselves to the north.

Chambrun.—Then war is inevitable, for we most certainly shall make the attempt. When I said that I was inclined to think that the chances were in favour of war, I spoke much too undecidedly. Peace seems to me to be possible only in one of three contingencies; one, that he makes his spring on Italy instead of on the Rhine; another, that you let him do whatever he thinks fit; the third, that his career be cut short by a ball or a dagger. The first, perhaps, may bring on the third, which is a sufficient reason for his not adopting it.

Something he must do. His prestige is gone; he cannot afford to let himself be opposed by you, treated as a child by Cavour, denounced as a false friend by his protègè, Francis of Naples, and excommunicated by his other protègè, the Pope. The reproaches that most injure a sovereign have been showered on him : cowardice, irresolution, falsehood, treachery, selfishness, and, what is a hundred times worse than all the rest put together, stupidity.

We think that he made the war because he was afraid of the Carbonari, that he made the peace because he had brought his army into a position of extreme peril, that he allowed the peace to be broken because he was afraid of Cavour, that he deserted Francis II. because he was afraid of England, and that he will now desert the Pope, because he is afraid of Prince Napoleon. War *may* destroy him, peace *must* destroy him. Prepare yourselves, therefore, for a *duel à mort*, or to give up the Rhine.

Chambrun was followed by General Changarnier.

Changarnier.—Ellice has passed through Paris, and has gone to tell everybody in London that we are going to war with you, to punish you for having encouraged Italian unity.

Senior.—Not precisely so. He tells us that you are furious against Italian unity ; and that you are furious against us, because you think that we have contributed to it. But he does not say that you are going to war with us. He knows that you have nothing to do with peace or war. That that question, like every other, is decided for you by a wiser head than any of yours.

Changarnier.—Well, I do not believe that that wise head intends war—at least for the present. Few people know him so well as I do. I have seen him in all situations. Though we do not meet now, I have intimate friends who are about him. From all that I hear of what he is doing and what he is saying, he does not wish for war.

Senior.—Perhaps not for its own sake. The Russian and Italian wars may have cured him of that. But may he not be resolved to obtain objects to which war may be incidental?

Changarnier.—*He* may be ; but *we* are not. And

if we can preserve even the shadow of free discussion which we now have, it will be difficult for him to make a wanton war. The Chambers hold legally the purse-strings. They would refuse the budget for an unnecessary war.

Senior.—May he not abolish them? May he not make use of the clause in the Constitution, enabling him to appeal from the Chambers to the people?

Changarnier.—I do not think that he would do that. It would be too slow and too doubtful. I think him more likely to make another *coup d'état* if the Marshals will help him, which is by no means certain.

I think it still more probable that, if he wants war he will make it when the Chambers have been prorogued, *et quand il nous aura lancé dans les événemens,* will defy us to refuse the supplies.

Thursday, April 4th.—Beaumont* came to Paris yesterday, and he and Circourt, Chambrun, Madame Mohl, Hayward, and Waldegrave, breakfasted with us.

We talked of the removal of the ashes of Napoleon from the chapel in which they have lain during the

---

* Gustave de Beaumont, a great friend and adherent of Tocqueville, whose biographer he became. He wrote several other works, one upon Ireland, another called *Marie; ou l'esclavage aux Etats-Unis,* &c. He was for a short time Ambassador in England in 1849. He was an affectionate and sincere friend, and a delightful converser, full of animation and energy. He died in 1866.—ED.

last fifteen years, to a vault under the dome of the Invalides. It took place yesterday, privately.

Circourt.—Louis Napoleon has spent millions in preparing an Imperial tomb at St. Denys. The Bonaparte dynasty was to be interred during the next thousand years by the side of the Capets.

All the bishops were to attend in vestments of violet, brocaded with gold, and embroidered with pearls. Twenty or thirty bishops *in partibus* were to be created for the purpose. The procession was to be lighted by 100,000 torches, and to reach from Montmartre to the cathedral.

All has been spoilt by the quarrel with the Church. The Emperor got angry. ' *Mettez le dans un trou,*' he said, ' *et ne m'étourdissez plus les oreilles.*' This has literally been done. He has been put into a hole, over which is a sarcophagus of sandstone, as ugly as the rest of the tomb, which the Emperor believes to be of porphyry.

Circourt is recovering from influenza. He has been kept silent for a week, and his pent-up talk overflowed in indignation against us.

We were wicked for not stopping the war with Austria; we were wicked for not forcing Louis Napoleon to force Victor Emmanuel to observe the peace of Zurich; we were wicked for sending Garibaldi to Naples; we were wicked for sending the French fleet from Gaeta; we are wicked for allowing Prussia to attack Denmark. In short, as it is in our power to keep the whole world quiet, it is our fault that it is all in uproar, and we shall be punished by seeing the French flag flying from Mayence to Antwerp, the Greek flag at Corfu and the Green flag in Dublin.

Our French friends seemed to think all this very friendly and very wise.

Beaumont dined with us.

I attacked him about the suppression of Tocqueville's ' *Révolution.*'

Beaumont.—I think myself bound to act as I believe that Tocqueville would have acted. I am certain that if he had known that he was dying, he would have burnt that manuscript. He was a great thinker, but still more, a great artist. He was an artist in his books, in his letters, in his speeches, in his despatches, —even in his conversation. He worshipped ' *La Forme*' perhaps even more devoutly. than ' *La Substance.*' He used to say that an idea not produced in its very best dress, was injured. He had another idol,—his own reputation. No motive could tempt him to appear before the public, or even before his friends, *en déshabille.* Often when I have tried to make him speak in the Chamber, he has answered, ' I cannot ; I am unprepared.' I have remonstrated. I have said that considering the state of the debate a few sentences from him might give it a turn which would be useful. It was in vain : he never would speak unless he could speak his best. This defect made him useless to his party as a debater.

We passed on to politics.

Beaumont.—The few persons whom I have had time to see in Paris, do not expect war. They say that our finances, good as they may be made to appear, are in a bad state : that the Emperor's civil list owes 80,000,000 (3,200,000*l*).

In the country, at least in my province of Sarthe, the horror of war is indescribable. The wars of the last five years, and the enormous conscription even in peace, are ruining our agriculture and our labourers, and desolating our families. As the day of balloting approaches, you see everyone *triste* and *préoccupé*.

When it comes, it sometimes takes every able-bodied young man who is subject to it, and even then does not give the number required from us. The people say, ' What is the use of balloting when every one has to go ? ' Those who serve, count the days till they can escape. Every month I am requested to intercede with a general in order to get a man discharged before his time. Sometimes I succeed, more frequently I fail.

Senior.—Changarnier tells me that the reluctant conscripts make the best soldiers.

Beaumont.—Changarnier, and Lamoricière, and our other successful generals, all delight in the conscription. It gives them every year a crop of from 120,000 to 150,000 strong, healthy young men, who are, I dare say, more orderly and more obedient soldiers than the rascals who can be hired as *remplaçants*. Their *métier* leads our officers to treat war as

the great object of human existence, and the conscription as the readiest means of supporting it.   Those
only who live in the country as I do—live familiarly
with the country people—know what are its horrors.
If a peasant or farmer complains, he is sent to prison
—perhaps to Cayenne.

We boast of *égalité*. What can be more unequal
than a tax, paid in money or by service, which ruins
the poor and is not felt by the rich?   If one of my
sons were taken, it would cost me 80*l*., and I should
be free for ever. To one of my tenants, 80*l*. is a year's
income. He must pinch himself for years to raise it.
To a labourer it is a fabulous sum. He never has
possessed, or will possess, a quarter of it. He gives
instead of it, the six best years of his life—often his
life itself.

The management, too, of the conscription is harsh.
We are in the hands of the Gendarmerie, who hate or
despise the peasants as *péquins*. Not long ago, one
of my peasants—a soldier on furlough—was required
to join. The gendarme came to me at ten o'clock in
the morning, and desired me to send him off by the
train which starts at two. 'If he does not report
himself in Paris,' he said, 'to-morrow morning, I am
ordered to arrest him as a deserter.'

'It is impossible,' I answered. 'I do not know
where to find him. He shall go by to-morrow's train.'

'That won't do,' he replied ; 'if he is not off by
the two o'clock train to-day, I must arrest him.'

I sent out in every direction, found him by accident

three miles away, lent him a horse to gallop to the station, which he reached just before the train started. It he had been two minutes later, he would have been arrested, and his chance of promotion, or of early discharge, destroyed.

The conscription is almost equally unpopular among the employers of labour. Our agriculture is languishing, both from the want of hands and from the extravagant wages demanded by the few who can be hired.

Twenty years ago the population of Beaumont la Chartre was 900. It is now only 650. This indeed is partly owing to the growth of the towns and to the enormous public works.

An intelligent Russian said of this Government that it is ' *condamné à travaux forcés à perpétuité.**

For the mere purpose of giving employment, the towns are forced to demolish and rebuild whole quarters ; the railway companies are required to make unremunerating lines and branches. A week's interruption of the building trade would terrify the Government. The north-west district of Paris is now to be pulled down and renewed. When that has been

---

* The *mot* was first said by M. de Rozière to me. I was so charmed with it I told it to the Baron d'Uxkühl, a Livonian ; he carried it to Petersburg, and two years afterwards a Russian told it to me as coming from thence ; he said it as we were looking at some building going on, and I said what will be done when all this building is at an end.—(*Note by Madame Mohl.*)

done, the operation must be repeated towards the north-east. The workmen are feeling their power. There is a strike now among the masons in my neighbouring town of Chartre. Such a thing was not heard of two years ago.

Senior.—Is a strike legal?

Beaumont.—Certainly not. It is severely punishable, but the Government is afraid to interfere. I am building ; my workpeople, who used to be satisfied with 35 sous (1*s*. 5*d*.) a-day, asked three francs (2*s*. 6*d*.) 'We want,' they said, 'the prices of Paris.' 'If I am to pay,' I answered, 'Paris prices, I will send for Paris workmen, who will do twice as much in the same time.' I have been looking out in vain for six months for a *fille-de-ferme*. I used to pay 80 francs a-year. I offer 200 and cannot get one.

Senior.—What do you pay for your higher servants,—to the man, for instance, about your person?

Beaumont.—I used to pay 300 francs a-year. I now pay 400 (16*l*.) ; but that is clear profit to him, as I provide him with clothes and washing.

Formerly our conscripts, when discharged, returned to us. Now we may never hear of them again. Those who do not die establish themselves elsewhere : those who do return are deteriorated as workmen, they have lost part of their skill, and more of their industry. A garrison life makes a man *dégourdi* and intelligent, but idle, *flâneur*, and often drunken.

Senior.—They are taught, I suppose, to read and write?

Beaumont.—Seldom. There are regimental schools, but they are not forced to attend them.

We passed on to the Papal question.

Beaumont.—The quarrel with the Pope has not yet produced much effect in the provinces. In fact, it is not known. While the Pope and the French soldiers are in Rome, the people take for granted that he is under our protection.

My maire, an excellent Papist, received Prince Napoleon's speech. It delighted him. ' *Voilà*,' he said to me, ' *un qui défend joliment le Pape. Ah ils auront beau ménacer le Pape. L'Empereur est là pour le protéger.*'

But if the Pope leaves Rome, the veil will fall. Our people cannot conceive a Pope out of Italy, nor can they conceive Catholicism, or even religion, without Papacy. All the absurdities, all the inconsistencies, all the miracles, and all the vices of Catholicism, are to them parts of their religion. It can scarcely indeed be otherwise, for, being forbidden to inquire, even if they had the necessary leisure or knowledge, they are in the hands of their priests, who are as uninformed as they are, and perhaps still more prejudiced.

If they cease to be Catholics, they will cease to be Christians. To distinguish between the different parts of a creed, and retain one, rejecting the other, is impossible to an ignorant, unreflecting people. To make them Protestants, you must first make their priests Protestants, as the early Reformers did. But they had no prejudices to contend against. Luther was a monk, and spoke to his brother monks a language which they understood. Protestant doctrines are unintelligible to most of our clergy ; and those who could understand them are fortified against them by obstinate prejudice.

But if our peasants lose their religion, they will become savages. It is their only restraint, their only intellectual exercise. Their intercourse with the priest alone raises them above barbarism.

Senior.—Has their intercourse with the school-master no effect?

Beaumont.—Scarcely any. They leave school so early that they forget in a year or two the little that they have learned. Scarcely any of my tenants can read, though some of them pay me as much as 2000 francs a-year. The masters are not much better scholars. There ought to be a normal school in every department to train masters. But when I applied to the *soi-disant* normal school of the department of La Sarthe, they told me that they trained none. They sent me one, some time ago, ignorant and drunken. I got rid of him, and am forced to trust the school to two Sisters of Charity—good people, but not real teachers.

Senior.—Could any one open a private school in Beaumont la Chartre?

Beaumont.—He might, if he had patience enough to go through the requisite formalities, and could obtain the requisite certificates, and the requisite permissions, which would not be easy. If he were an Imperialist, the bishop would refuse his consent; if he belonged to any other party, the prefect. But he would get no scholars. First, because our peasants care nothing for education, and, secondly, in a country so *administré* as France, a private establishment cannot compete with a public one.

In fact, however, I never heard of the attempt being made.

Friday, April 5th.—Hayward was sitting with me this morning when Beaumont came in. We talked of the *morcellement* of property in France.

Beaumont.—It does not extend. Real property is so desired in France, that the construction of estates goes on as rapidly as their dissolution. Our conveyancing system, though very expensive, is simple. To be a land-jobber—a *marchand de terrain*—is a considerable profession. It is so easy to buy and sell, that the land of the country is supposed to change hands on an average once in twenty years. This is one of the reasons which make it difficult to get tenants or farm-servants. If a man has capital, he had rather spend two-thirds of it in buying a farm, and the other third in stocking it, than employ the whole on another's land. I have not a servant who has not his field. To have none is a degradation. My labourers are constantly telling me, 'I cannot come to-morrow, as I have to sow my barley. I cannot come another day, because I have to dig my potatoes.'

Hayward.—This is John Mill's favourite system of peasant proprietors.

Senior.—That system used to be praised as a preservative against revolution.

Beaumont.—To be sure, it has not saved us from dynastic or political revolutions ; that is, from revolutions affecting the depositories of power, but it has saved us from Socialist ones. The affection of the proprietors for their little cottages and fields, often intense in inverse proportion to the size of the property, occasioned the return of the Constituent Assembly in 1848—one of the best that we ever have had.

Senior.—I should have thought that the man with only one acre would have liked a scramble, out of which he might get two.

Beaumont.—He was wiser. He thought, with La Place, that a certainty of one acre was better than an even chance of two.

Guizot now came in. He was delighted to see Beaumont, not only for his own merits, but as a member of the Academy, in order to canvass for Reynouard, who is candidate for a vacancy to be filled up a fortnight hence. Reynouard was Procureur-Général at the time of the *coup d'état*, and

signed the order for the arrest of Louis Napoleon.
It is a curious trait in Louis Napoleon's character,
that while destroying by thousands, and tens of
thousands, his enemies in the lower classes, he has
left untouched, indeed unnoticed, those belonging
to the aristocracy of birth or of talent. It is said
that Reynouard will be elected, though a single
whisper from the Tuileries would make it impossible.

Guizot asked me for political news.

Senior.—I know none, and I have given up
conjecturing.

Beaumont.—No one has any policy; every one
lives *au jour le jour*.

Guizot.—Except Cavour. I honour him as the
only man living who has an object, and pursues it
straightforwardly through every danger and every
difficulty. I believe his object to be an unattainable
one, and, indeed, a bad one if it could be attained.
Italy ought not to consist of less, at the very least,
than four kingdoms — Piedmont with Lombardy,
Parma and Modena, the Popedom, Tuscany and
Naples. Even if France be weak enough to allow
this new composite kingdam to be formed, it will
tumble to pieces from the mutual repulsion of its
elements. But when I think only of the skill and
boldness of his means, I am carried away by my
admiration.

Beaumont.—So am I. He will ruin his country
with consummate ability. What a contrast there is

between his vigour and decision and the vacillation of our master!

Guizot.—Not only of *our* master, but of every other sovereign, except Queen Victoria.

Beaumont.—And Queen Victoria, as represented by Lord John Russell, is not a model of consistency.

Guizot.—The inconsistency was rather in words than in acts. A minister who has to obey the will of the people in Italy, and to defy it in Ireland, Corfu, and Hindostan, cannot always talk the same language.

I mentioned to Guizot Beaumont's account of the state of education in La Sarthe.

Guizot.—There must be some great fault in the authorities. In Normandy we have nine hundred schools. The normal school of my department, Calvados, gives from ten to twenty masters and mistresses a-year; so it is in that part of the *midi* which I know.

Senior.—Do the clergy take much part in education in Normandy?

Guizot.—None. It would be unpopular. Our peasantry respect the clergy, but keep them strictly within their spiritual functions. Education is not one of them. No one would send a child to a school managed by a priest.

Senior.—And yet they interfere in the elections. The Bishop of Coutances returned at the last election one of the deputies for La Manche.

Guizot. — That could not have happened in Calvados.

St. Hilaire, Saturday, April 6th.—I breakfasted with the Mohls and St. Hilaire, and walked with him to the Institut. He is anxious and depressed.

Barthélémy St. Hilaire.[*]—I feel convinced that our

---

[*] Barthélémy St. Hilaire, a learned philosopher and member of the Institute, was born in 1815. During the Restoration he belonged to the Court of Exchequer. In 1833 he renounced politics for a time, and held professorships in the École Polytechnique and the Collége de France. At the revolution of February he joined the Government, and, as deputy for Seine-et-Oise, voted with the moderate party. He supported the Ministry of Odillon Barrot, but went over to the Gauche when the party of the Elysée seemed to favour a counter-revolution. M. St. Hilaire protested against the *coup d'état*, refused to take the oath, and renounced his professorship and the direction of the Collége de France. After 1854 he devoted himself entirely to learned pursuits, and took an active part in the discussions at the Académie des Sciences morales et politiques. In 1858, he was one of the Commission charged to study the question of the Suez Canal, and published in *les Débats* an account of his visit to Egypt in the company of M. Lesseps. Mr. Senior was of this party, and kept an interesting journal of all he saw. M. St. Hilaire has translated into French the entire works of Aristotle; he studied Sanscrit, and has written for the Académie papers on the Vedas and Budhism. He remained in Paris throughout the siege in 1870-1, and was elected a member of the National Assembly by an immense majority. M. St. Hilaire accepted the office of ' Chief of the Cabinet' during the Presidentship of M. Thiers, to whom he was a devoted friend, and he exercised great influence in the Government. He has always been a consistent Republican.— ED.

master feels that from the dangers which are closing
round him war is the only issue. He cannot allow
the parliamentary discussion of his policy to continue,
for it is killing his reputation. He cannot prohibit
it; that would be a sign of weakness. It would be
running away from a dog who barks at you. He
cannot safely keep the Pope in Rome. It is an opposition to Italian unity, which neither our revolutionary party nor the Italian Carbonari will tolerate.
He cannot safely drive him or frighten him out of
Rome. Even now, though Imperial soldiers guard
the Vatican, and protect the patrimony of St. Peter,
the disgust occasioned by Louis Napoleon's refusal
to defend the rest of the Pontifical States has shaken
his throne. It is the principal cause which is driving
him to seek support from his old enemies, the Rouges.
What will be the storm if he turns from a feeble
friend of the Pope to a real enemy? At present he
is suspected by everybody — by the *parti de l'ordre*
and by the revolutionists; by those who wish for
peace, and by those who wish for war; by the
friends of religion, and by its enemies. He must
choose. He will cast in his lot with the revolutionary,
the anti-Papal, the war party. It is the most active,
the most energetic, and the least scrupulous party.
Fleury, his confidant—if he has one—said the other
day to a friend of mine, ' By this time next year we
shall have the Rhine, and the world will be astonished to see how easily we shall get it.' If you
are quiescent, if you do not interfere until it is too

late, Fleury is right. And the *Chauvinist* feelings
of gratified ambition and gratified vanity may render
him strong enough to silence or destroy the Chambers,
drive the Pope into exile, and perhaps make himself
head of a schismatic Gallican Church.

. But if you come instantly to the assistance of
Germany, if a maritime war be as calamitous to
us as it has always been, if our commerce be ruined,
our harbours blockaded, our squadrons taken, and
the war drag on for six months, he is ruined. The
revenue will fall off, the conscription will be intolerable, the increase of the National debt will frighten
even our ignorant bourgeois—who now look on a
loan only as a *placement*, good, and therefore popular,
in proportion as it is improvident—and he will be
hooted out of the country, as his uncle was. But
how frightful it is to think that the most probable
escape from this despotism is through the humiliation of France. As has often been the case of
late, our destinies depend on your wisdom and your
courage. If you are wise enough to appreciate your
danger, and to provide the means of resisting it, and
bold enough to proclaim that you will use those
means, he may be deterred. A war with England,
fully prepared and exerting her full force, is a war
which he fears. He may seek to please the revolutionary party by other expedients. I think that he
will fail. I think that he will be overthrown if he
remains at peace, that he will be overthrown if he
makes an unsuccessful war, and that the only

chance of his continuance in power is a successful one.

I called on Circourt.

Believing, as every one. else that I have seen does, that war is imminent, he thinks that it will fall on Austria. He saw a letter yesterday from the governor of Temeswar to his wife in Paris, in which he begs her not to come with the children to Hungary. As far as he can ascertain, the governor says, the revolutionary party can command a force of 60,000 men, which is about the number of the Austrian troops.

Senior.—What will be the pretext of the war?

Circourt.—It will probably be brought on by Garibaldi. A large force obeying his orders is scattered over Piedmont and Lombardy. I believe that he will throw them, by the paths that wind among the spurs of the Alps to the north of Verona and Bergamo, into the plains watered by the Tagliamento, and excite revolutionary movements to the east of Venice. Austria will complain. Cavour will say that he is *débordé*, that he bitterly laments and strongly disapproves the invasion, but cannot control the popular movement. Austria may lose her temper, as she did in 1859, defeat the Garibaldians, and enter Lombardy; and then we interpose to protect the treaty of Villa Franca. Louis Napoleon may find another pretext, by summoning Austria to execute her part of the treaty, by giving a separate and

Italian administration to Venetia, withdrawing all foreign troops, and putting the country into the hands of a native army. 'I,' he will have a right to say, 'have performed my part. I have recalled my army, I have endeavoured to force Piedmont to perform her part. Her refusal does not release me from my engagements to the people of Venetia. I promised them freedom—even independence. Perhaps, when I consented to consider your engagement to give them a separate Italian administration as a performance of my promise, I scarcely kept faith with them. But I should be utterly faithless if I did not keep you to that engagement. I summon you, therefore, to withdraw within fourteen days all non-Italian troops from Venetia. If you refuse or neglect to do so, I am bound, as a man of honour, to remove them myself.'

Senior.—With what feeling will Prussia hear that such language has been used to a German power?

Circourt.—With delight. Her hatred of Austria is such that she will rejoice in her danger and in her humiliation. Bavaria, Wurtemberg, Hesse Darmstadt, and perhaps Baden, will stand by Austria. You, according to your practice, will temporise, wish us to be beaten, as you did in 1859, but spend nothing and risk nothing for the purpose. We shall beat Austria, allow Venetia to decide her destinies by universal suffrage, and take the Palatinate as our reward.

Prussia meantime will be fighting with Denmark,

and trying to absorb, first Schleswig Holstein, then
Oldenburg and Mecklenburg, and at last Hanover
and Saxony.

One of the worst fruits of 1848 was the delivery
of Jutland and Zeeland into the power of the mob.
The King, a dissolute coward, quailed before the
Copenhagen rioters, and gave them a radical constitution. They have used it, as might have been
expected, in tyrannising over the part of their fellow-
citizens with whom, as not being Jutes, they have no
sympathy. Holstein is altogether German. Schleswig
is inhabited by Jutes, Frisians, Angles, and Saxons,
the Jutes predominating only in the northern portion.
It had for centuries been, for the purposes of government, united to Holstein. They have had the same
states, the same courts, the same laws, the same
revenue, and the same administration. The Copenhagen radicals wish to alter all this. They want to
separate Schleswig and Holstein, to radicalise them
both, and to Danify Schleswig.

Schleswig and Holstein deny the power of the
Copenhagen mob to abolish their provincial constitutions. They say that the fact that the same person
who is sovereign of Schleswig and Holstein is also
king of Jutland does not authorise a Jutland mob
to dispose of provinces which, though under the same
sceptre, are as independent of Jutland as England
was of Hanover. Holstein is resolved to break off
from Denmark, and to become German. Schleswig
refuses to be separated from Holstein. Prussia wishes

to annex them both, and this attempt alone will occupy her sufficiently to prevent her assisting Austria, even if she wished to do so.

I called on Mme. Cornu,* and found there M. Maury, of the Academy of Inscriptions. He is assisting Louis Napoleon in his work on Julius Cæsar. I asked after its progress.

Maury.—Much is finished, and the materials for the rest are collected. He is still on his introduction, and is now at the times of the Gracchi. But some subsequent portions are completed, particularly the story of Catiline.

Madame Cornu.—Catiline was always one of his favourites. He maintains that Cicero and Sallust were unjust to him. At one time he almost thought him a *patriot incompris*, until he found that he had pillaged Africa as governor, and escaped condemnation only by being defended by Cicero.

Maury.—He says, with truth, that if Catiline had been, as Cicero makes him out, a mere robber, who wished to burn and pillage Rome, he would have

---

* Madame Cornu was the wife of an eminent artist. Her mother was *dame de compagnie* to Hortense, ex-queen of Holland. She was bred up as a sister with Louis Napoleon, visited him every year during his imprisonment at Ham, and corrected his writings. She continued devoted to him until the *coup d'état*, when she broke with him, and in spite of his persistent advances, would not be reconciled to him for nearly twelve years. She died before the war of 1870.—ED.

raised the slaves. The Emperor treats him as the leader of a political party — an extreme one, a mischievous one, but not a band of robbers and assassins.

Senior.—Is the Emperor still absorbed in his literary work?

Maury.—As much as ever. To-day 'when I entered he was dictating a portion of it. He thinks much more about it than about Italy. He does not like the theatre, excepting sometimes farces that amuse him. He cares little for society. His delight is to get to his study, put on his dressing-gown and slippers, and work at his history.

Senior.—What sort of a scholar is he?

Maury.—In Latin, far above the average of educated Frenchmen ; perhaps on a par with educated Englishmen : he reads it without difficulty.

We continued to talk about Louis Napoleon after Maury had left us.

Mme. Cornu showed me a vase of jade, taken from the palace of Pekin, which he sent to her the day before yesterday. It came without the cover. This morning, Thelin, the Emperor's servant, who managed his escape from Ham, brought her the cover. 'The Emperor,' he said, 'spent all yesterday in looking for it.'

Mme. Cornu.—Louis Napoleon is a strange being. One who did not know him would think that he had enough to do without wasting a day in looking for the cover of a vase. But it is just like him. His mind wants keeping. A trifle close to his eyes hides from him the largest object at a distance. I have no doubt that what Thelin said was true, and that he did spend three or four hours yesterday hunting for the cover of that vase. He wished to send it to me, and, for the time, that wish absorbed him.

Senior.—What are your relations with him now?

Mme. Cornu.—We do not meet, but we correspond. I am his *intermédiaire* with many of the German literati. I get for him information for his book, as I did when he was at Ham for his book on artillery.

We lived together, from our births till I was about fourteen and he was about eighteen. During the first seven years of this time he was surrounded by all the splendour of a court. During the last eight he was in Germany, looked down on by the Germans—who would scarcely admit the Bonapartes to be gentry, and would call him Monsieur Bonaparte—and seeing nobody but his mother and her suite. Afterwards he lived in Italy and in Switzerland, among Italians or Swiss, but never with French people.

His long exclusion from the society of the higher classes of his countrymen, and in a great measure from the higher classes of the foreigners among whom he resided, did him harm in many ways. It is wonderful that it did not spoil his manners. He was saved, perhaps, by having always before him so admirable a model as his mother. But it made him somewhat of a *parvenu*—what you would call a tuft-hunter. He looked up to people of high rank with a mixture of admiration, envy, and dislike. The more difficult he found it to get into their society, the more he disliked them and the more he courted them. I had an odd proof in myself of his fondness for mere titles. I had been at a German court, where they proposed to make me a *dame d'honneur*.

'Impossible,' I answered, 'for I am not noble.'

'But,' they replied, 'we will make you noble.'

When I told this to Louis Napoleon, he said, 'Why did you not accept? You might have afterwards given up the office, and kept your nobility.' I could not make him understand my contempt for such artificial nobility.

The great progress in political knowledge made by the higher classes of the French between 1815 and 1848 was lost to him. When we met in 1826, after three years of absence, I was struck with his backwardness as to all political matters. While I had been learning he had been stationary. The works of his uncle, and the conversation of his mother and of her friends, all old imperialists, formed his political education. He learned something in Italy which was bad, and in Switzerland which was good, and more in England, the country that he likes best.

During his adult life he has taken a little from every country in which he has resided, except from France. In France he has never lived, except as a

child, a prisoner, or a sovereign. It will seem a
paradox to you, that it is to his want of sympathy
with the feelings of the higher classes in France, and
to dislike or ignorance of their opinions, that I
attribute much of his success. His opinions and
feelings are those of the French people from 1799 to
1812, as they were fashioned by Napoleon during his
thirteen years of despotism, war, and victory. Now,
those opinions and feelings, all modified or abandoned
by our higher classes, are still those of the multitude.
They despise parliamentary government, despise the
Pope, despise the priests, delight in profuse expenditure, delight in war, hold the Rhine to be our
rightful frontier, and that it is our duty to seize all
that is within it, and have no notion of any foreign
policy except one of aggression and domination. The
people and he, therefore, perfectly agree. It is not
that he has learned their sentiments—how could he
in prison or in exile?—but that they are his own.
I have no doubt that the little that he heard, and the
less that he attended to, from the persons whom he
saw between 1848 and 1852, about liberty, self-
government, economy, the supremacy of the Assembly, respect for foreign nations, and fidelity to
treaties, appeared to him to be the silliest trash.

So it would have appeared to all the lower classes
in France, so it would have appeared to the army,
drawn from those classes, and exaggerating their
political errors.

As soon, therefore, as he appealed from the aristo-

cracy and the bourgeoisie to the lower classes and
the army, as soon as the people and the army recog-
nised the tone, and the feelings, and the opinions of
the Empire, they rushed enthusiastically to his side.
I do not, as many persons do, admire him for having
shown quickness of apprehension in divining the
sentiments of the people, or even in conjecturing
them : he simply took them for granted. He supposed the Orleanists and Legitimists to be governed
by their prejudices, and the Parliamentarians by their
vanities or their interests, and all the rest of the
nation to be Bonapartist, to participate in the *Idées
Napoléoniennes.*

Those were *his* ideas. He naturally believed that
they were those of the people, and he was right.

Senior.—Do you believe that he intends war?

Mme. Cornu.—I do not. I believe that he intends peace. He will not seek war, though it may
be forced on him.

Senior.—From Hungary?

Mme. Cornu.—I think not. The Hungarians are
poor creatures. Prince Napoleon told me that after
Solferino the Emperor desired him to talk to Kossuth
and Klapka. They admitted to him that at that
time there were only 10,000 Austrian troops in
Hungary, yet they asked for the assistance of 30,000
Frenchmen to enable the Hungarians to rise.

Senior.—What has been the effect of the parliamentary discussion?

Mme. Cornu.—Good. He is delighted. It has

proved his confidence and his strength. His enemies
have shown how unfit they are to govern, and on
one important point, on which he is opposed to the
republican party, Italian unity, the nation has declared itself on his side.

I called on General de Fénélon, the son-in-
law of Marshal Randon, Minister of War, and
found there Admiral Fourichon. We talked of the
trireme.

Fourichon.—I think that with her 126 oars she
might make in calm water from four to five knots an
hour. A light wind, giving her some assistance from
her sail, without much sea, might help her a little.
The Emperor seems to have solved the problem of the
trireme. But what was a pentecontor? What were
the vessels propelled by oars, aud large enough to
carry six hundred soldiers, besides their rowers, and
provisions and water for ten days?

We talked of the demolition and rebuilding of
Paris, of the restoration of the Sainte Chapelle and
of Notre Dame, of the churches of Caen, and, at last,
of the Duomo of Milan.

Fénélon.—I was there for so short a time I
scarcely saw it.

Fourichon.—I hope that you will be there again
soon, and for much longer.

As he spoke these words he left us, and I asked

Fénélon if he thought Fourichon's wishes likely to be accomplished.

Fénélon.—No; the Emperor does not wish for war. No preparations are going on. Half the army is *en congé.* No one has better opportunities of judging than my father-in-law, and he utterly disbelieves in war, except in one event, an attack on us by Prussia.*

Senior.—That supposes the Prussians to be absolutely mad.

Fénélon.—It supposes them only to be *passionés,* for a nation under the dominion of passion ceases to reason. Here is a pile of Prussian pamphlets and newspapers, full of threats and of plans for dismembering us. Look at the motto of this pamphlet, written by a friend of mine: '*Frisch gewagt ist halb gewonnen.*' They admit that they shall be beaten for three years, but by that time their soldiers are to have become veterans, and they will have found out their generals. This, without doubt, is madness, but such madness is incidental to Germans. The Prussians of 1861 are not madder than their fathers were in 1805.

Senior.—Well, I do not share your fears of a Prussian aggression; my fears are from Italy.

Fénélon.—There, again, the only danger is from passion.

---

* I believe Fénélon said this on purpose to have it reported. —N. W. SENIOR.

Senior.—Is there none from interest? Does not France think it her interest to prevent the unity of Italy? May not the Emperor think it his interest to divert your attention from home affairs to foreign ones?

Fénélon.—Why should he? You live among his enemies, who have convinced themselves, and try to convince you, that he is unpopular. And so he is, among those whom he excludes from power. But that is not the case with the bulk of the nation. He has given to us security and tranquillity at home, he has restored to us our south-western frontier, and has replaced France, where she ought to be, at the head of the Continent. The debates on the address have shown his confidence and his popularity. The fullest liberty, the freest license, have been given; a liberty and a license, of which his uncle, in his best days, would have been afraid. And the result is a general ratification of his policy, at home and abroad. Of liberty we have as much as is fit for us, and as much as we wish for.

As to Italian unity, I see no objection to it. I think, that, for the next fifty years, the King of Italy must lean on us. I admit, that almost all Frenchmen, except the Republican party, dislike it as much as the Emperor does; but neither he, nor we, think its prevention worth a war. We do not believe, indeed, in its permanence.

Senior.—And what do you expect in its place?

Fénélon.—A *gachis.*

Senior.—A Murat in Naples?

Fénélon.—That would be giving Sicily to you.

Senior.—We would not take it.

Fénélon.—I did not mean that you would take it under your sovereignty, but merely under your protectorate. It is the most fertile country in Europe.

Senior.—What use would its fertility be to us, except for purposes of trade, and we can trade with Sicily without being encumbered by its protectorate? The Ionian Islands have cured us of protectorates. What will be the fate of the Pope in the '*gachis?*'

Fénélon.—We shall remain in Rome to protect him. To leave him in the hands of the Piedmontese would be to transfer to Piedmont the influence which we now possess, by holding in our hands the Head of the Church.

Senior.—And what will be the fate of Piedmont?

Fénélon.—If she has sense, she may keep what she has in northern Italy, down to the frontiers of Umbria and the Marches. If she is mad, and attacks Austria she will be disgracefully beaten. I have served two campaigns by the side of the Piedmontese army, and know what it is.

Senior.—When did you reach the Crimea?

Fénélon.—Just after the fall of Sebastopol. Your army became towards the end of the war a very fine one, equal to the best that I have seen. It excited the admiration of Lüders, the Russian general, to whom we gave a review.

Senior.—What was the Russian?

Fénélon.—I saw little of it. I went once or twice to Simferopol, the head-quarters. The men looked dirty and poor. Some of the officers came to visit us. About one in a hundred was a gentleman, and the gentlemen were distinguished men ; but the other ninety-nine were blackguards, ignorant and drunken. We soon found it necessary to refuse to see any who did not bring special recommendations.

Monday, April 8th.—I called this morning on D. E. F., and we went together to a great printing-house.

D. E. F.—I feel some doubt whether Louis Napoleon has gained or lost by the recent debates. He has changed his fulcrum. Till now he relied on the anti-revolutionary party, on those who were willing, nay, eager,

'Propter vitam vivendi perdere causas,'

whom *le Spectre Rouge* frightened into the sacrifice of freedom of action, of speech, almost of thought, for the sake of servile safety. All distrusted him, all feared him, many hated him, but they crouched under him for protection. The revolutionary party feared him, too, but their fear was mixed with hope. They thought that they saw war under his promises of peace, apostasy under his Catholicism, plunder and socialism under his conservative mask. He is now showing them that they were right. By quarrelling with the Church, by courting the revolutionary party in Italy and in Hungary, by admitting that the uneducated masses have a right to drive out their sovereigns and to change all the domestic institutions and all the foreign relations of their countries, by proclaiming, in fact, the doctrine of *Le peuple souverain*, he has gained the Revolutionists and necessarily lost the Conservatives. *Il a changé d'assiette.*

His new supporters are more active, more energetic, more unscrupulous than his old ones were. They make revolutions ; the *parti de l'ordre* merely submits to them. But they are far more *exigeants*, more impulsive, and less consistent ; and what makes them more formidable, they are honest. Their objects are often ill chosen, for their knowledge is superficial, and their prejudices and their passions are violent, but they are willing to sacrifice whatever they have, often not much more than their lives, in the pursuit of them. They sympathise with Louis Napoleon in most of his hatreds. They hate the Pope, they hate the bourgeoisie, they hate the aristocracy, they hate parliamentary government. They sympathise also with many of his desires. They like an insolent, interfering, aggressive foreign policy ; they like to see treaties torn up, international law laughed at, the rights and interests of foreign nations disregarded, in short, every restraint on the will or the caprice of France broken through. They like to see all this begun and maintained by an enormous army and a profuse expenditure.

They differ from him in some respects. He is

opposed to Italian unity ; they have set their hearts on it. Garibaldi is their hero. They would precipitate a war with England; he is, I think, determined on having one, but would defer it.

Senior.—What are your grounds for thinking that he is determined on a war with England ?

D. E. F.—My grounds are his maritime preparations. I hear that they are working day and night at Toulon ; the tone of his newspapers, the care which he takes to keep open or to create subjects of quarrel with you. He never will settle with you the question of the Newfoundland fisheries. He is trying to irritate France against you on the Syrian business. We care nothing about Syria ; we have no subjects there, or commerce, or even travellers. But for him, we should never have heard of Druses or Maronites. He claims for France the protectorate over the Maronites. I believe that he himself excited the Druses against them, and them against the Druses. His papers accuse you of being the protectors of the Druses ; they publish the most extravagant lies about the massacres of the Maronites. They accuse you of having occasioned those massacres, and of trying to screen your instruments, the Druses. I have been requested to become a member of a society over which the Archbishop of Paris presides, the object is to relieve the sufferings of the Christians in Syria. The Archbishop sent word to me that my presence would be useful, as it would show the sympathy of the Republicans with the Eastern Christians. I consented, partly because it was difficult to refuse such an appeal, and partly because I hope to be useful in preventing their mixing politics with their benevolence. But I fear that I may have to retire.

Your only real friends are the Constitutionalists, among whom I include the Republicans. We, the Republicans, prefer a republic to a constitutional monarchy. My expectation is, that Louis Napoleon will be overthrown by an unsuccessful war. My wish is, that he should fall under the hatred and contempt which are accumulating against him in peace.

Senior.—But you admit that the Conservatives do not make revolutions?

D. E. F.—No, but the Republicans do. There are 400 men in the *atelier* which we have just quitted; I could carry every one of them to die behind a barricade. Between us and the Revolutionists is the common bond of honesty, of a real wish to serve the people, and a real determination to meet danger in their cause. By our writings, by our conversations, even by the parliamentary debates, poor as they are, we hope to instruct the Revolutionists. If their eyes are opened they and we together will shake down by a single effort the imperial structure which nothing but their ignorance, and the passions produced by their ignorance, allowed to rise.

Tuesday, April 9th.—I called this morning on Vuitry. He is Vice-President of the Financial Committee of the Conseil d'ètat.

I asked him as to the state of the French armaments.

Vuitry.—They are on their usual establishment, except that our 25,000 men in Rome, 12,000 in China, and 13,000 in Syria, require an excess of 50,000 men. But after these extras, our army amounts to only 400,000 men.

Senior.—And is not that 100,000 too much? Louis Philippe had not more than 300,000.

Vuitry.—I quite agree with you, 300,000 men would be ample. But our master likes to be feared, and to arrange the affairs of Europe as it may suit him. He has gratified his ambition, and now wishes to gratify his vanity.

Senior.—And what is the object of his maritime preparations? Are they also mere scarecrows, to frighten without being used?

Vuitry.—His maritime preparations are made merely in obedience to the Report of the Naval Commission of 1849. It recommended seventeen millions extra a-year to be employed in the transformation of our fleet from sails to steam. We are doing no more than was then decided on, with the assent of the Assembly which was certainly pacific.

Senior.—But your *vaisseaux blindés* are in addition to this sum.

Vuitry.—No; they are included in it; we make only two a-year. You are right in preparing yourselves; but I see no symptom of warlike intentions here. If war were probable, the Emperor would not

set on foot these enormous public works, nor would
capitalists be found to carry them on.

Senior.—What is the revenue of the city of
Paris ?

Vuitry.—110,000,000.

Senior.—And the debt ?

Vuitry.—270,000,000 (about 11,000,000*l.* sterling).
We consider our Parisian finances as flourishing,
especially by comparison. Marseilles owes 38,000,000,
and is borrowing 38,000,000 more. Amiens is deeply
in debt ; so, indeed, is every large town. I own that
I look on all this with alarm. A building crisis in
Paris, though not imminent, seems to be certain.
The prices of labour, and of materials, and of land,
are constantly rising. Unless the price of houses
rises too, there must be a loss. As yet the rise in
rent and in price has kept pace with the increased
expense of construction. But the supply of large
houses must in time overtake the demand. Péreire
alone has entered into building contracts to the
amount of 40,000,000, (1,600,000*l.*) The aggregate
of the engagements of smaller men must be much
greater. All the houses are mortgaged. As soon as
the supply exceeds the demand they will cease to be
worth the mortgage money. 1000, or 10,000 houses,
may be put up to sale in one day. 50,000, or 100,000
men may be suddenly out of work. There will be
wide private ruin, and perhaps public danger.

Senior.—What is the state of your other trades ?

Vuitry.—The silk trade is suffering from the bad

state of the American market. No ribbons are bought, and St. Étienne is starving. The cotton manufacturers are frightened by the treaty. They are not afraid, they say, of English competition in ordinary periods. They can make a profit at the price which gives a profit in England. But if a commercial crisis comes, if vast masses of English or Scotch goods must be sold for what they will fetch, however below the cost of production, the market may be spoiled for months. They may have to reduce wages, to work their mills at short time, and even at short time to accumulate stocks. The strong would get through such difficulties, the weak would sink. The trades that are in the best state are the metallurgic trades.

Circourt, the Mohls, Simon, D. E. F., and St. Hilaire, breakfasted with us. M. de Chambrun came in late. He had been in court, where his claim for the value of a house, that had been taken for one of the new boulevards, was disposed of this morning.

M. de Chambrun.—The jury has given me all that I asked, 250,000 francs, about twenty-five years' purchase, which is good for house property. When it was over, one of the jurymen said to me, 'You might have had twice as much, if you had asked for it. We gave yesterday 5000 francs for a cottage worth 2000. We think that the only way of stopping this mania of demolition is to give whatever is asked.

Simon.—I am not sure that such a treatment will

cure the malady.   Madame Haùsmann, the wife of the
Préfet de la Seine, said to a friend of mine, ' No one
is safe.   Not less than twenty-seven houses belonging
to my husband have been pulled down, many just
after he had bought them.   It seems to me that his
placements in houses are a source of constant plaguè.
No sooner does he buy a house than it is demolished.'

Senior.—I hear that Madame ———'s beautiful
house in the Champs Elysèes is to be pulled down.

Circourt.—Hausmann has nothing to do with that.
You know that Madame ——— and Morny have long
been in partnership.   When his marriage put an end
to the connexion, the accounts were settled by arbi-
tration.   A balance was awarded to her, but much
less than her claim.   She went crying to the Emperor,
and said that she was ruined, that the arbitrators
had favoured Morny as a great man and a friend of
the Emperor's, and that she could not live in her
house.   The Emperor cannot refuse any application;
so he told her that if she must give up her house, he
would get her a good price for it.   But he found that
it could not be easily sold standing—at least, for a
price above its value.   So it was resolved to make it
a case of *expropriation pour cause d'utilité publique.*
For this purpose a vast space around the *rond point*
is to be cleared, including, of course, the site of
Madame ———'s house; and large hotels are to
be built, with gardens in front of them.   She will
get for her house twice what it cost her; it will be
pulled down, and the site become a grass plot.

St. Hilaire.—The history of Billault's house is amusing. The Emperor gave it to him—at least, the money to build it. He was living in it when he became minister. Whereupon he said, ' As minister, I must be lodged by the Government. I do not wish to give trouble, or to create expense. I am satisfied with the modest house which I inhabit. I will let it to the Government, and have no objection to continuing to reside in it.'

D. E. F.—I wish that the greatest crimes of the Government were its jobs. I could bear its prodigality, if it refrained from positive oppression.

Senior.—What is the sort of oppression to which you allude ?

D. E. F.—Its interference with the course of justice between man and man. An humble friend of mine, a watchmaker, is married to a woman who is a *chemisière*. She received an order from the wife of the Marquis ———, a man high in the Emperor's favour, for some dozens of chemises and window-blinds, much worked, for they were to cost 3800 francs. They were sent home. The Marchioness was much pleased with them, and without paying for them gave a further order. The two orders amounted to 6000 francs. The woman consulted her husband. Six thousand francs was about half the amount of her capital, the fruit of twenty-five years of saving; and she feared being out of it for some time. The husband joined in her fears, and resolved not to execute the second order until the first was paid for. When the bill was sent to the Marchioness, she referred my friend to her husband. The Marquis looked at it, and said, ' My good friend, I am very sorry for you. You have lost your 3800 francs. I give to my wife a monthly allowance, quite sufficient for her just wants, and I make it perfectly well known that I never pay her debts. If I acted otherwise, she would ruin me.' My friend first argued, then implored, and at last said that he would not be *volé impunément.*

' You call me,' said the Marquis, ' *un voleur.* If a witness were present, you would spend the rest of your life in prison.'

My friend went to the *juge de paix,* and made his complaint.

' Are you aware,' said the judge, ' of what you are doing ? That you are proposing to bring an action against a man *haut placé, et dans la faveur de l'Empereur?* Even if you could succeed, you would be ruined, for what *honnête homme* would employ you or your wife after you had made such a scandal ? But you will fail, and you will go to prison for the costs.'

' *Bien,*' said the watchmaker, ' *alors je saurai ce que c'est que la justice en France.*'

' *Quoi,*' said the judge, ' *vous injuriez la justice? Savez-vous que c'est une affaire de la police correctionelle ?*'

' *Je n'injure pas la justice,*' said my friend, ' *je dis seulement que je saurai ce qu'elle est.*'

My friend is a resolute man. He has stood behind a barricade, and has moral as well as physical courage. He is of the stuff of which martyrs are made. The action was brought and failed. My friend, as I said, is a martyr. Foiled in a civil action, he resolved to prosecute the Marchioness for *escroquerie*. But a new difficulty arose. No advocate of any eminence would undertake his cause. I applied to several; to men whom their liberal sympathies would, as I weakly supposed, have made eager to support a poor man in his contest with a rich and powerful robber. Not one of them has sufficient leisure. The whole bar seems to be overwhelmed with business. At last we have obtained the services of a man, not eminent enough to have much to risk—but we shall fail. Not only will my friend be ruined, but his oppressor will escape exposure. The trial will not excite interest. it will be ill-pleaded, and the journals will not be allowed to report it.

Madame Mohl.—I do not wonder at the refusal of the advocates. Such is the base servility of our judges, that the Government can always ruin any advocate by whom it has been offended. *Le mot d'ordre* is given to them that his clients shall always fail. This is soon found out, and his practice is gone.

St. Hilaire.—I have known many such instances. No prudent man takes legal proceedings against a friend of the Government. No prudent advocate will plead such a cause.

Senior.—What is the cause of the Emperor's em-barrassments ? With more than a million sterling a-year, how has he managed to owe three years' income ?

Circourt.—Profuse liberality and unlimited *gas-pillage.* Almost everything that he, or any of the court, have touched, or looked at, becomes perquisite. Perquisites are the sieves through which the revenues of great houses leak. Toward the end of her reign, the Empress Catherine found that the civil list of her son Paul was much in debt. She sent for the accounts, and found a charge for some thousands of bottles of brandy for her son's own use. She was alarmed, and talked to him about it. He assured her that he never touched brandy. She sent for earlier accounts, and still found charges for brandy, which were at last traced up to the day of his birth. It appeared that when he was born, there were some slight excoriations on his legs. The nurse had sent for a glass of brandy as a lotion for them. From that time a bottle of brandy was sent to him, or, at least, charged to him, every day.

April 11th.—Madame Cornu, Mrs. Grote, Madame Mohl, Circourt, Target, Duvergier, and Lèonce de Lavergne,* breakfasted with us.

---

* Léonce de Lavergne, a well-known politician and writer on political economy and agriculture. In early life he was one of the chief editors of the *Revue du Midi.* In 1842 he went to

Circourt told us that he had acquired a new neighbour—the Emperor—who has purchased Malmaison, and a considerable tract all round it, and is busy planting and gardening.

Circourt.—He comes to Malmaison once or twice a-week, pointing out, indeed writing on little tickets, with his own hands, the place for every shrub. He is a most considerate purchaser, pays liberally, and is anxious that no one should suffer inconvenience by removal. A strange contrast to the indifference with which he turns tens of thousands into the streets, to make a boulevard or a square.

Madame Cornu.—I have often said of him *qu'il a la sensibilité dans l'œil.* He is deeply affected by any distress that he actually sees. He is indifferent to any that is not brought before him in detail. One day I found him at Ham in great grief. The man who waited on him had died the day before, leaving a wife and family in distress.

' I gave them,' he said to me, ' three hundred francs, but that will do little.'

Paris, entered the Conseil d'Etat as *Maître des Requêtes*, then became sub-director in the Ministry for foreign affairs, and deputy in 1846. After the Revolution of 1848 he resigned office, and wrote, for the *Revue des Deux Mondes*, articles on contemporary history, political economy, &c. In 1855 he succeeded M. Léon Faucher as Member of the Académie des Sciences morales et politiques. In 1871 he was elected a member of the National Assembly by a majority of 30,115 votes, and sat on the Right Centre ; but his health has prevented his taking much part in politics. He is a member of the Senate.—ED.

'How much have you left?' I asked.

'Sixty,' he answered. 'I can manage with that for a fortnight, until my next remittances come. The Government must lodge and feed me.'

While we were talking, the man's daughter—a girl of about fourteen—came in to thank him. She was weeping, and he began to sob too. Suddenly he went to his *escritoire*, took out the sixty francs that he had left, and gave them to her.

'It is lucky,' I said, 'that I have 100 francs more than my journey home will cost me.' So I gave them to him, or I should have left him utterly penniless.

Senior.—How came he to be so poor? I was told that when he was taken at Boulogne he had 160,000 francs, which were deposited with the Maire, and returned to him after his trial.

Madame Cornu.—He had much more than that. His coat was lined with banknotes. It disappeared with its contents; but, as you say, the 160,000 francs were returned to him. He sold, too, almost all the little property which he had; but nearly all went in buying up the pensions to which the old servants of his mother were entitled.

He said to them, 'I am condemned to imprisonment for life. With my active habits, imprisonment will kill me in a few years, and my will may not be respected. You had better take the value of your pension, while I am allowed to pay it to you.'

Almost all that remained he spent in allowances to those who had accompanied him in his expedition, and were in different prisons. Persigny had a great deal. The result was, that during the latter part of his imprisonment he was very poor, and had the utmost difficulty in getting together the money which was necessary for his escape.

April 13*th.*—Count Zamoyski* called on us. He is looking anxiously on the Polish movement.

Zamoyski.—The only results of the last insurrection were thirty years of misery and servitude. It is

* [This note has been kindly given to me by a Polish friend.]

General Count Ladislas Zamoyski, one of the most eminent of the Poles of the last half century, was aide-de-camp to the Grand Duke Constantine previously to the commencement of the revolution of 1830–31, in which he took a leading part. After the revolution was suppressed he proceeded to Cracow, and thence to Paris, where he took up his residence with his uncle, Prince Adam Czartoryski. He was frequently employed by the Prince on diplomatic missions, and the skill and ability which he displayed on these occasions gained him a high reputation among the European governments. When the Crimean war broke out he proposed to Lord Palmerston that a Polish legion should be formed in England for the purpose of assisting the Poles to recover their independence, which, he urged, would far more effectually cripple the power of Russia than the destruction of Sebastopol. Lord Palmerston declined this proposal, saying that he did not ' wish to make an enemy of Russia;' but he permitted the formation of a Polish corps in Turkey, under the name of the Cossacks of the Sultan, as a contingent to the British army in the Crimea. The close of the war after the capture of Sebastopol dashed the hopes of the Poles. Count Zamoyski, however, did not relax his efforts to serve the cause of his country, and to the day of his death he neglected no opportunity to bring the Polish question before the parliaments and the governments of Europe. He was well known and respected among our statesmen of some twenty years ago as an able negotiator and a warm-hearted patriot, animated with a chivalrous spirit which is too seldom found in the political men of the day.—G.

a proof of the wonderful vigour of Polish nationality, that those thirty years have not Russianised us. The higher orders might have been expected to retain their Polish feelings, but the lower classes might have been forgiven if they had adopted the sentiments and habits of the great nation with which they have been incorporated—if they had become Russians, as the Alsatians have become French, and the Scotch and Welsh have become English. But it has not been so. The lower classes are as anti-Russian as the higher. A thousand peasants, with scythes and pitchforks for arms, crowded to Warsaw as soon as they heard the firing. The Polish *employés* have given up their situations. Every document printed in Russian is ignored. The streets are full of people, quiet and unarmed, who chant prayers for deliverance to the Virgin—the Queen of Poland. Gortschakoff asked the crowd what grievance they had to complain of. ' That you are here,' was the answer.

Senior.—Have they refused to pay taxes?

Zamoyski.—Not as yet. After the insurrection of 1831, Nicholas thoroughly disarmed the country. There cannot be a civil war, as the Poles have no means of fighting. I rejoice in this. It is almost a compensation for all the misery that Nicholas inflicted on us.

Senior.—But if you pay your taxes, and remain quiet at home, what harm does your passive resistance do to Russia? It is a mere protestation.

Zamoyski.—It injures the prestige of Russia. Government, you know, is a matter of opinion. No sovereign could reign if his subjects were unanimously disaffected. Now, as far as the Poles are concerned, this is the case with Russian Poland. They make no specific complaint, they ask for no redress, they do not promise that on any conditions whatever they will be good subjects; their only answer to expostulation is, 'We want to undo the partition; we want restitution; we want a wicked injustice to be redressed. We have been kidnapped; we want to be set free.' No concessions, no reforms, no favours, will satisfy this demand. We do not ask for good government, we require self-government. As Russia will not voluntarily grant this, and we cannot force her to do so, I cannot see my way to any solution of the Polish question, unless France and England, or one of them, interfere. Prussia is hostile to us, Austria is hostile to us; even Hungary, though we have a common enemy, does not sympathise with us.

Senior.—In what capacity were you in Hungary during the insurrection?

Zamoyski.—As a spectator, I was sent thither by my uncle. He wished one of his family to watch what was taking place.

Senior.—What impression did Kossuth make on you?

Zamoyski.—That of a very great speaker, and of a very great rogue. He seemed to me to be a man without moral sense—without any perception of the difference between right and wrong. When he was on his way to England, he made a violent anti-English speech at Marseilles. Some days after he panegyrised England at Southampton. When we met, I alluded to the difference between the two speeches. ' Of course,' he answered, ' the character of a speech depends on the character of the audience.' I was returning to France, through Turkey, when he was there as a refugee. He sent word to me that he was unwell, and begged me to visit him. I found him with Batthyany and Perczel.

Senior.—Who are they?

Zamoyski.—Batthyany is the brother of a man whom you must know in England. He was one of Kossuth's ministers, and highly valued by him. He said that if he could give a king to Hungary, it should be Batthyany. Perczel was their best general.

Senior.—I thought that Gœrgei had been their best.

Zamoyski.—No. Gœrgei is a good general of division, but not a great commander. He is a rascal. He was put at the head of the Polish army, in order to capitulate, as the Russians would not treat with Kossuth. Instead of capitulating, he surrendered at discretion—perhaps I ought not to say at discretion, for he made one stipulation, and only one — it was for his own personal safety. The Russians shot twelve generals, his companions in arms, the next day. Well, when I found Kossuth, Batthyany, and Perczel, they sent me a paper, drawn up by Kossuth, which they had signed, and sent to the Porte. It was to offer Hungary to the Sultan.

' We find,' it said, 'that we were mistaken as to the Turkish Government. We find that it is liberal and enlightened, and in the name of Hungary we request that she be incorporated in the Turkish dominions.'

The Hungarian movement can come to no good. The Magyars, Slavs, and Germans, will never coalesce. As soon as they are released from the weight of the Austrian throne, they will split into fragments. I hear that the inhabitants of the military colonies — the refuse of all countries, thieves and murderers—are now requiring their nationality to be respected.

I dined at the Embassy, and met Lord Clyde. Just as I was going thither, M. de Chambrun brought me the Duc d'Aumale's letter to Prince Napoleon.*

---

* The following are some passages from the Duc d'Aumale's letter to Prince Napoleon.

'One thing astounds me, and that is, that my grandfather found no favour in your sight: for you, like him, sat on the left side of a Republican Assembly. There, indeed, the resemblance stops, for he expiated his fault. He left the National Convention to mount the scaffold, while you descended from the benches of the Mountain to enter the splendid mansion in which the Duke of Orleans was born. When the Bonapartes threaten to shoot people, their word may be relied upon. And note this, Prince, that of all the promises made by you and yours, that is the only one upon which I could rely. For it must be admitted that the present French Government, all fortunate as it has been in many respects, is less successful as regards the fulfilment of promises than in other things. One man only swore to the

' It has just appeared,' he ˜said, ' and of course will be seized as soon as the authorities have heard of it.'

I took it with me to the Embassy. We looked at it before dinner, and Lord Cowley rather laughed at Chambrun's expectations.

Lord Cowley.—It is forcible, and would be worth suppressing ; but it will be republished in London and in Belgium, and the seizure would only advertise it.

He sent, however, for half a-dozen copies, as I have done; but the answer to our messenger was, ' *Saisie.*'

After dinner I had a long conversation with Lord Cowley. I asked his opinion as to Louis Napoleon's plans.

Lord Cowley.—I believe that he has none. He feels that he is in a great scrape in Italy—sees no issue, and waits till events open one. The last campaign has sickened him of war. It has shown him vividly its calamities and its dangers ; and of

---

Republican Constitution, and that man was the author of the 2nd of December. The same man said, The Empire is peace : and we have had the wars of the Crimea and Lombardy. In 1859 Italy was to be free to the Adriatic ; Austria is still at Verona and Venice. The temporal power of the Pope was to be respected : we know what has become of that : and the Grand Dukes are still waiting for their restoration which was announced by the Peace of Villafranca.'—ED.

all wars, that which he most dreads is one with
England. 'I believe that he agrees with me in
thinking an invasion impossible, except in the event
(which also appears to me impossible) of his having
the command of the sea.

When we were talking one day of his naval
armaments, he said, 'I know that as against you
they are useless. I know that you will always be
our superiors at sea, and I would reduce our naval
armaments if I could. But the French have set their
hearts on being at least the second maritime power,
and I do not venture to disappoint them. I know,'
he added, 'that with the new artillery, neither your
arsenals nor ours are safe. *Corvettes blindés* and
canons rayés could destroy either, or both of them.
And this would be to the advantage of those who,
at the beginning of a war, are masters at sea.'

Senior.—Was he sincere?

Lord Cowley.—I think so. I do not believe him
to be false of malice prepense, though he often appears
to be so. He is a bad politician ; he has no advisers
whom he ought to trust, or does trust. He is a man
travelling without a guide or a map in a country
which he imperfectly knows. Such a man may announce that is he going to a particular place, and
may fully intend to do so ; but he may take the
wrong road, or he may find on his way a mountain
or a river of which he knew nothing.

When Drouyn de Lhuys left office he told me
that he knew of no one to put in his place.

He asked my advice. I did not venture to give any.

Later in the evening I talked to J. K.

J. K.—While Drouyn de Lhuys was in Vienna I saw Louis Napoleon every day. He was at that time anxious for peace.

' I do not know,' he said, ' what is thought of the English generals, but ours seem to me to know little of European war, and this double command is fatal. Why cannot the English take the command of the united fleet, and we of the united army? Let their contingent to the army be one-fifth, and let us supply one-fifth of the naval force.'

' I see,' I answered, ' only one difficulty. The general who commands the English contingent, and all under him, will obey implicitly every order of the French commander-in-chief. But not a captain of a French gunboat will obey the English admiral.'

It was, I think, on a Sunday that I heard that Drouyn de Lhuys and Lord John had arranged a peace, and he sent for me on Tuesday. He was walking and smoking in the garden, and he asked me to walk up and down, and talk the matter over.

' I think,' he said, ' that it is a good arrangement. What think you ? '

' Well,' I said, ' it does not appear to me that the Russian predominance in the Black Sea will be materially affected.'

'Not,' he replied, 'by our having now a right to keep an equal force there?'

'She is to keep Sebastopol,' I answered. 'Her fleet will be at home, and will always be there. France and England will be tired of keeping large fleets far from all their resources in a dangerous sea. In a year or two Russia will be as much mistress of the Black Sea, and as dangerous to Constantinople, as she was when we went to war in 1854.'

'I will talk the matter over again with Drouyn de Lhuys,' he answered.

I said, from a sudden impulse which I am not sure I was right in following:

'Would there be any objection to my being present?'

He looked a little surprised, and then said, 'Certainly not;' and he appointed an hour for the next day.

When I arrived, Vaillant was in the ante-chamber, and Drouyn de Lhuys with the Emperor.

'The game is up,' I thought. 'Drouyn de Lhuys has gained the Emperor's ear.'

We were soon introduced. The Emperor begged Drouyn de Lhuys to explain the grounds of his arrangement.

Drouyn de Lhuys did so at considerable length. I think that he talked for nearly half-an-hour. The Emperor seemed to go along with him, and when he had finished said to me:

'Are you not satisfied?'

'My only answer,' I said, 'is to beg your Majesty to ask Marshal Vaillant whether he thinks that this arrangement will really effect the purpose of the war —the putting an end to the preponderance of Russia in the Black Sea and the Bosphorus.'

The Emperor turned to Vaillant.

'I am not a politician,' said Vaillant, 'but I know the feelings of the army. I am sure that if, after having spent months in the siege of Sebastopol, we return unsuccessful, the army will not be satisfied.'

The Emperor then turned to Drouyn de Lhuys, and said :

'Write to Vienna to break off the negotiation.'

The next time that I saw the Emperor he showed me a letter of Drouyn de Lhuys, written on the very evening of the conference, tendering his resignation ; an answer by himself, begging him to reconsider his determination ; and a reply from Drouyn de Lhuys, somewhat dry, repeating his resignation.

Senior.—Then you and Vaillant were the real causes of the continuance of the war?

J. K.—All turned upon Vaillant's presence. Louis Napoleon was pleased with the peace, and would have adhered to it if Vaillant had not frightened him.

I talked to Lord Clyde about the French army.

Lord Clyde.—The troops of the line are good, though not peculiarly good. The Zouaves are perhaps for an attack the most formidable troops in the

world. Their capture of the Austrian battery at the
Naviglio was an astonishing feat of arms. They are
men who value life only for its excitements, care
little for the future, nothing for the past ; their
courage is that of a gamecock—fierce, uncalculating,
and, in fact, instinctive, but all the more dangerous.
How they would act on the defensive I cannot
say. French officers have confessed to me that
their men, if they had been in our places at Inkerman, could not have resisted the repeated Russian
attacks.

I have an intimate friend, General Vinois. He
was willing to expose not merely his life, but his
military position, for me. We had orders one evening
to clear away the Russians from the banks of the
Tchernaya. I set out before daybreak, the ground
being covered with deep snow. It was only by my
intimate knowledge of the ground, so that I could
tell what valley or what eminence we were on, that
I could pick my way. Several of my ammunition
waggons and some pieces were upset, and some of
my own detachments lost their way to me. All the
separate corps, English and French, who were to
have supported me, lost their way, or were recalled.
Among those recalled was that commanded by
Vinois. When he got up in the morning, he could
see us on the hills in our position ; he instantly,
without waiting for orders, sounded his bugles, collected his men, and marched them without their
knapsacks to my relief. Of course, we could not

execute our manœuvre, but this assistance enabled me to retire without molestation.

On the day of the assault on Sebastopol I found myself placed where I could obviously do nothing. Two bodies of men were before me, and I was ordered not to interfere with them. I went to Vinois, who commanded the body that was to tack the Malakoff.

'I have nothing to do,' I said, 'but I will put into your hands a friend whom I request you never to part from.'

'Well,' he answered, 'I will take charge of him if he is willing to run our risks.'

It was a new revolver. When I saw him the next day he was almost too hoarse to speak. He told me that they had no difficulty in getting into the Malakhoff; it was almost empty, as the Russians did not expect an attack, but that they had had the utmost difficulty in maintaining themselves in it, and could not have done so, if the Russians, fearing that we might break through their lines and enter from behind, had not closed it all round. They brought up column after column to assault it on the side next the town, while the French could receive no reinforcements. His men, he said, re-entered three times.

Senior.—What do you mean by re-enter?

Lord Clyde.—That they left the parapet for an instant, and had to be rallied and brought back.

Senior.—And did any Russians get in ?

Lord Clyde.—No, but they were very near doing so. They certainly would, but for the discovery of ammunition left by the Russians. The French ammunition was expended. They forced the Russian prisoners to show them where the reserved stores were. The bore of the Russian musket is smaller than that of the French, so that it could be used ; had the reverse been the case, the Malakoff would have been retaken, as the Redan was.

April 14*th.*—I went in the morning to hear the Père Félix preach at St. Clotilde. The whole nave and aisles of the great church were full. There must have been four or five thousand auditors. It was a charity sermon for a society which takes care of young workpeople when they first enter the factories. It has at present 10,000 young persons under its protection. The preacher told us that the ' *classes ouvrières* ' were the masters of France ; that the higher classes, the middle classes, and the army only registered their decrees.

' The fate of the country,' he said, ' is in the hands of the working-classes, and the working-classes are led, not by their older members, who are timid, not by their middle-aged members, who are prudent, but by their youngest members, who are governed, not by their timidity, not by prudence, but by passion, by the love of excitement, by caprice, by envy. You have heard of the *enfant terrible;* the *enfant terrible* is the *gamin de Paris.* All our revolutions have been made by children.

'Now what is the training which we give to these children who are the masters of our destinies? Is it moral? is it religious? What is its creed? what is its catechism? It is this.

'What is God?

'God is nature; God is the highest power in nature, the human mind. God is in yourselves.

'What is Satan?

'A scarecrow.

'What is duty?

'The pursuit of happiness.

'What is happiness?

'The satisfaction of our desires.

'What is heaven?

'This world, if you are happy in it.

'What is hell?

'This world, if you are miserable in it.

'What is the object of government?

'Equality.

'What is equality?

'That no man have an undue share of the means of happiness.

'What are the means of happiness?

'Wealth.

'How is equality to be produced?

'By taking from the rich and giving to the poor.

'Such, my brethren, is the catechism which the

unprotected child learns in the *atelier*. The object
of our society is to protect it from these maleficent
influences ; to arm it with the knowledge, the feelings, and the habits, which may enable it to detect
the sophistry, despise the folly, and abhor the
wickedness, of its misdirected companions. If you
wish to save society from a revolution more
frightful than any that has preceded it, if you wish
to save the happiness of the higher classes and the
souls of the lower, give your time and your money
to this holy work. And with these words I put my
sermon under the protection of the Immaculate
Mother of God.'

From St. Clotilde I went to breakfast with
Merimèe. I gave him a sketch of the sermon.

Merimée.—There is much truth in Père Félix's
remark that our revolutions are caused by children.
On the 23rd of February, 1848, I was in the Rue
Richelieu. A battalion was marching down the
street. Three boys stood across it ; they cried out
that the troops should not pass without killing them.
The men hesitated, the officers were afraid of responsibility, and, in fact, the battalion halted for a
quarter of an hour, and then retired.

Senior.—Were they National Guards ?

Merimée.—No, troops of the line. The *gamins*
were armed and utterly indifferent to life, whether
their own or that of others. They would have shot
three men of the first rank, and the soldiers, if they

had killed them, would have been execrated as the butchers of the citizens.

We talked of the Duc d'Aumale's pamphlet.

Merimée.—The speech and the pamphlet are a scolding match on each side. What royal house is there that has not had among its members tyrants, profligates, and fools? The House of Hanover is respectable, yet Thackeray's lectures do not show the Georges to have been edifying models.

Its publication was cleverly managed. The *Procureur Général* of Versailles is an imbecile. The last two pages, which are generally left open, were closed, he did not see them, and therefore did not see the signature. The title had nothing alarming, so he passed the pamphlet as a matter of course, and 5000 copies had been sold before its nature was discovered.

Senior.—Was it wise to suppress it?

Merimée.—It was not worth while as far as the *Salons* of Paris are concerned. The suppression has probably added to the number of readers. But if cheap editions had been circulated by thousands in the provinces and in the army, it might have done harm. The popularity of the Duc d'Aumale and the unpopularity of the Prince in the army, would have given to it a weight far exceeding the intrinsic importance of its contents. Altogether, such a publication from such a man is a grave event.

Senior.—You heard the Prince's speech; how was it delivered?

Merimée.—Admirably. Though he had prepared the substance, he had left the words to the inspiration of the moment. Though often vehement, sometimes excited, he never lost his thread. There was scarcely ever, I suppose, a more remarkable first speech. The stenographer left out one or two phrases. The Prince said, ' *Que des Légitimistes ou des Republicains fassent une descente sur nos côtes, nous les fusillerons bel et bien comme des chiens ;*' the words '*comme des chiens*' were omitted in the report. What adds to its merits as a work of art is the nature of the audience. There never was one to which it is more difficult to speak with energy. I have heard peers complain that the atmosphere of your House of Lords is be-numbing ; it is warm and exciting compared with that of our Senate. The senators are few, they are stupid, they are ignorant, they are inattentive, they are unsympathising ; it is a moral ice-house. When a man attempts to be vehement there, he puts me in mind of an old H.B., in which Lord Brougham stands gesticulating in a fog to a sleeping house.

Senior.—Considering the anti-papal tendency of the speech, was the Government wise in adopting it ?

Merimée.—Quite wise ; there is no Papal feeling among the people. Louis Napoleon's hostility to the Pope had added greatly to his popularity in all quarters, except among the Bourbonist parts ; and the Papalism and Ultramontanism of even the Or-leanists is, like their affection for the Italian pre-tenders and their hatred of Italian unity, rather a means of opposition than a real feeling. At least, I hope so, for I should be grieved to think that a large portion of educated Frenchmen are really the friends of superstition and of misgovernment. Their best friends must hope that they are insincere; and as insincerity is one of the worst reproaches that can be made to a party, the Emperor must be glad to see his enemies avow opinions so opposed to liberty, to progress, to good sense, and to good feeling that those who utter them can be excused only by supposing that they do not believe what they profess.

Prince Napoleon sent, a few days ago, to ask me to visit him to-day. I found several people in the ante-chamber. We were called in one by one, but no one's audience lasted more than three minutes, except mine, which was prolonged to five. He seemed anxious and absent—to use a French phrase, 'préoccupé.'

He told me that he had heard from an authority that could scarcely be mistaken that Lord Derby and Lord Palmerston had coalesced—that Derby was to be Premier and Palmerston Foreign Secretary, and that Gladstone had joined the Radicals.

'It is a most dangerous combination,' he added, 'and disturbs me, who, as you know, am a steady friend to the English alliance. With such a ministry, and this painful Syrian question, *tout est possible*.'

'*Tout est possible*,' I answered, 'except the story itself.'

But I did not convince him. So he told me that 'Sa Femme' hoped that I would dine with them that day, and bowed me out.

At dinner I found Lord Henry Lennox and several other persons, none of whom, except Michel Chevalier, I knew.

The dinner was stiff and silent. Between me and the Prince sat Mme. de ———. He talked to her much in a half-whisper. I found afterwards that it was about the letter.

'I am sorry,' he said, 'that the Emperor has suppressed it, as now I cannot answer it.'

Immediately after dinner we went into the smoking-room, where the Prince took his usual arm-chair by the fire. He was bitter and cynical. We talked of the Pope.

Prince Napoleon.—What I wish is to get rid of him altogether; and if all the bishops and priests follow him, so much the better.

Senior.—Yet your imperial highness has lately been recommending a bishop, Monseigneur ———.

Prince Napoleon.—I told the Emperor that ——— was not quite so bad as the rest; so he was made bishop. But there is little to choose among them. I have seen priests of every kind. They are bad in Germany, they are bad in Italy, but they are nowhere so thoroughly bad as in France. Perhaps, however, I ought to except Ireland. When I was in Ireland last year, the priests crowded round me.

But they had no knowledge or common sense. I found them highly disaffected; but when I asked for their grievances, they could not explain to me that they had any. On their own showing, Ireland is as free, as well administered, as lightly taxed, and as impartially governed, as any country in Europe.

Senior.—They had one grievance, though they did not choose to complain of it—that they have no public provision.

Prince Napoleon.—I scarcely call that a grievance. No priests ought to be paid by the Government. The real grievance is, that the large majority, and the poor majority, of the Irish have to pay the priests of the rich minority. It is bad enough to have to pay a priest whom you believe.

He talked much of English politics: said that Palmerston was a Tory, Gladstone a Radical, and —— a fool, and would not allow that any one had any political honesty except Lord Grey.

The smoking party broke up very soon, and the Prince merely walked through the drawing-rooms, and disappeared.

The Princess looked smiling and happy. Probably she was the only person present who had not heard of the Duc d'Aumale's letter.

April 15th.—General Changarnier, Lord Clyde, M. de Bourke, Duvergier, the Duc de Broglie, Mr. Grey, Secretary of Legation, and Lanjuinais, and one or two others, breakfasted with us. The meeting between Lord Clyde and Changarnier was very cordial.

We talked, as every one does, of the Duc d'Aumale's letter.

*　　*　　*　　*　　*　　*

Lord Clyde.—When I was returning from India the Emperor wished to see me. His manner is very good, but perhaps not quite frank. His voice is low and pleasing, but somewhat artificial. We got on a subject on which a military man can seldom keep his temper. I called baggage *le diable.* He said that in Italy, marching on the *chaussées* raised high over the flooded rice-fields, his advance had sometimes been separated from his rear by baggage-waggons, which it was impossible to pass, or to get rid of in any way, unless they had been thrown off the *chaussée* into the water. He got almost excited by the recollection, and certainly his voice differed much from the subdued, equable tone with which he began.

Lord Clyde outstayed the rest of the party.

Lord Clyde.—My military friends tell me that the Emperor is popular in the army. He has done much for them, and only the higher officers know that he made great blunders, and exposed the army to great risks.

Senior.—I am told that he never was really under fire.

Lord Clyde.—That is not true. At Magenta he was under fire for some time. Viennois tells me that when, for want of the Piedmontese, on whom he reckoned, he was outnumbered, he was more calm than those around him. 'At the worst,' he said, '*nous mourrons en soldat.*' The danger, perhaps, was still greater at Solferino. My friends say that towards the end of the day the vastly superior Austrian cavalry, if they had charged, would probably have decided it against the French; but they were ill commanded, and did nothing. Their African experience gave the French an enormous advantage. They never lost their presence of mind.

April 16*th.*—I dined with M. de Parieu, Vice-President of the Conseil d'ètat. Among the company were Michel Chevalier and the Marquis de la Grange, senators.

The titles granted by Napoleon were not hereditary, unless connected with a *majorat* (an entailed estate). They have long been claimed by descendants without a *majorat*, and it is proposed to legalise the claim.

Chevalier.—The matter was sharply debated till four o'clock, the time at which the whist party meet at the *Cercle.* So many of the Senators belong to it that the Chamber was rapidly emptying, and the Senate, therefore to accommodate the whist-players, got rid of the question by referring it to the Minister of Justice.

Parieu alluded to a remarkable difference between English and French aristocracies.

Parieu.—The highest classes in England are all politicians. They are among the best speakers in both Houses, they are the leading men in the provinces, they are hard-working cabinet ministers. Ours are men of pleasure, or of society, or of literature, but scarcely ever statesmen. And yet our politics are quite as exciting as yours.

Chevalier.—Our aristocracy is governed by traditions, and idleness is one of them. Under the *ancien régime* a man who belonged to the higher noblesse, to the *noblesse de l'épée*, could only be a soldier or a diplomatist, or, if his family could command for him a high ecclesiastical dignity, a churchman. Those who belonged to the *noblesse de la robe* could be judges. All other careers implied loss of caste. And this prejudice continues. The education of our young men, too, by private tutors, or in colleges under ecclesiastical superintendence, makes them averse to the struggles and roughness of political life. Then the smallness of our families, for in the higher classes there are not two children to a marriage, and the law of equal partition, secures to every one enough to live on, and prevents any one from having the fortune and position which give to your elder sons the means of entering Parliament, and almost impose on them the obligation of doing so.

If we had retained the constitution of the Restoration, with its hereditary peerage and its narrowly

rcstricted suffrage, a race of men born and trained t
politics might have grown up. The Legitimists
forming perhaps a majority of our aristocracy, aban
doued public life in 1830 ; the Orleanists did so ˙
1848 ; the Republicans did so in 1852. I think tha
they were all wrong. I think that they ought no
to have abandoned the destinies of the country t
lawyers, soldiers, bankers, or *aventuriers,* unfitted b
knowledge or by habits to direct them. They ough
not to have left the Emperor so unprovided wit
men of political ability and political experience tha
his ministers are unable to defend, or even to explain
their own measures.

But though I see the end, I do not see the cure
unless we revert to the government by parliamentary
majorities virtually nominating the ministers, an
reducing the *chef de l'état* to a puppet. Such a form
of government may be a better one than our democratic absolutism ; but it is abhorred by the people,
would not be submitted to by the sovereign, an
is not desired even by the bourgeoisie, whom i
would make our masters.

A gentleman sat next to me high in the French
Foreign Offiee. He told me that he was engaged in
preparing, in concert with M. Waddington, the Home
Office Under-Secretary, a treaty of extradition.

'Under the present treaty,' he said, 'there is no
extradition on your side. Your judges do not
understand, or at least do not act on, its first prin-

ciple. That principle is, that extradition is to take place if there be ground sufficient to put the accused on his trial. Your judges virtually insist on trying him themselves. As they have not the witnesses, as they know nothing of our law, and not much of our language, the sort of trial which takes place in England costs an enormous sum, and always ends in a declaration by your judges that the case is not within the treaty. The consequence is that we have ceased to attempt to enforce the performance of the treaty by you. We are satisfied with ridding ourselves of your malefactors, which we do without putting you to any expense, and we allow you to keep ours. A fraudulent bankrupt, or a clerk who has robbed his employers of a million, or a husband who has poisoned his wife, if he can once reach England, may enjoy his spoil or his freedom in safety.

'By the treaty which M. Waddington and I prepared, any Frenchman was subject to extradition, if we proved that there was sufficient ground, according to French law, to put him on his trial. *You* were not to try him ; you were not to say, " According to our rules the evidence is insufficient." That was to be our affair, not yours. You were not to say, " Your laws are irrational : we will not surrender a man to a court in which he may be required to criminate himself, or be convicted on the mere ground of the public notoriety of his guilt."

' But the bill necessary to carry the treaty into

effect was brought in by Lord Malmesbury, who did
not understand it, was opposed by Lord Monteagle,
who, if he understood it, misrepresented it, and was
lost because your House of Lords could not, as our
Corps Législatif can do, call on M. Waddington, as
Commissaire du Gouvernement, to explain it.'

April 17*th.*—Rémusat* returned to Paris from

---

* Le Comte Charles de Rémusat, born in 1797, was a writer
and politician. He studied law in Paris, and was called to the
bar. In 1820 he published *De la Procédure par Jurés en matière
criminelle*, a short work of great merit, which was translated into
Spanish. In 1830, under the new *régime*, he took an active part
in politics, but though of liberal principles he endeavoured to
restrain the abuse of liberty. In 1836, he was made under-
Secretary of State for home affairs. In the following year he
joined the Opposition, and was amongst the supporters of
M. Thiers, under whom he served as head of the home department. Again, in opposition when Thiers left office, M. Rémusat
during the seven succeeding years distinguished himself by
speeches which were remarkable for their lucidity and caustic wit.
During the Guizot ministry, he gave himself up to literary and
philosophical labours, till in the last days of the Monarchy, he
was, with M. Thiers, again called to the Ministry. After the
Revolution of February 1848, he represented the Haute-Garonne
in the Constituent Assembly, always voting with the *droit*. The
coup d'état induced him to renounce politics and devote himself
solely to literature. Amongst his chief works on political economy
is one called *Du Paupérisme et de la Charité légale*. He wrote
many critical and philosophical works, contributed largely to
reviews, and translated five of Schiller's plays.

In 1869, during the Ollivier Ministry, he again became a
politician, and founded a Liberal newspaper at Toulouse. In

Italy yesterday. He called on me this morning. I asked him about the state of Rome.

Rémusat.—When I left Rome, three months ago, it was tranquil. The people, though disliking the Papal government, will not attempt to overthrow it, but they will not defend it. The Pope, a man of literature and society, hates business, and consequently does not understand it. He sees little of Corcelle, or Antonelli, or Mérode, and if politics are talked of turns aside the conversation. His policy is to temporise, and to trust to Providence. Antonelli is shrewd, and has some Italian feelings, but little knowledge. Mèrode and Talbot, the other advisers of the Pope, are foreigners. They have no sympathy with the Italians, and think solely of the Pope, to whose temporal interests and spiritual power they would readily sacrifice the liberty and nationality of Italy, or indeed of Europe.

Mérode is an agreeable companion, gay, lively, and pococurante; thinks that the Madonna can and will protect the Pope, without the aid of the French; and is always at war with Goyon. As Minister of War he has the means of teasing us, and tries to make Rome so disagreeable that we shall take a huff, and quit it. And I am inclined to think that if the Corps Législatif had not checked the Emperor, we

---

1871 M. Thiers offered to him the post of Ambassador at Vienna, which M. de Rémusat refused. He was then appointed Minister for Foreign Affairs. He died in 1875.—ED.

should have done so already.` When I last saw
Goyon, he said that he did not think that the French
could remain if the Pope left Rome. There would,
in fact, be no pretence for it. It would excite the
jealousy of Europe and the indignation of the
Italians.

When I last saw Antonelli he said that the Pope
could not remain in Rome unprotected by the French
garrison. If the French went, the Pope must go.
But while each is waiting on the other, they may
remain there for an indefinite time.

Senior.—What is the state of feeling in the Roman
provinces?

Rémusat.—Excited. They are delighted by their
escape from ecclesiastical rule.

Senior.—But do not the increased taxation and
the conscription disgust them?

Rémusat.—No. The taxation may be heavier,
but it is less vexatiously exacted ; and they submit,
as far as I could perceive, to the conscription as
a means of Italian unity. It is not half so severe
as that of France. I did not see much of Naples ;
but though unquiet, it is far less disturbed than
Paris was during the earlier part of Louis Philippe's
reign. The great danger to Italy is Garibaldi. On
the other hand, the great safety to Italy is the reten-
tion of Venetia by Austria. While that continues, a
common danger and a common enemy will keep
together the Italians. If they get Venetia, they will
split up.

Senior.—How did you find the French clergy?

Rémusat.—As respects the inferior clergy, not so opposed to the Emperor as is generally supposed. Ultramontanism is a mere feeling. It is the adoration of a principle. But fear of the Rouges, gratitude for past benefits, and the hope of future ones, are practical. Ultramontanism enables the bishops to gratify their vanity by issuing *mandements*, by disregarding the censures of government, and enjoying the gratitude and praise of the Pope. But the curés, who cannot play a part on the European stage, whose hopes and fears are inspired by the préfet or the maire, are getting tired of making a barren sentimental opposition to the dispensers of money and patronage.

Senior.—Do you believe in war?

Rémusat.—Not from hence. I do not think that the Emperor has any plans. He is allowing the country to drift. He is now in one of his torpid fits.

The liberal party are not without fears that when the separation of the Northern and Southern States in America has been completed your commercial interests may lead you to abandon the glorious war which you have waged for more than half a century against slavery, and to unite yourselves closely with the Southerns.

Senior.—I have no doubt that we shall discountenance, perhaps forbid, the renewal of the African slave-trade; and what more can we do?

Can we advise them to emancipate, and cast on their own resources four millions of slaves?

Rémusat.—No ; but you may advise them to facilitate, instead of prohibiting, partial emancipation. You may advise them to repeal the wicked laws which forbid the education of slaves and the preparing them for emancipation.

Senior.—And they may advise us to make a provision for the Roman Catholic church in Ireland, and to redress the wicked law which, by making the priest dependent on his flock, forces him to confirm their prejudices and aggravate their evil passions.

I suspect that they would receive our advice with about the same kindness with which we should accept theirs. The only free trade that does more harm than good is free trade in advice.

Thursday, April 18*th.*—I spent the evening at A. B. C.'s, and met M. Cintrat, Directeur des Archives at the Foreign Offiee.

I talked to Cintrat of Madame Cornu, with whom he was once intimate, though they have quarrelled.

Cintrat.—The information which I obtained from her as to the early years of Louis Napoleon was very useful to me. I believe his character to be unchanged. She taught me how to manage it.

Senior.—And what is your estimate of it?

Cintrat. — Romanesque, impulsive, bizarre, idle, inconsistent, good-natured, selfish, vain, fearing and hating all superiors. She told me that he always liked best the worst children.

A. B. C.—The *fonds* of his character is selfishness. If he wanted to boil an egg, and the only fuel at hand were bank-notes belonging to you, he would light the fire with them. If there were none of yours, he would light it with his own. The form which his selfishness takes is vanity, and his vanity is vulgarly commonplace. It is love, not of esteem, but of notoriety ; not of the approbation of the wise, or of the sympathy of the good, but of the astonishment of the mob. As a child, he liked bad children ; as a man, he likes bad men.

Senior.—Could he abandon the warlike policy of the last seven years ?

A. B. C.—I have no doubt that he could. The only warlike party in France is the Revolutionary party, and it is found almost exclusively in the large towns ; the peasantry and the bourgeoisie are pacific. The army is conservative. Of course it likes war— all armies do—but it hates revolution. If *Celui-ci's* Government were wise and moderate at home and abroad, he might retain his power for life, and perhaps transmit it.

But he will not be long wise or moderate. It is not his nature. He likes noise. He had rather beat a drum than fiddle as well as Paganini ; and rather fire a cannon than do either. At present he is *engourdi* and pacific, but he will not remain so.

Success has reanimated his early Carbonaro feel-

ings. His first war was conservative. So was the
peace of Paris,—so was the peace of Villa Franca ;
but from that time he has been drifting more and more
in a revolutionary course.

I do not think, however, that he will commence
another war, but he will foment one, and when the
fight has begun, he will take part in it.

Senior.—Will he break utterly with the Pope?

A. B. C.—I think that he will. He will make
himself Pope of the Gallican Church and make the
clergy tools of the Government.

We talked of the Duc d'Aumale's letter.

Senior.—In England a peer would refuse to fight
in defence of words spoken in the House of Lords,—
to do so would be to surrender the privileges of the
House.

A. B. C.—We do not take the Senate *au sérieux.*
Even a member of the Chamber of Deputies, important as that assembly was, could not have ventured
to maintain its privileges at the expense of what
would have been called his own honour.

I fear that these letters will be mischievous, not
only to the Empire, but to the Monarchy. The
people will say, as Henri IV. did after he had sat in
a court of law and heard the counsel on each side
plead, '*Ventre St. Gris, ils ont raison tous les
deux.*'

Senior.—Has the Emperor gained or lost by the
discussion of the address?

Cintrat.—Lost. He has been forced against his

wish to change his policy and keep the troops in Rome.

April 19*th*..—Mr. Kinglake has to allude in the introduction to his work on the Crimean war to the *coup d'état*, and has written to ask me to get information as to the executions in cold blood, said to have taken place after the 3rd and 4th of December, 1851. Most of the persons whom I have consulted say that they firmly believe that such was the case ; but that as no one at that time ventured to speak or to write, they have no evidence.

I called this morning on Jules Simon, and put the question to him.

Simon.—I *have* some evidence,—not that I saw any massacres of prisoners,—I saw men and women killed in the streets on the 3rd of December. The troops, as they were passing along the principal thoroughfares, stopped opposite to the cross streets, ordered the people to disperse, and immediately fired. A woman was killed close to me, in a little street crossing the Rue Montmartre. There is no doubt that they were ordered to kill indiscriminately armed men, spectators, and even passengers. But the cold blood massacres took place at night. After the terror of the first few days had subsided, people began to look for their friends. Many had disappeared.

A young man named Lacour was missing. His friends applied to me. I found that Madame Carnot was intimate with one of the *juges substituts*, who might know whether he was in prison or not, and she begged him to meet me at her house. I was excited, and spoke of the events of the 3rd with indignation.

'I have a right,' he said, 'to be far more indignant than you are. You have seen only slaughter in hot blood. I have seen men taken by violence, not from behind a barricade, or in a street, but out of the protection of justice. As *juge substitut*, I was ordered on the 5th and 6th of December, to go to the prisons to examine those accused of having taken part in the insurrection, and either discharge them or remand them for trial.

'While I was engaged in performing this duty, officers and sous-officers, even sergeants and corporals, entered the prisons, seized the prisoners whom I was examining, or had examined, and looked at their hands. If they were blackened by powder, the men were carried off.'

'*Menés où?*' I asked.

'Not to prison, for they were in prison already.'

'*Mais où?*' I repeated.

'*Où?*' he replied, 'to be *entassés et parqués* till night in a guard-room, and at night shot in the Champs de Mars or the Place des Invalides.'

I called afterwards on the Peyronnets, and asked the same question.

Peyronnet.—No one knows, or ever will know all

that passed during that week. Many people were hiding. The newspapers were silenced. Few dared to talk. I have always believed that massacres took place in cold blood, but I have no direct evidence. We lived at that time in the Champs Elysées.

We heard, during the nights of the 4th and 5th of December, and never before or after, firing from the other side of the water, which we supposed at the time, and still suppose, to have been fusillades of prisoners in the Champ de Mars, or near the Invalides, but I cannot prove it.

I called in the afternoon on M. Bloemarts, the watchmaker, whose lawsuit with the Marquis de ———— I have mentioned. I asked him what he knew of the massacres of 1851.

Bloemarts. — Nothing from my own senses. But some friends of mine who live in the Rue de Fleurus, which looks over the Garden of the Luxembourg, told me that during the night of the 5th of December, they heard many discharges of musketry, which sounded like platoon firing, it was the only time that they ever heard such firing. They might have supposed that the men were firing off their muskets for the night, but after each discharge they heard cries and sobs, and men imploring mercy. One voice cried out, ' Ma mère ! Ma mère!' till it was stifled in a scream. They have no doubt that these were massacres of prisoners.

I asked him to tell me the story of his lawsuit with the Marquis de ———.

Bloemarts.—I believe that the Marquise de ——— is recklessly extravagant, and that the Marquis finds it difficult to keep her within bounds. He is avaricious and litigious, but vain,—likes the expense of his wife, but hates paying for it. When we met before the *juge de paix*, he said, ' M. Bloemarts shall not lose a farthing. I will pay the bill and the costs —*mais il me faut un procès.* I must make it notorious that I do not pay the Marquise's debts.'

I expected, therefore, an amicable suit. But in his defence he attacked me and my character with violence, and accused me of being the accomplice of his wife in the endeavour to ruin him.

I obtained a verdict for the price of the window curtains ; it was held that they were for the benefit of *la communauté* (the husband and wife considered as one person), but I failed for the rest. The Marquis had for him, not only his favour with the Emperor, but also with the *Procureur Impérial.*

As for his wanting ' un procès,' I found that mine was his eleventh!

Senior.—You are prosecuting him, also, penally, for fraud?

Bloemarts.—I have two such prosecutions. Last year he brought an Englishwoman from Boulogne, lodged her in a fine hôtel in the Rue de Lille, carried her about in his carriage to order furniture, went with her to shops, where she ordered silks and jewellery, and brought her to my wife to order linen. This was the first beginning of our acquaintance. It was followed immediately after by the order given by the Marquise. One day the English lady disappeared, taking away (as it is said in the fourgons of the Marquis) all that was portable, and leaving her bills unpaid.

I prosecuted the Marquis as her accomplice; but instituted the proceedings, not only in my name, but in that of the *Procureur Impérial.*

This is a precaution frequently taken, as in that case the costs falls on the Government.

Six months passed without the prosecution appearing to advance. I went to the *Parquet* from time to time, and saw the *juge d'instruction,* who always said he was inquiring into the matter. At last I lost patience, and told him that I would proceed in my own name alone. 'That,' he said, 'you cannot do. The *Procureur Impérial s'est saisi de l'affaire,* and you cannot proceed without him; and I will tell you in confidence that he is of opinion that you have no case against the Marquis, and that you had better quietly withdraw your complaint.'

'Well,' I said, 'if I am to submit quietly to be robbed in *this* affair, I will not in another. The Marquis and his wife have robbed me of 3000 francs. *Je les assignerai moi-même à la Police Correctionnelle.*'

'*Vous voulez donc,*' he said, '*faire un scandale. vous vous en repentirez. C'est alors que j'ai dit que je verrais ce que c'est que la Justice en France,*' and that he threatened to punish me, '*pour avoir injurié la justice.*'

This is the prosecution which is still pending. This is the prosecution in which I found difficulty in obtaining an advocate. At length I have obtained Emmanuel Arago. But with the Marquis for my opponent, the *Procureur Impérial* for my enemy, and my well-known republican opinions, I do not expect success.

Senior.—How stands the Emperor at present?

Bloemarts.—Well with the *peuple*, in consequence of his quarrel with the priests. With the *bourgeoisie* he has been losing ground for the last four years, principally from the denial of justice, as to which my case is only one of thousands. No redress can be obtained against any one in power, or connected, or supposed to be connected, with any one in power.

A watchmaker, a friend of mine, had to repair a watch belonging to the *bonne* of a *commissaire de police.* She called for it, but he refused to let it go until he was paid. Soon afterwards the *commissaire de police* came to his shop, said that he had heard that his register was not properly kept and required to see it. It was placed before him, and he looked at the names and numbers till he came to the name and number of the watch of his *bonne*. He asked for the watch and tried to put it into his pocket. The watchmaker resisted.

'Do you venture to resist the *commissaire*—to resist an officer of police? There are many irregularities in your register. I shall take it away with the watch as *pièces justificatives*.'

The only redress against an officer of justice is to complain to his superiors. The watchmaker went to the *Procureur Impérial*. He referred him to the *Procureur Général*, the *Procureur Général* answered :

' Address to me a complaint on stamped paper, and if you have been wronged, I will do you justice.'

My friend departed, convinced that the *commissaire* would be dismissed. But months have passed, and the only answer that he can get is, that the *Procureur Général* has not had time to look into the matter.

And this is the only answer that he ever will get, unless it be that if he gives any more trouble he will be prosecuted for having kept an irregular register. The result is that he has given up business.

Senior.—But this has always been the case. No Frenchman has ever been allowed to proceed against an officer of the Government, without the permission of the superiors of that officer.

Bloemarts.—Unhappily this *has* always been the law. But if such things as my friend's, or as my case, could have occurred under any other *régime*, we should have published it in the newspapers. If the newspapers had refused to insert it, we should have had it denounced from the Tribune of the Chamber. And the fear of exposure prevented such an occurrence. Now, if we complain that we are plundered, we are insulted, perhaps ruined.

Sunday, April 21st.—Guizot breakfasted with us. We talked of the Syrian business.

Guizot.—I find with regret that our transports are really leaving Toulon, to bring back our troops. You will soon hear that the massacres have recommenced. The Druses, protected by the Turks, are resolved to extirpate the Maronites. Our troops will have to return to Syria, and the only result of their temporary withdrawal will be six months or a year of bloodshed and devastation.

You were wrong in requiring us to withdraw; we were wrong in consenting to do so. We were wrong indeed in consenting to occupy Syria for so short a time and with so small a force; we ought to have landed 24,000 men, to have stationed 8000 at Beyrout, 8000 in Damascus, and to have kept a movable column of 8000 between the two cities. We ought to have proclaimed our determination to have stayed there five years, ten years, even twenty years, if the safety of the Christians required it.

Senior.—Such an occupation would have cost you about a couple of millions sterling, and some thousands of lives, a-year; would France have been willing to make such sacrifices?

Guizot.—Certainly; there is no folly for which France is not ready, provided it be a military folly. Think of the Chinese expedition; what interest had we in China? We get all our tea through you; but it was a war, therefore it was popular.

You would probably have objected, for you object

to everything. You think that wherever we send an expedition we mean to make a conquest, and that every conquest increases our strength. I believe that when we sent our expedition to Syria we no more intended a conquest than we did when we went to China. And I further believe that the conquest of Syria will enfeeble us, just as that of Algiers has done.

Were I an English statesman, intent as most of your statesmen are on weakening France, I should be delighted to see her distant conquests increase. If our army were as dispersed as yours is, if our vulnerable points were as numerous as yours are, we should be as timid and as peaceful as you are.

Palmerston and Thiers made each of them a great mistake in 1840. Your mistake, mischievous to yourselves and fatal to Syria, was the taking Syria from Mehemet Ali; our mistake was the not accepting your offer to let Mehemet Ali be the independent ruler of Egypt. We asked for all or nothing, that he should be the Sovereign of Egypt or only an hereditary pacha.

Senior.—Your great mistake was the stopping Ibrahim Pacha, after he had gained the victory of Nezib. If you had allowed him, he would have gone to Constantinople, and reformed and reanimated Turkey.

Guizot.—But at whose instigation did we stop him? At yours. You wanted to keep alive, or at least standing, the Ottoman *cadavre;* you wanted a desert between the Turks and the Egyptians. You have had your wish, and see the result.

I do not wonder, however, at Palmerston's conduct. The support of the integrity of Turkey is a traditional English folly. Nearly a hundred years ago Lord Chatham said, that if any Englishman thought Turkey might, without great danger to England, be allowed to fall in pieces, his friends ought to remove him to Bedlam.

Senior.—What think you of giving Syria to Abd-el-Kader?

Guizot.—I should be delighted to do so. He is a soldier and an administrator; he could hold the country, and could pacify it.

April 22nd.—I took a long walk with L. M. He is an Alsatian.

Senior.—Do your German or your French sympathies predominate?

L. M.—My French sympathies; but I take great interest in Germany. Thoughout Alsace and Lorraine German feelings and German interests are strong. If they had been separated from France in 1815 they would have acquiesced without much repugnance. What made them French was not identity of language or of race, or even any similarity of character, but simply the abolition by the Constituent Assembly of the feudal rights of the nobles, and the distribution of their property among the people. While there was any fear of those rights being re-established, or

of that property being resumed, they were enthusiastically French. They are now almost indifferent to
France.

Senior.—E., who is from Lorraine, tells me that
his sympathies are all with Lorraine, that he does
not feel himself a Frenchman.

L. M.—Well, *I do* feel myself a Frenchman, but
also a German.

Senior.—If your countrymen were separated from
France, would they wish for independence ?

L. M.—No ; they would join Prussia.

Senior.—But the Prussian government appears to
be very bad. They seem to be ruled by what is
much worse than a despotic king—a despotic police.

L. M.—That is true, but Germans are fit for
nothing better ; they desire nothing better. They
are like the French ; their eyes are fixed on foreign
politics, not on domestic ones. They want to be a
great, or, indeed, the great nation of the Continent.
For that purpose they all gravitate towards Prussia
as the greatest German power. Holstein has determined to join Prussia, so has Schleswig, though the
Danish government and the Danish constitution are
far superior to those of Prussia. Prussia is destined
to absorb all the other Protestant states. Baden
would have joined her six months ago, if France had
not declared that she would oppose the union, even
by a war.

Senior.—Do you propose to add to your kingdom
of Germany the Austrian Germans ?

L. M.—No, nor Bavaria—they are Catholics. If, however, as seems to be probable, Papacy dies out, and the Catholic Church separates itself, as the Greek Church has done, into many different ecclesiastical bodies, each governed by its own Synod, or Patriarch, or Assembly, it is possible that Protestantism and Catholicism may cease to be important distinctions. And the whole German race, whatever be its form of Christianity, may unite to form one empire.

It will be a great blessing to Europe, for it will be unaggressive ; it will keep you, and France, and Russia in order, and being no longer intent on foreign affairs, will try to obtain, what no German has ever enjoyed, liberty at home. The great tyrant, the police, and the smaller tyrants, the kings, and grand dukes, and nobles, and guilds, and corporations, will have to untwist the innumerable Lilliputian strings by which the German giant is pinned to the earth.

Senior.—If Papacy is to be thrown off, where will the revolt begin ?

L. M.—In France.

Senior.—My French friends tell me that in that event you will become not Protestants, but infidels.

L. M.—I do not think so. The working-classes in the towns are infidels, but the higher and middle classes respect Christianity as an institution certainly most useful, possibly divine ; and the peasantry are undoubting believers. We shall make a Christianity and a Church of our own, perhaps with Catholic forms and ceremonies, with Protestant morality, and with dogmata about which no one will trouble himself.

April 23rd.—Lord Clyde, Merimèe, the two Chevaliers,* Kergorlay, Parieu, and Drouyn de Lhuys, breakfasted with us. We talked of the debate.

A. Chevalier.—The two good speeches were Keller's and Prince Napoleon's. The Prince's was the best delivered. Keller's was rather recited than spoken. His voice was monotonous, and so was ·his action, merely raising and sinking his right arm. Neither had a favourable audience. The Corps Législatif, though it hates the Piedmontese, does not love the Pope. And the Senate sympathises little in the Prince's Italianism. While he was speaking in one of the *bureaux*, MacMahon said something in an under voice, the Prince cried out, 'Everybody ought to speak openly; I wish the Duke of Magenta to repeat what he has just said.'

'It was a mere trivial remark,' said MacMahon.

'Then,' said the Prince, 'there can be no harm in repeating it. I insist on hearing it.'

'If your Imperial Highness insists,' said Mac-Mahon; 'it was this : *Je me moque de lui et de son Italie.*'

---

* Auguste Chevalier was Louis Napoleon's private secretary up to the *coup d'état:* he died several years ago. Michel Chevalier is too well known to require a note.—ED.

A prize of 10,000 francs, provided by the Emperor, is to be given by the Institute every other year, for a literary work or a scientific discovery. It is proposed to give it this year to Madame Dudevant (Georges Sand).

M. Chevalier.—I shall vote for the proposition.

Merimée.—And so shall I. It is certain that if Madame Dudevant were really Georges Sands, she would be a member of the Académie Française.

We talked of the probabilities of war.

A. Chevalier.—I believe that both the Emperor and the country are pacific. The revolutionary party in the towns wishes for war, because it likes noise, and bustle, and excitement, and glory. But it is vain rather than ambitious, and it dislikes the burthens that war brings ; the peasantry hate the conscription, and care little for glory ; the higher classes in both town and country desire nothing but quiet and safety ; the Emperor has gained his laurels, and does not wish either to endanger them, or to let any one else wear rival ones.

Kergorlay.—The great danger is from Garibaldi. The Austrians know well how unpopular Cavour and Italian unity are in France. They are burning to revenge themselves on the Piedmontese, and they think that if Garibaldi's insolence and violence give them a fair excuse for attacking him, or, after having repelled his attack for pursuing him, we shall allow them to do so. My fear is, that they may presume too much on our anti-Italian feelings, and carry reaction so far as to force us to interfere.

A. Chevalier.—At all events, whatever be the pacific appearances, I recommend you to keep up your armaments. England disarmed, in the state in which she was ten years ago, is not merely useless for the purpose of keeping the peace, but as a great defenceless prize, is an excitement to war. England armed, able and willing to interfere in favour of those who are attacked, might render European war impossible, and ought to do so.

Senior.—We are told that blessed are the peacemakers; but it seems that peace-making is an expensive, and not always a safe employment.

Parieu.—The greatest peace-makers are the Bourse and the Stock Exchange.

Senior.—Does any one know how Rothschild is operating?

Drouyn de Lhuys.—I do not think that much can be inferred from his operations. He never looks beyond a month.

M. Chevalier.—Parieu and I were present some time ago at a council held in the Tuileries to consider a proposal made by the Minister of Finance, that the bank should pay to the Government one hundred millions, and receive an extension of its charter for thirty years. We had all spoken except Rothschild. The Emperor turned to him, 'Your opinion, M. le Baron,' he said, 'will be peculiarly valuable.'

'*Sa Majesté*, answered Rothschild, '*veut-elle que je m'exprime franchement?*'

'Of course,' said the Emperor.

'*Eh bien donc*,' said Rothschild, '*puisque votre Majesté veut que je m'exprime franchement j'ai l'honneur de dire que je trouve le projet excellent.*'

'*Mais*,' said the Emperor, '*c'est une opinion très importante, mais peu motivée.*'

'*Sa Majesté*,' replied Rothschild, '*veut-elle que je m'exprime franchement?*'

'*Mais sans doute.*'

'*Eh bien donc puisque votre Majesté veut que je m'exprime franchement, je dis donc, que je trouve le projet excellent. Seulement, je crois que c'est mauvais pour la Banque, que c'est mauvais pour le trésor, et que c'est mauvais pour le commerce.*'

As he said this he looked round, and seeing the author of the project making a facè, he added, '*Excellence, j'espère que je n'ai dit rien d'inconvenant.*'

A. Chevalier.—You may have observed that Rothschild never says, '*Pardon*,' nor '*mille pardons.*' He always says, '*Millions de pardons.*'

We talked of the Duc d'Aumale's letter.

A. Chevalier.—It has killed the fusion, if the fusion had any life to be killed. The Legitimists are angry at the praise of 1830, at the allusion to the throne as then vacant, at the claiming for Louis Philippe the conquest of Algiers. The free traders dislike the sneer at the Commercial Treaty, and the liberals the sympathy expressed for the Pope. On the whole, however, its publication is an important event. It has given a blow to the Emperor, and a wound to Prince Napoleon.

Merimée.—It gave Prince Napoleon a great opportunity. If he had instantly fought the Duc d'Aumale, he might have become popular.

Senior.—It would have been a dangerous experiment.

Merimée.—Those are dangers which a man who accepts the title of General, and rides about on a charger with a sword, is bound to encounter.

Senior.—His habits of life have not prepared him for such trials.

I spent the evening at Montalembert's.

Montalembert.—I still find among your countrymen men who trust in the honour, or in the friendship, or, at least, in the good intentions, of *Celui-ci*, who still think that Queen Victoria and the Emperor Napoleon can be permanently allied. I hope that they may remain at peace, for peace depends on mutual fear ; but allies, except for some one special enterprise, such as the Russian war, they cannot be. An alliance supposes some community of feelings and of purposes, and nothing can be more opposed to all your sentiments than his are. You are sober, pacific, traditional, legal, honest. He hates all law, all tradition, all established power, even all established opinions, all that is sober, and all that is honest.

The world is governed by two classes of motives.
One class is yours. It contains — reason, habit,
honour, truth, fidelity, affection, generosity. The
other class is his. It contains — passion, desire of
change, vanity, hatred, selfishness, ambition, rapa-
city. His success is mainly owing to his absolute
indifference to the first class of motives, and therefore
his absolute freedom from the restraints which they
impose, and the intensity with which the second
class impel him ; almost possess him. Between him,
therefore, and the vast majority of his countrymen,
there is . perfect sympathy. They have the same
prejudices, the same hates, and the same desires.
But what sympathy can there be between him and
you, except, indeed, your common dislike of the Pope?
The Pope's is the oldest sovereignty in Europe.
When *Celui-ci* has destroyed that, he will try to finish
the destruction of the next oldest, the Roman empire.
Surely your countrymen cannot intend to be his
allies in that ?

Senior.—Our alliance ended with the Russian
war, and I do not think it probable that there will
be again a real alliance between England and France
until France is again constitutional.

Montalembert.—Constitutional, in your sense of
the word, we shall never be. Thiers' maxim : ' *Le
roi règne et ne gouverne pas,*' was never accepted by
prince or by people. We should treat a really constitutional king as King Log. *You* think that Louis
Philippe interfered too much. The *French* thought

that he interfered too little. They grudged him his civil list, though it was not a third of what this man is allowed, without a murmur, to receive and to waste. They accused him of avarice, whereas his fault was, that he was too careless of money, that he laid out for public purposes so much of his own, that he was in debt when he left France. If, like *Celui-ci*, he had delighted in show, and noise, and ostentation; if he had had the tastes of a *parvenu*, instead of those of a gentleman, the people would have applauded his extravagance. My countrymen make me almost a misanthrope. They are to be governed only through their bad passions, or their servile passions. They are hounds. They enjoy nothing but a hunt, and respect nothing but a whip.

April 24th.—I went with Lord Clyde to call on Changarnier. We talked on our way of the new weapons.

Lord Clyde.—The Armstrong gun is too delicate an instrument for a field-piece.

Senior.—Yet it stood well in China.

Lord Clyde.—Yes, for there the roads were soft, or rather, it was all soft, flat ground without much road. If Armstrong guns had to be rattled over bad roads on rocky ground they would soon get out of order. As for the new muskets, we found in India that the charge of the Enfield fits too closely. It took in that climate too much exertion to ram it down. I do not attach great importance to the rifle, except for light infantry and skirmishers. When two lines of men are advancing towards one another, much aim is not taken. They never actually meet; the line that is least steady turns.

We committed a great mistake before Sebastopol. We sent detachments into the trenches in which men of different companies, sometimes under officers of different regiments, were put together. This should never be done. I was most careful in India never to separate from one another the men who had been used to serve together, or to put men under the command of any but their own officers.

We found Changarnier in his dressing-gown, sitting at work in a little boudoir adjoining his *salon*. I asked what he was writing.

Changarnier.—My memoirs. Falsehood is so often required from the French press and truth forbidden, that I think it my duty to leave a record of the much that I have seen and the little that I have done.

We talked of Prince Napoleon's refusing Bastide's challenge and declaring that it was Lamartine whom his speech attacked.

Changarnier.—Lamartine has moral, but not physical courage. Ou the 16th of April, 1848, when I went to the Hôtel de Ville to see what preparations the Provisional Government had made for repelling the 100,000 *ouvriers* who were assembling in the Champ de Mars for the purpose of attacking and deposing their rulers, he was trembling and helpless. When I asked him what was to be done, he could answer only, '*Les Révolutions ont leurs péripéties.*' In fact, the danger was great, for there were no soldiers in Paris. The National Guard, though it had been appointed and had chosen its officers and received its arms, had not yet met. No one knew whether it would turn out at all, or with what feelings or intentions. Marrast was the only other member of the Provisional Government present.

I asked if they would give me power to act for them. 'You may take it,' answered Marrast. I dictated to Marrast a letter to be copied and sent to the different legions of the National Guard, requiring their immediate presence at the Hôtel de Ville, and indicating their line of march. 'If you have to fight,' the letter added, '*tirez juste, et tirez bas.*' Marrast, however, would not write these words, so that I was forced to write them in my own hand.

Well, the Emperor resembles Lamartine ; he is bold when he is planning, timid when he is executing.

Senior.—I am told that at Magenta he was the person who showed the greatest coolness in danger.

Changarnier.—He was not in immediate danger. The battle did not actually begin till about two in the afternoon. The Emperor crossed the Ticino by the Buffalora bridge some hours earlier, but did not remain long on the other side. He left his troops there, returned to the right bank, and remained there during the rest of the day. He was not within two miles of the real fighting. To this extent he was in danger, that if MacMahon on hearing our firing had not turned to the right and marched on Magenta without orders, or if the concentration of the Austrian army in and near Magenta had not been prevented by the interference of Hesse with Giulay, the French troops on the left bank of the Ticino must have been beaten, and he might have had to gallop for his life.

I spent the evening at Thiers', and met there a North American.

Thiers is only passing through Paris. He joins in the general opinion that Louis Napoleon does not at present intend to take the initiative in any war, though he believes him to be fomenting war everywhere else, in Poland, in Syria, in Hungary, and in Bulgaria.

Thiers.—I admire much the Duc d'Aumale's letter. It is admirable in design and execution. Perhaps he could not avoid publishing it. Perhaps he could not remain silent when his family were so furiously calumniated. But I fear that all these attacks on royalty may turn to the profit of the revolutionary party ; *that* is the party to be dreaded, for it will soon be the Imperial party. The object of Louis Napoleon's hatred is, whatever is established—religion, morality, international law, treaties, institutions, aristocracies, and sovereigns. If he could, he would leave nothing in Europe standing but a despot, an army, and a mob. If his mad career be not cut short, the decisive struggle between all that is conservative in Europe and all that is destructive may come. If France fail, she may be dismembered; if France succeed, the Cæsarian *régime* may follow. The throne of France may again and again be the prize of an usurper, reigning by the grace of the army and of the people.

Senior.—Up to 1848 every revolution has produced, or at least pointed out, its great men. The long despotism of Louis Quatorze and Louis Quinze trained the men of 1789 ; the despotism of Napoleon trained the men of the Restoration and of Louis Philippe ; but 1848 has produced nobody.

Thiers.—Nor will 1852. There is no Young France, at least, in politics ; if there were, Keller would not pass for a speaker. We justify, perhaps, our degradation by submitting to it so quietly.

He spoke with great regret of the dissolution of the American union.

Thiers.—It is a great misfortune to the whole world, and peculiarly to France.

American.—I do not believe that it is to be averted. I do not believe that even a previous war can be averted.

Senior.—But how will that war end ? You may beat the South, I believe that you will do so, but can you conquer it? If you conquer it, can you rule it as a conquered country? If you force it to re-enter the Union, can you force it to become a loyal member of your confederation? Will you be stronger or happier for having your Hungary, your Poland, your Venetia, your Ireland?

If separation is to be the ultimate result, would it not be better to let the result which, sooner or later, will be obtained, be obtained peacefully?

American.—You do not take into account, or you do not sufficiently take into account, the effect on the separate states of such an example. To quietly allow the South to secede on such a motive as this, would be to proclaim that the states of the Union are united by no special bond—that the Union is a mere voluntary and temporary compact, not a marriage, but a cohabitation to be dissolved on any whim or caprice. For what pretext can be more monstrous than that by which the present secession is defended —the election of an obnoxious President? On such terms no confederation, indeed no state, can expect to retain its integrity for more than a few years.

We see to what a state of semi-barbarism disintegration has reduced Spanish America. English America must be saved from such a fate, and it can be saved only by making secession a difficult and dangerous attempt.

In Europe you hold every individual who endeavours to separate a province from the monarchy of which it is a part, guilty of treason, and you hang him whenever you can. We cannot hang our seceders, but we must inflict on them the only punishment that can be inflicted on states—war. We shall ourselves suffer a great part of that punishment, but we shall remain a nation, that is to say, a permanent body, with a past and a future. If we abandon our duty, if fear of the sufferings which we must endure and inflict leads us tamely to acquiesce in this separation, we shall become virtually a mere collection of settlers, friends to-day, perhaps strangers to-morrow, and enemies the day after.

Thursday, April 25th.—General Trochu* called on me. We talked of different armies.

Trochu.—In our own, the best troops are the infantry of the line, taken from the plough. They

---

* General Trochu was born in 1815, and educated at St. Cyr. He became a captain in 1843, and was attached to the army of Marshal Bugeaud in Algeria. He was aide-de-camp to St. Arnaud in the Crimea, appointed Brigadier-General in November 1854, and commanded in that capacity to the end of the war. He was General of Division in the Italian campaign in 1859. In 1861, when he was appointed *Grand Officier de la Légion d'honneur,* he counted twenty-five years of active service, and eighteen campaigns. His work on the French army in 1867 went through seven editions. He was appointed Governor of Paris in 1870, and during the siege he held the command and directed the operations of all the troops within the walls. In 1871 he was elected a member of the National Assembly, and sat in the Right Centre. He retired into private life in 1872.—ED.

are sober, docile, brave, proud of their country and of their profession ; and though anxious to return to their friends and to their little properties, perform zealously their duties.

Senior.—We hear much more of the Zouaves.

Trochu.—The Zouaves have wondeful *élan ;* they are a useful portion of our army ; but I doubt whether they are worth what they cost. They are ill disciplined and marauders, and so set a bad example. They are taken from different regiments, which are thus deprived of their most active and energetic soldiers.

Senior.—What think you of the Piedmontese ? Fènélon described them to me as good third-rate.

Trochu.—So I should have called them, from what I saw of them in Italy. In the Crimea they did nothing. But now, swamped as it is by a rabble of Tuscans, Romans, and Neapolitans, the Italian army can be worth little,—I had almost said, nothing.

The best troops in the world are the English, and the best portion are the infantry and artillery.

Never in the history of war did only two guns do such service as Major Dickson's did at Inkerman. Never did troops stand such attacks as your Guards did on that day. Ours could not have done it. I saw the field. There was an uninterrupted line of dead Guardsmen,—every man seemed to have fallen at his post. It is fortunate that your army is so small. If it were as large as ours is, it would conquer the world.

Senior.—What are the Russians ?

Trochu.—Very good indeed, but they have no generals. It seems an absurdity ; but one cause of their failure at Inkerman was their superiority in number. Their columns were so crowded that they interfered with one another, had not room to deploy, and were ravaged by our fire.

The Austrians, too, are very good. But with the exception of Benedec, who is excellent, they were miserably commanded. Hesse was an excellent general in 1854, but he has lost his decision and his presence of mind. He saved us at Magenta by stopping the march of the Austrians on the 2nd of June. Giulay never had any merit. Their commissariat was worse managed than our own, which was not brilliant. Both at Magenta and at Solferino we made prisoners of regiments who had not eaten during the day. The first thing that they did was to ask for food.

The Austrian soldiers began the war under great disadvantages. They expected to be beaten. They believed our troops to be much more superior to theirs than they really are. We equally exaggerated their inferiority. Our confidence and their despondence had a great effect on the campaign.

As for the two Emperors, they were about equally useless ; but the Austrian exposing himself to fire and interfering, did perhaps the most harm.

Senior.—Did not Louis Napoleon expose himself?

Trochu.—Not in the least. In the morning of the 4th of June, he crossed the Ticino, by the Buffalora bridge, and found that the enemy were in force at Magenta, on the other side of the Naviglio. He maintained that it was only a reconnaissance, and returned to the right bank, where he remained during the rest of the day, three miles from the battle.

I was with my brigade—part of Canrobert's division —at Novara, in the rear, about sixteen miles from Buffalora, and twelve from Trecate, where we were to sleep. When we reached Trecate, we received orders to advance as quickly as we could to Buffalora. We reached Buffalora in the evening in some disorder from the haste of our march. I found the Emperor before the door of a house, near the bridge, walking silently up and down, and smoking. I asked him for orders, and he answered that I had better cross the bridge and advance towards the Magenta. There the battle was going on, but the Austrians were losing ground.

I found several generals, but nobody who could give me any orders, and at last I was advised to attack a village to our right. I did so,—drove out the Austrians, and established myself there for the night. At about three in the morning, I was attacked myself, but unsuccessfully.

Senior.—That seems to prove that your victory at Magenta was not complete. A thoroughly beaten army does not attack within a few hours.

Trochu.—Certainly ; and so they seem to have thought at head-quarters. For though we were highly praised, and twelve crosses were given to me to be distributed to my officers, the fact that we had been attacked was carefully concealed. You will find no mention of it in the bulletins or general orders.

As for Solferino, I can tell you but little. Canrobert's division formed the extreme right of our army, and was ordered to protect it against Lichtenstein, who, with 40,000 men, had left Mantua the night before, and was supposed to intend to attack us. A few regiments of his cavalry did indeed come near enough to charge us, but they were easily repulsed and left the field, and he himself was never within sight of us. I am inclined to think that under such circumstances Canrobert ought to have moved toward our left, and taken part in the attack on the Austrian centre. He received no orders, however, and remained stationary.

As for the Emperor, it is certain that not one of about 250 persons who were about him was touched. He can scarcely have been under fire. He says, as I know, that he found a battle a very different thing from what he expected. He thought that it would consist of manœuvres, scientifically planned and carefully executed. He found it a wild scene of disorder, difficult to understand, and governed more by accident than by skill. I do not believe that he wishes to command again.

Senior.—I am told that the cavalry on both sides was ill managed?

Trochu.—Very ill. Ours did little, and the Austrians did little. My brigade was in a field, insulated, at some distance from any support. I

Lichtenstein's cavalry had attacked us in force, they might have cut us off. In fact, if Lichtenstein had come up as he ought to have done, or if, without waiting for him, the Austrians had attacked our right, consisting of Niel's and Canrobert's divisions, as they came up, they could have overwhelmed us with their superior forces and taken in the rear Baraguay d'Hilliers and MacMahon during their attack on Solferino.

If they had beaten us, it would have been a far more decisive victory than ours was. When we had taken Solferino, they leisurely retired and recrossed the Mincio without loss. We should have had no good line of retreat open.

General Trochu was followed by General Fènélon. I gave him an outline of our conversation.

Fénélon.—I know nothing of Magenta, for I was in the rear. Trochu knows little of Solferino, for he was not allowed to take part in it. If Canrobert had received the orders which he ought to have received, and come to the assistance of our centre as soon as it became clear that there was nothing to fear from Lichtenstein, we should have taken 30,000 prisoners.

I do not know whether the Emperor exposed himself at Solferino. He certainly gave some orders. He pointed out Solferino as the key of the enemy's position. He ordered it to be made the one point of attack,—it was so : it was taken, and the victory was gained.

Trochu says that if the Austrians had vigorously attacked our right before Medola, our centre might have been taken in the rear and defeated. It is possible. The Austrians had 30,000 men more than we had, and might have used them against us with effect.

But these are only suppositions. In war we must judge by the result. The Emperor did more than one man in a hundred, perhaps one man in a thousand, seeing actual war for the first time, and commanding 200,000 men, would have done. He has great military qualities, and if he had begun sooner, would have been a distinguished general. He is decided, he is *tenace*, and, above all, he is not afraid of responsibility. I am not sure that he will not command again. It is a *métier* which one easily learns to love passionately, especially when one has the power to produce great results. Nothing can be conceived so interesting as a field of battle, though it is, as Trochu says, wild and disorderly. Even the horses lose their natural timidity. They will carry you fearlessly over the field while the fight is going on. The next day they would shy at every dead body or dismounted gun.

April 26th.—I called on Lord Cowley.

He agrees with the opinion of the great majority of my friends, that Louis Napoleon does not at present intend war. One war, perhaps, was necessary to him. He has had two, and is satisfied.

'How do you explain, then,' I asked, 'his great armaments?'

Lord Cowley.—Early in his reign he said to me that he was determined not to fall, as Louis Philippe had done, by an ultra-pacific policy ; that he knew well that the instincts of France were military and domineering ; and that he was resolved to gratify them. As for his fleet, he admits to me that it is absurdly large ; that his rivalry with us is a race of expense in which he cannot win.

' I know,' he said, ' that in a naval war you will have the command of the sea, and be able to burn my arsenals. But the present expenditure is only carrying out the recommendations of a committee of the Legislative Assembly ; and though I think them wrong, I must follow them.'

Have you heard what passed at the *Conseil des Ministres* on the Sunday after the Duc d'Aumale's pamphlet appeared? They all came open-mouthed, exclaiming against its calumnies and lies.

' *Mais, messieurs,*' said the Emperor, ' *il n'y a pas de quoi crier contre la calomnie et le mensonge. Tout est vrai dans la brochure.* The only mistake is, that I am described as conferring with the republican chiefs while my mother was with the King, whereas I was then kept in bed by a quinsy.'

I mentioned to him my conversation with General Trochu.

Lord Cowley.—Canrobert has often talked to me in almost the same words. Trochu has long served under him, and they have the same opinions. Can-

robert told me that when the Russian attacks had all
failed, and he and Lord Raglan stood together on the
edge of the cliff below the two-gun battery looking
at the Russians in retreat, Lord Raglan proposed
to him to follow them up in force, and to try to
enter Sebastopol with them, and finish the siege that
day. 'I hesitated,' says Canrobert. 'The attempt
was, of course, dangerous ; but on the whole I regret
that I did not follow his advice : the chances were
in our favour.'

April 26th.—Lord Clyde, Captain Hore, our naval
attaché, and Captain Lynch of the Indian naval service, breakfasted with us. We talked of the French
naval budget.

Hore.—It is a mere prospective estimate made
eighteen months in advance. It is a minimum, but
very far from a maximum. The naval budget for the
last year was five millions sterling. The actual
expenditure was eight millions.

Senior.—Do you think that we are sufficiently
ahead of them?

Hore.—We are. But we have no ship actually at
sea equal to the *Gloire*. The *Warrior*, however,
when we get her, will be superior to her.

Senior.—She is not, like the *Gloire*, invulnerable?

Hore.—No ; but she is incombustible, which the
Gloire is not. The shell of the *Warrior* is iron, that
of the *Gloire* is wood. The thing most to be feared
now is fire. We shall discharge shells filled with

melted iron.   Her plating will resist them, but one of them may enter a port ; and if such a shell bursts in her, she must take fire.

Senior.—Then she cannot use her main-deck guns if there be any sea.

Hore.—That would be a great defect if she were intended for sea-going purposes ; but in the Channel she may bide her time, and come out only in a calm. In a calm she would be a match for four, or perhaps five, ships of equal size.   The undefended parts of the *Warrior* are in water-tight compartments, and no men would be there in action.   Not much damage could be done to her.   Her screw shaft is too deeply immersed to be exposed.   No shot can penetrate ten feet of water.

Lynch.—Could not her rudder be exposed?

Hore.—That is deep too.   But this is unavoidable in all ships.

Lynch.—I think that if she were mine I should either strip off her armour, which weighs about 2000 tons, and thereby give her greater speed, or take down her masts and rigging, so as to avoid the danger of their being shot away and fouling her screw.   In fact, I would have only two sorts of ships —invulnerable unrigged vessels, which cannot be very swift, for the attack and defence of the Channel, moved only by steam, and very large and swift frigates, unplated, for more distant service.

Hore.—It may be necessary to send the *Warrior* into the Mediterranean.   As the French will have plated vessels there, so must we. For that purpose she must be rigged, in order to economise her coal. I admit that for Channel purposes, and generally for the attack and defence of ports and harbours, unrigged invulnerable floating batteries will be necessary.

Senior.—It seems to me that whoever has the command of the sea at the beginning of a war must keep it, as he will be able to destroy his enemies' docks and arsenals.

Lynch.—He would be able at least to destroy all the wooden ships in his harbours. An invulnerable ship could steam into Cherbourg, and destroy all that was afloat within the Digue—perhaps the forts on the Digue.

Hore.—We shall have to build invulnerable fortifications at some points. To do so will be expensive, but it must be practicable, for their armour may be as heavy as you like.

Senior.—Shall we build any more line-of-battle ships?

Lynch.—Certainly not. I doubt the wisdom of even completing those that are on the stocks. Single deckers have more speed, and in steam warfare speed is everything.

Senior.—I have often heard the opinion that the best vessel for Channel purposes will be a gunboat carrying only one, or at most two, very heavy guns.

Lynch.—That may turn out to be the case.

Senior.—What do you think of rams?

Hore.—Of course, if a very heavy steamer could strike her enemy on her quarter, she might run her down : but the chances are so much against her having the opportunity, that I do not think that ships ought to be built for that purpose.

Senior.—Shall we continue to build large wooden ships?

Hore.—I doubt it. Besides the enormous danger of fire, a wooden ship is quickly injured by the vibration of the screw. An iron ship lasts longer without repair, and is more easily repaired. On the other hand, an iron ship cannot be coppered—the two metals corrode one another. She therefore fouls quickly. We are trying paints, and probably shall in time find something that will prevent or diminish fouling.

Senior.—In a contest depending on iron, we ought to beat the French, for ours is much cheaper.

Hore.—Yes, but worse. Theirs is made principally with wood, ours with coal. Our great superiority is in men. They have not 80,000 sailors, including fishermen. We have four times as many. And fishermen, of whom a large portion of their sailors consists, are bad man-of-war's men.

Senior.—How long does a sailor last?

Hore.—He is not good after thirty-eight ; but as they begin at eighteen, that gives twenty years' service. In fact, they begin as boys at thirteen or fourteen ; and the best sailors are those who have been trained in the Queen's service as boys.

Lord Clyde.—A soldier is best at the age of twenty-eight. He, too, is generally too old at thirty-eight.

Senior.—You lose them at their best, for at twenty-eight their ten years' service has expired.

Lord Clyde.—Many of them re-enter; but it is a misfortune that they seldom re-enter in their old regiments. They have been boasting, perhaps, to their companions that they should soon be free, or they want change. Whatever be the motive, such is the fact.

April 28*th.*—I breakfasted with D. E. F. We talked of the letter.

D. E. F.—It has most affected the bourgeoisie and the army. The higher classes do not require to be reminded of the crimes or the vices of the Bonapartes, or of the glories of the Bourbon race. The *ouvriers* —that is, the working men of Paris—do not like it. It speaks respectfully of the Pope, of the Neapolitan royal family, and of the *ancien régime*, and slightingly of Italian unity. Here is a letter from an intelligent working man. He begs me not to distribute it among his fellows.

But it is popular with the army, in consequence of their traditional affection for the Duc d'Aumale, and popular with the bourgeoisie, who are engrossed with their own affairs, and look back with regret to the quiet times of the government of the house of Orleans, and with earnest hope to its restoration.

There are, in fact, only two important parties in France—the Liberals and the Revolutionists—for the only other large party, that of the servile Legitimists, is powerless. Under these two great divisions are comprised many who profess to belong to other parties. Thus, among the Liberals are Legitimists, Orleanists, Republicans, and even Imperialists. I could cite among our common friends men of every denomination, who yet are Liberals, Thus, Circourt, Corcelle, and Chambrun, are Liberals, though Legitimists. The Chevaliers, Kergorlay, and Drouyn de Lhuys, are Liberals, though Imperialists. The great majority of the Orleanists are Liberals, and perhaps half of the Republicans. On the other hand, the party which I term revolutionary comprises also Legitimists, Orleanists, Republicans, and Imperialists. The difference between the two parties consists, not so much in the form of government which they respectively prefer, as in the objects which they respectively wish that Government to pursue.

The Liberals desire law, peace, constitutional government. They feel humiliated and degraded by their impotence. Even when they approve of the results of their master's policy, they dislike the means. Many of them are free-traders, but they are ashamed to have free-trade forced upon them by a trick. All are pleased to get Savoy, but they wish that they had been consulted as to its acquisition. Many dislike the temporal, and many the spiritual

power of the Pope ; but they all abhor the hypocrisy
and treachery with which he has been deceived,
robbed, and oppressed. In many cases they detest
the end almost as much as the means. The majority
are Protectionists ; the majority are Catholics, from
belief, or because they think . Catholicism useful.
Then the lavish expenditure, the constantly increasing debt, the conscription, the corruption, and
the illegality of this *régime* offend them all. They
know that every foreign country is arming against
us; that we are the disturbers of Europe; that the
second Empire is following the course, and preparing
the disasters of the first, or perhaps worse disasters.
Hatred of military rule, hatred of an aggressive
foreign policy, and of a corrupt, despotic, wasteful,
irrational administration at home, and an earnest
desire to control and direct their Government, are
the bonds which unite all the liberal party.

The revolutionary party wishes for despotism
everywhere. It wishes France to be despotic abroad,
and its ruler to be despotic at home. For these
purposes it would destroy every foreign power which
is a restraint on France without, and every institution which checks her master within. A Legitimist
king — *le premier gentilhomme de France*, or a Constitutional king — *le premier bourgeois* — would be
equally objects of its detestation. It hates the
noblesse, it hates the lawyers, it hates the clergy, it
hates every superiority of rank, or wealth, or education, or refinement. Of this party Louis Napoleon is

making himself the head. It is active, and it is unscrupulous; but it is a minority, and in quiet times it is a diminishing minority.

The Revolutionists of Louis Philippe's time, and of 1848, are getting older and soberer; as they die out they are not replaced. Every year the more sensible men of the party detach themselves from it. They feel the dangers of its foreign policy, and find out the mischief of its home government. In 1854— two years after the *coup d'état*—though Louis Napoleon had then the support of the Conservative party, he was falling. He had recourse to war.

War instantly withdraws our attention from our home affairs. We think of nothing but victory and defeat. The only questions asked are, How such a general, or such a division, or such a regiment, has behaved? What are the prospects of the campaign, and what profit is to be made out of loans and contracts?

A voice denouncing the oppression or the corruption of the Government, or demanding reforms or free institutions, is no more heard than the preacher would be if a drum were beaten in the church during his sermon. With the peace of 1856 the reaction against the Imperial system recommenced. It grew till 1859, when he stopped it again by the Italian war. With the peace it has begun again. It is going on now; it is stronger than it ever was. This is shown by the debates on the address, by the boldness with which the Emperor is denounced by the clergy; and, above all, by the enormous success of the Duc d'Aumale's letter.

I believe that Louis Napoleon now wishes for peace, that he will defer war, and especially war against you, as long as he can. But as soon as he thinks that he has to choose between war and dethronement, or even between war and constitutional government, he will decide for war.

Senior.—To the north, or to the east?

D. E. F.—That may depend on the facility of the enterprise, or perhaps on the caprice of the moment. A war for the Rhine, or a war with you—and probably one would bring on the other—would be the more effectual diversion. We care comparatively little about distant wars. No one ever mentions Cochin China. But, of course, it would be the more dangerous war. If it were unsuccessful, he would let out on us the wildest Socialism. He would probably perish in a tempest. In the face of these dangers, he will keep making preparations, but defer and defer the war—perhaps defer it too long. Disease of body or of mind may overtake him. He has no substitutes.

The ablest military men,—such as Changarnier, MacMahon, Lamoricière, and Trochu,—are Orleanists.

April 29*th.*—I paid some visits of adieu—among others, to Madame de Circourt. We talked of Madame de Lieven.

'She was very agreeable,' said Madame de Circourt, 'in her own salon, but dull out of it—a peculiarity which I have often remarked among women distinguished *dans l'art de tenir salon.* They are so accustomed to direct the conversation—rather to make others talk than to talk themselves, and to be constantly *dans un état de représentation*—that they feel awkward and dispirited, or else indifferent, when they leave their thrones.'

April 30th.—We left Paris.

[IN the summer of 1861, Madame de Tocqueville invited some of her late husband's intimate friends to visit her at Tocqueville. My father and I were among the number, and we met M. and Madame de Beaumont and M. Ampère. The journal kept by Mr. Senior during this visit is published at the end of the *Conversations and Correspondence with Alexis de Tocqueville*. We next proceeded to Switzerland, where we intended to visit the De la Rives, M. Marcet, and other friends, but were stopped at Ouchy by the serious illness of my father.—ED.]

Hôtel Beaurivage, Ouchy, near Lausanne, August 29th.—We left Tocqueville on the 20th, spent a couple of days in Paris, and started on the 23rd by the 7.30 p.m. train for Lausanne, which we reached at about 12.30 the next day. The sun had just risen when we arrived at Macon, where we left the Lyons railway for that which struggles and twists through the Jura to Geneva. The road from Ambèrieux to Culoz runs through a succession of deep, narrow valleys, traversed in the beginning by the little river Albérine. We saw it very ill through the windows of a railway carriage, blinded by a fierce sun and tired by twelve hours' travelling ; but to anyone who could walk, or ride, or even drive through it, it must be enchanting. The hills on each side rise from 1500 to 24,000 feet, sometimes precipitous, but generally covered by pasture or forest. The narrow strip of level ground along which we rushed, passing from valley to valley through long tunnels, was green and well wooded, and the hill-sides were studded with picturesque villages.

At Culoz we met the Rhone, and kept it in our sight till we reached Geneva. About Bellegarde the Rhone is about 200 feet lower than the railway, is contracted to about sixteen feet in breadth, and is forced to fight its way through passages which it has eaten for itself in the limestone rock. That the whole lake of Geneva, forty-five miles long, six miles broad, and 900 feet deep, should escape by a passage only sixteen feet wide, seems impossible ; but such is the case. In the midst of these wonders we, poor railway travellers, could only know that there was glorious scenery all around us which we could not examine.

At Bellegarde we left France : this was shown, not by any demand of passport or examination of luggage, but by the immediate improvement in the houses, the gardens, the fields, and the general appearance of the population. I remember having been struck, when I posted from Geneva to Dijon, twenty-four years ago, by the deterioration as soon as I crossed the French frontier. The road, which had been excellent, suddenly became execrable, country-houses disappeared, the villages became untidy or ruinous, no houses were being built or even repaired, the population was squalid — civilisation seemed to have receded a century.

The difference between Switzerland and France is now perhaps rather less ; but still it is very great.

We are here in one of the magnificent new hotels with which the railways are filling Switzerland. This hotel, just overlooking the lake, with a garden joining M. Haldimand's* grounds of Denantou, was opened in

---

* M. Haldimand was a man of great cultivation, refinement, and benevolence. His sister was Mrs. Marcet, the distinguished authoress of *Conversations on Political Economy, Conversations on Chemistry, Willie's Seasons,* and many other delightful books for young people. In 1860, M. Haldimand had already attained a great age, and had lost the use of his limbs ; but his conversation was as agreeable as ever, and his hearing unimpaired.—ED.

Since the above paragraph was printed, I have received the following note from Mr. Frank Marcet :—

M. Haldimand's father was of Swiss origin, but established in England since the middle of the last century, and the head of a well-known commercial house in London. His son William, born in 1784, was appointed Director of the Bank of England at the early age of twenty-five; and greatly contributed, by his knowledge of Political Economy and the evidence he gave before a Select Committee of the House of Commons, to the abolition of the Bank Act of 1797, and the resumption of cash payments.

At the general election of 1820, Haldimand obtained an independent seat in Parliament for the Borough of Ipswich. He

the spring, and is found far too small. It can accommodate, the landlord tells me, 192 *maîtres*, and on the morning that we arrived he had already had to turn off sixty families, and expected to have to refuse as many in the evening.

I hear that all the inns are equally crowded. If I ever come to Switzerland again, it shall be in May or June, not in the touring season of August and September. At this time the accommodation is not half equal to the demand. Our landlord purposes to

---

was renominated by a small majority in 1826; but his health, which had been declining for some time past, and the chances of a petition against his return with which he was threatened, decided him to retire altogether from public life. He was soon after induced, by the advice of his physician, to leave England, and take up his abode at Ouchy, near Lausanne, in one of the prettiest villas of that neighbourhood. He passed there the remainder of his life; his health improved, and he lived surrounded by friends, both English and Swiss, for whom he kept, so to speak, open house for many years.

His popularity at Lausanne was extreme. He founded and maintained at his expense during his lifetime, and by a munificent legacy (20,000*l.*) after his death, the well-known Asylum for Teaching the Blind, for which the town of Lausanne granted him the '*Bourgeoisie d'honneur.*' He also founded a hospital for the poor at Aix-les-Bains, which bore his name, until Queen Hortense having, with his consent, contributed a small sum in order to increase the number of beds, her name was substituted for that of the original founder.

Haldimand, during the latter part of his life, was attacked with paralysis, and completely lost the use of his legs; but his faculties remained unimpaired until his death, which took place in September 1862.—F. Marcet.

build a new hotel, close to this, to accommodate four
or five hundred guests, in smaller rooms, and less
luxuriously furnished than those of this vast palace.

We drove, on the evening of our arrival, to Bois
Céry, about three miles from Lausanne, where
Duvergier de Hauranne has a small house, in a
beautiful country, seven or eight hundred feet above
the Lake. We found the family preparing for an expedition next day to Zermat, which is to occupy a
week.

The day had been oppressively hot. I felt so unwell at night, that I was forced to send for a Lausanne
physician, Dr. Ricordon. I have been ever since in
his hands, and have been unable to do more than
walk from the hotel to M. Haldimand's, about half
a mile off, and back.

The weather is sultry, seldom less than 78° in our
rooms, and 98° to 100° in the sun. The nights, however, are not unpleasant, as there is generally a breeze
from the Lake. My sleeping apparatus consists of one
sheet, spread over the elastic mattress, and another
above me, and the window open. We are forced to
close the blinds, indeed the shutters, all the morning.
We do not, however, lose much, for, until the afternoon, [the mountains on the opposite shore of the
Lake, here about six miles wide, are covered by haze.
Towards the evening it clears away, their fine outlines
become clear and defined, we can distinguish pastures
on their sides and slightly inclined green *plateaux* on
the tops of those nearest to us. On the sides of those

above Vevay and Villeneuve there are still some patches of snow.

Later in the evening, as the sun sinks behind the Jura, the Savoy mountains are in shadow for about half their height, but reflect the red rays from their summits. Later still they are of a uniform dark blue, and at night they look like low, black hills, divided from us by a narrow strait. The eye, not having light enough to judge of distance or of size, under-values both the width of the Lake and the height of the mountains.

The pleasure-grounds of Denantou are unrestrict-edly open to the public. They are not extensive, but are planted with great taste. Here M. Haldimand was visited by Queen Hortense, who brought with her her second son, Louis Napoleon.

Directly he came he sat down to sketch. 'Now,' said his mother, 'he is thoroughly happy. All his pleasures are those of country life and country scenery. He has solemnly promised me never to take any part in politics. And in fact he has no taste for them.'

'Was the Queen,' I asked, 'pleasing?'

'Charming,' he answered; 'very handsome, intel-ligent, and simple, and *très grande dame*. She put you at ease at once. The Prince was silent, and I thought even awkward.'

August 30th.—We were to have gone to M. De la Rive's at his pretty country-house near

Geneva to-day, but I am not yet well enough for visits.

I have been reading the Vaudois Constitution; it professes to be a democratic republic. The Evangelical, that is to say, the Calvinistic, creed is the national religion. All children are to be educated in the principles of Christianity and democracy. The legislative authority is the *Grand Conseil*, consisting at present of 194 members elected for four years by universal suffrage. They are paid thirty *batz* (fifteen pence) for every day on which they attend the meetings of the *Conseil*, and five *batz* (twopence halfpenny) a-mile travelling expenses to Lausanne, including the expense of returning. A majority of the whole number is necessary to make a house.

The executive authority is the *Conseil d'État*, consisting of nine persons chosen by the *Grand Conseil* out of its own members. The present *Conseil d'État* consists of two surveyors, one notary, and six lawyers. It is appointed for four years. As a general rule, it has the exclusive power of proposing laws to the *Grand Conseil*, but the *Grand Conseil* may request it to propose a law, and if it neglects for one year to do so, may propose it itself. The judges are named by the *Grand Conseil*, and are irremovable except by judicial sentence.

M. Haldimand called on us.

Haldimand.—I believe that this is the most prosperous community in the world. The great body of the people are proprietors, and they work on their own lands with a vigour, a perseverance, and a pleasure unknown to the hired labourer.

Senior.—I suppose that their families are small.

Haldimand.—There are about three children to a marriage.

Senior.—Paucity of children seems to be éssential to the welfare of peasant proprietors in an old country. If you had four and a half children to a marriage, as we have, and your population doubled, as ours does every fifty years, you would soon cease to be mainly agricultural.

How is your aristocracy of the Rue du Bourg going on?

Haldimand.—Going down. There is a strange difference between the aristocracy of the Pays de Vaux and that of Geneva. In Geneva they take to science, to literature, and to politics. The De la Rives, Marcets, Prèvosts, De Saussures, and others whom I could name, are not only among the oldest, but among the most distinguished families in the Canton. The Lausanne aristocracy does nothing. It inhabits its spacious, ill-kept houses in the Rue du Bourg, lives in a clique, wastes its property, and is dying out.

Senior.—I suppose that there is the usual republican jealousy of the higher orders?

Haldimand.—Certainly. *I* am forgiven because, as an old bachelor with few wants, I give to the public the use of my place and of a great part of my fortune. Still, I am scarcely popular. The other day a friend of mine listened to the conversation of the boatmen who were rowing him across the lake. One of them did me the honour of calling me ' *un brave homme !*' ' *Mais si c'est un brave homme,*' said the other, ' *pourquoi a-t-il tant de domestiques ?*'

A friend of mine, M. de Hauteville, who has a large property above Vevay, wished to add a field to it. It was for sale, and he offered more than its value, but the owner would not sell to him. '*En effet,*' he said, ' *nous ne voulons ici des sommités hors le Dent de Jaman.*'

Chief Justice * and Lady Erle arrived this morning, and drank tea with us in the evening.

August 31*st.*—The hot weather of the last week has knocked up Lady Erle. Sir William drank tea with us.

September 1*st.*—I will throw together my conversations of the last two days with Sir W. Erle.†

---

* Sir William Erle was appointed, in 1844, one of the Judges of the Court of Common Pleas ; in 1846 he was transferred to the Court of Queen's Bench ; in 1859 he was promoted to the Chief Justiceship of the Court of Common Pleas, on the elevation of Lord Campbell to the Woolsack. He retired into private life, taking his farewell of the Bench on November 26th, 1866.—ED.

† These conversations have been corrected by Sir W. Erle.— N. W. SENIOR.

I mentioned that in all the Swiss constitutions trial by jury in criminal matters was required.

Erle.—And very wisely.

Senior.—Wisely for the purpose of keeping power in the hands of the people ?

Erle.—Wisely for *all* purposes.

Senior.—Including the discovery of truth ?

Erle.—Including the discovery of truth. I believe that a jury is in general far more likely to come to a right decision than a judge.

Senior.—That seems to me strange. The judge has everything in his favour,—intelligence, education, experience, and responsibility.

Erle.—With respect to intelligence, a judge is certainly superior to an ordinary juryman ; but among the twelve there will generally be found one, often two men, of considerable intelligence, and they lead the rest. As to education, the jury have decidedly the advantage. The education of a judge, as far as relates to deciding fact, is the education of a practising barrister who is immersed in the world of words, and removed from acting in the commercial, agricultural, and manufacturing facts which form the staple of contest. He is so accustomed to deny what he believes to be true, to defend what he feels to be wrong, to look for premisses, not for conclusions, that he loses the sense of true and false—*i. e.* real and unreal. Then he is essentially a London gentleman ; he knows nothing of the habits of thought, or of feeling, or of action in the middle and lower classes who supply our litigants, witnesses, and prisoners. And it is from barristers thus educated that judges are taken.

When tried by a jury, the prisoner is tried by his peers, or by those who are a little above his peers, who are practically accustomed to the facts adduced as probantia, and can truly appreciate their value. I have often been astonished by the sagacity with which they enter into his feelings, suppose his motives, and from the scattered indicia afforded by the evidence conjecture a whole series of events. For, after all, the verdict, if it be a conviction, must always be a conjecture.

Experience the judge certainly has. As counsel or as judge he has taken part in many hundreds of trials. The juryman may never have served before. But this long experience often gives the judge prejudices which warp his judgment. The counsel who are accustomed to plead before him find them out and practise on them.

I was counsel in a case of assault. My client had had three ribs broken by a drunken bargeman. The opposite counsel cross-examined as to whether since the accident he had not been a field preacher, whether he had not actually preached from a tub. He admitted that he had. I did not see the drift of this, for though a man could not easily preach directly after his ribs had been broken, he might when they had reunited. The judge summed up strongly against me, and my client got nothing. I afterwards found that the judge had an almost insane hatred of field preachers. It is true that each jury-man may have prejudices equally absurd, but they are neutralised by his fellows, and, above all, they are not known. They cannot be turned to account by counsel.

As for responsibility, a judge being a permanent officer, especially a judge sitting alone, is more responsible to public opinion than any individual juryman, who is one of a body assembled only once and immediately dissolved. But I believe that the feeling of moral responsibility is much stronger in the case of the juryman, to whom the situation is new, whose attention is excited, who for the first time in his life is called upon to exercise public important functions in the face of all his neighbours, than in that of a judge who is doing to-day what he has been doing perhaps every day for ten years before. I have seen dreadful carelessness in judges. Again, a judge is often under the influence of par-ticular counsel; some he hates, some he likes, some he relies on, and some he fears. It is easy for a judge to be impartial between plaintiff and defendant, indeed, he is almost always so; it is difficult to be impartial between counsel and counsel.

Senior.—I have felt that myself, but in general the feeling of dislike was stronger than that of liking. There were men on whose side I could decide only by an effort; they were so false, so sophistical, so anxious to dress up a cause which was sufficiently good if merely clearly and simply stated, that I was almost ashamed to decide for them lest I should be supposed to have been deceived. But I do not recollect having had favourites.

Erle.—Perhaps you had them without knowing it, and attributed solely to the argument a force which was partly due to your good opinion of the speaker.

Senior.—Just as a juryman who had been in court during the whole sitting at Liverpool congratulated Scarlett on having been always employed by the side that was in the right. What class give you the best jurymen ?

Erle.—The respectable farmers and the higher shopkeepers in the country towns. The men from the great cities, accustomed to excess in trade speculations, are inferior to them, especially in an honest sense of duty. The worst juries that I have known came from such places. Their adventurous gambling trade seems to make them reckless. At one time they appeared to have a pleasure in deciding against what they supposed to be my opinion, which I counteracted by seeming to give more emphasis to the reasons in favour of the decision to which I was opposed. One of the things which used at first to surprise me, is the very small motive which is enough to lead men to commit atrocious crimes. Smethurst's* motive, for instance, was a small one.

---

* Dr. Smethurst was accused of marrying Miss Bankes during the lifetime of his wife. He caused her to make a will in his

Senior.—You hold Smethurst guilty?

Erle.—Certainly I do. If the evidence against him was insufficient, almost all circumstantial evidence must be insufficient, for it ·scarcely ever is stronger.

Senior.—Sir George Lewis was partly influenced by the want of motive.

Erle.—Do you recollect the Buckinghamshire groom, who murdered his fellow-servant because she would not give him a glass of beer?

Senior.—You would have convicted Vidil * of the attempt to murder?

Erle.—I have no doubt that he did attempt to murder, and I think that I should have convicted him.

---

favour, and she died soon afterwards of slow poison. He was convicted and sentenced to execution, but Sir George Lewis, who was Home Secretary at that time, did not consider the evidence sufficient, and granted him a free pardon. Smethurst was afterwards tried, convicted, and imprisoned for bigamy.—Ed.

* The Baron de Vidil made an attack upon his son with a loaded whip while they were riding together in a lane near Orleans House, Twickenham. The Baron alleged that his son's injuries were caused by an accident on the road. In his deposition the boy said that his father had struck him twice on the head; at the police examination, however, he refused to give any information tending to criminate his father. Immediately after the occurrence, the Baron fled to Paris, where he was apprehended and tried. As the son still refused to give any evidence against his father, the jury could find the prisoner guilty only of unlawfully wounding. The Baron was sentenced to twelve months' imprisonment with hard labour.—Ed.

Senior.—Would he have been hanged ?

Erle.—I think not. I recollect no case of an execution for a mere attempt. He would have been sentenced to penal servitude for twenty-five years, which means twelve and a half years if the prisoner conducts himself well. His present sentence of one year's hard labour is severer while it lasts. The men in penal servitude live apart, each in his cell, and employed in trades. Great importance is attached to keeping up their weight. As their work does not promote the development of muscle, their weight is retained by fattening them. I saw a set of convicts at Dartmoor. Every one of them had thrown out a bow window. Nothing could look more absurd than a line of sixty or seventy men, each adorned by this prominence. Its reformatory effects, however, will be great. They will be guilty of none of the thefts which require agility.

Senior.—I am not sure of that ; Falstaff was a highwayman.

Erle.—Yes ; but he admitted that he could not rob a-foot, and no one can rob now on horseback.

Senior.—And how will Vidil's punishment differ from penal servitude ?

Erle.—It will not be separate, he will be mixed with common felons. He will probably have to sleep on an inclined plane fifty or sixty feet long, and six feet broad, running along the side of the room, among twenty or thirty other convicts, those on each side of him separated from him by only an imaginary line.

He will have to work with them and live with them.
To a man of any refinement, and he must have some,
it is a horrible sentence. And think what will be his
position when he is released. I had much rather be
hanged.

Senior.—Do you believe that many innocent men
are tried ?

Erle.—I believe that many men are tried, and
that some are convicted, who are innocent of the
crime of which they are accused. But I also believe
that *almost all* those who are wrongfully accused, and
that *all* those who are wrongfully convicted, belong
to the criminal class. An honest man always proves
an *alibi*, but a professional thief is constantly employed in some breach of the law. If, from a mistake
of identity, the great cause of erroneous prosecutions,
he is accused of some crime of which he is not guilty,
he too can prove an *alibi ;* but that very *alibi* would
show his participation in some other crime. He prefers the risk of a false conviction to the certainty of a
true one. He will not defend himself against the
charge of having stolen A.'s sheep, by showing that
at that very time he was breaking into B.'s house.

Senior.—You have pleaded the cause of juries in
criminal cases. What do you say to them in civil
causes?

Erle.—Even in civil causes I prefer juries to
judges. The indifference to real and unreal, and so
to right and wrong, which besets a barrister bred in
the world of words rather than of facts, often follows

him to the bench. Besides this, I have known judges, bred in the world of legal studies, who delighted in nothing so much as in a strong decision. Now a strong decision is a decision opposed to common sense and to common convenience.

Senior.—Such, for instance, as Lord Eldon's; that if a book be mischievous you have a right to pirate it.

Erle.—A great part of the law made by judges consists of strong decisions, and as one strong decision is a precedent for another a little stronger, the law at last on some matters becomes such a nuisance, that equity intervenes, or an Act of Parliament must be passed to sweep the whole away.

Senior.—As was done as to the construction of wills.

I am told that Cockburn regrets that he has changed the bar for the bench.

Erle.—So do not I. Both are laborious, and both are anxious; but the labour of the bar to a man in great practice is overwhelming. My great delight is my farm at Liphook. I cannot explain to you the soothing influence of agricultural occupation. As soon as I get there, I run to look at my colts and my calves, and my other stock, even my pigs. I care much more about my turnips, which are of no real value, than about my salary. When I am going away I get up an hour earlier to go round the farm once more.

Senior.—I have no doubt that farming is an

agreeable and interesting amusement; but is it not an expensive one?

Erle.—I do not think that my farm costs me more than two hundred pounds a-year. It is the money which I spend most profitably.

September 2nd.—Baron Marochetti * is at Évian, on the opposite side of the Lake. Steamers cross in half-an-hour, three and four times a-day. He breakfasted with us this morning, bringing with him a Captain Lutyens, an amateur artist of such excellence that Marochetti has advised him to quit the army and take to painting as a profession; and I think that he will do so. We talked of the present French school. Marochetti surprised me by not admitting De la Roche or Scheffer to be great painters.

Marochetti.—They were both of them men of great talent and industry, and having taken to painting, they succeeded; but they would have done anything else as well, and many things better. They had that which can be attained by labour—such as

---

* Baron Charles Marochetti, the well-known sculptor, was born in 1805 at Turin, of naturalised French parents. He studied and resided in France until the Revolution of 1848, when he came over to England and obtained great success. The statue of Richard Cœur de Lion in front of the Houses of Parliament is by him, as well as the altar-piece in the Church of La Madeleine in Paris. His *chef-d'œuvre* is the statue of Emmanuel Philibert at Turin. He died in December, 1867.—ED.

accuracy of outline, proportion, perspective ; and they had what is given by intelligence. Each of them conceives well, and represents well his story. Scheffer's Mignon tells her whole history. But the power of colouring is not to be got by labour or by by imitation. It is a gift from Nature to those whom she intends to be painters, and neither De la Roche nor Scheffer had it.

Senior.—Whom do you put at the head of the French school ?

Marochetti.—Delacroix, and perhaps Ingres and Meissonnier.

Senior.—And whom at the head of the English?

Marochetti.—Landseer and Watts. Landseer I put first, because, though his line is not the highest, he has attained the highest rank in it, and because he owes so little to others. If Watts had not seen the great Italian painters, he would not have been what he is. If neither Rubens, nor Paul Potter, nor Schnyders, had lived, Landseer would probably have painted as well as he does. Landseer borrows nothing from them, indeed has no motive to borrow from them, for they have nothing so good as what is his own.

Watts has taken much from his great predecessors, and great as he is, has not equalled, or nearly equalled them. In his best works there is always something wanting. In his portrait, for instance, of Miss S——, an admirable picture—perhaps the best that he ever painted—the colouring is defective. It is too flat, and the figure is too thin. He is not fond of portrait-painting, but he would be unwise if he were to give it up. It is necessary both to keep him from mannerism and to keep him from deviating, in search of beauty, from real nature. At one time he painted much without models, and his figures, as you may see on the walls of Lord Somers' house in Carlton Terrace, lost reality and individuality. But with all his faults he is really a great painter—the greatest that you have had since Gainsborough and Sir Joshua.

Senior.—Do you not rank Callcott and Stanfield high?

Marochetti.—Callcott is a pretty painter of still-life, but he is feeble. He will scarcely live. Stanfield belongs to the French school of landscape-painters, and there are several that are superior to him—Gudin, for instance.

Senior.—What do you say of Martin?

Marochetti.—That he is à man of genius, ruined by mannerism, and by neglect of the details of his art. He never took the pains necessary to know how to paint the human figure. He is a great master of perspective. He is a great architect of the Egyptian School. His imagination revels in miles of colonnades, and sphinxes, and colossi. The boldness, the originality, the vastness, and the real merit of his Belshazzar's Feast, delighted, and almost awed, the spectators. But when it was found that every Martin resembled every other Martin, and re-

sembled nothing else, they ceased to interest. They
came to be considered as tricks, as is the usual
result of mannerism when pushed, as Martin's was,
to its utmost extent.

September 3rd.—We] breakfasted with the Duvergiers at Bois Céry. Lausanne is placed at about
the centre of the Jorat, a sort of Appennine,
which rises above Vevay, and runs in a westerly
direction towards the Jura, which it joins at Sarras,
above Cosonay. Its ridge divides the waters which
fall into the Mediterranean from those which fall into
the Atlantic—those which flow down its northern
side reach the Lake of Neufchâtel, and thence the
Rhine: those which flow down from its southern side
going by the lake of Geneva into the Rhone. When
I was in this country some years ago, I was shown,
I think near Cosonay, a spring, whose waters flowed
out of the well-head which they had filled in different directions—about one-half into the Mediterranean, the other half into the Atlantic.

Bois Céry is situated on the side of the Jorat,
seven or eight hundred feet above the lake, and
perhaps three hundred feet below the ridge of the
Jorat, immediately above it. The house covers a
good deal of ground, and is cut up into small rooms.
A covered portico—the charming appendage to
almost every Swiss house—runs round it.

The whole property, containing about fifty
acres, cost 4000*l.* The land is let off for 80*l.* a-year.

As the house cannot be wòrth more than 1000*l.*, Duvergier gets about two and a half per cent for his investment.

Land is very dear. M. de St. Julien, a Lausanne friend, told us that three per cent was the *beau idéal* of an investment, and that two and a half per cent was more common.

Madame Duvergier:—We were in Switzerland in the summer of 1848. The instability of the Republic alarmed us. If the Rouges had seized the power, and more than once the chances seemed to be in their favour, our property, and perhaps our lives, would have been in danger.

This place, very bad as a house, but capable of holding us, was to be sold, and we bought it as a retreat in a neutral territory, and as we have it, we spend a few weeks here every other year. Thirty years ago it stood in a forest; now the greater part of the wood has been cut, and the land reclaimed, but there are still some shady walks, and the views around are splendid.

After breakfast we drove to Vernant, a château with a large park belonging to M. de Blonay; we left our carriages near the château, and walked over a great part of the park. It is large. Duvergier, Target, and I walked for about a mile in it, but Madame Target, the young Duvergiers, and my daughter, who left us, must have walked three or four, for they were absent at least two hours.

It is about 300 feet lower on the Jorat than Bois Céry. The land is finely tossed about, scooped into deep glens, well timbered, and intersected by rapid streams. Every knoll or promontory commands a view of the lake and the Alps. The Blonays are the Montmorencys of Switzerland. Our conversation, at first occupied by the scenery, soon turned to French politics. We began by discussing the chances of the Imperial dynasty.*

Target.—If this man lives, and retains his power for a dozen years longer, the little prince may succeed. But no one believes in a regency. Whom could they take? The Empress would be impossible. Prince Napoleon has talents, and, in political matters, boldness; but the army would not tolerate him, or even the peasantry.

The conversation passed to the first Napoleon.

Duvergier.—Did Rémusat ever mention to you his mother's journal?†

Senior.—No.

Duvergier.—It is a most curious record, but full of such details affecting living persons that it cannot be published for many years. Her husband, Rémusat's father, was high in Napoleon's household.

---

* The first part of this conversation relates to so many persons now living, that I am obliged reluctantly to omit it.—ED.

† This Journal has lately been published.—ED.

As a specimen, I will tell you the history of the first meeting of Napoleon and the Countess Walewska.

When Napoleon was on his way to Warsaw, he wrote to Duroc, who managed those things for him, and desired a house to be taken for him outside of the town, and a Polonaise to be provided, *jeune, intelligente, et d'une des premières familles.*

There was some difficulty about the last article, but a lady was found, intelligent and young, and recently married to an old man.

As soon as he arrived, he asked if they had got the Polonaise.

' Yes,' he was answered.

' *Bien*,' he said, ' *qu'elle m'attende.*'

The rest of the story she thus related to Madame de Rémusat.

' Several hours passed, and at last the Emperor entered the room. He came straight to me, and said,—

' " Is it true, Madame, that you belong to one of the first families?"

' " Yes," I said.

' On which he sat down to the writing-table, and questioned me for more than two hours as to all the Warsaw people, their connexions, their characters, and their political opinions, and filled page after page with notes of my answers.'

Senior.—What became of Madame ——?

Duvergier.—Her Polish husband died, and she married again, and lived for many years, and was very well received in society. *Jupiter savait dorer la pillule.*

Thursday, September 5th.—We breakfasted at La Grangette, the country-house of the Comte de St. Julien, and met there Comte de la Motte, a Swiss who has been long in the Prussian service, and the Duvergiers and Targets.

Though about 700 feet above the Lake, and therefore nearly 2000 feet above the sea, the St. Juliens pass the winter at La Grangette. There is seldom, they say, snow for any long time, and never fog, and the Jorat screens them from the Bise. The neighbourhood of Geneva is much colder,—the Bise there, blowing down the whole lake, is frightful. Mrs. Marcet never ventured to pass the winter at Malagny.

M. de la Motte had often been at Gräfenburg, once for more than six months. He spoke very highly of Priessnitz, to whom he thinks he owes his life. The St. Juliens are remarkably pleasing, with all the polish, the ease, and the simplicity of the *ancien régime.* They are Parisians by birth, though long settled here.

In the evening we called on M. Haldimand.

We talked of the expense of living near Lausanne.

Haldimand.—You could not comfortably spend ·more than 1500*l.* a-year. I doubt whether Mrs.

Marcet spent that, though she had a fine place, received much, and had an apartment in Geneva in the winter. I doubt whether Frank Marcet, living in what the Swiss call very loud style, spends 1200*l.* a-year.

Senior.—Of course you leave out the rent of Malagny?

Haldimand.—Of course I do. But that rent cannot be put down at more than 200*l.* a-year. I have a charming place, called 'L'Elysée,' close to my own, which I let to M. de Cerjat for 150*l.* a-year. He has four daughters, keeps horses and carriages, and is one of our rich men, and I do not think that he spends 1000*l.* a-year, after paying his rent.

Senior.—How do you account for this cheapness of living? for general prices cannot be lower than in England.

Haldimand.—The price of services is rather less. You pay your physician 8*s.* for a single visit, and much less if, as I do, you employ him by the year. But the great difference is the absence of ostentation. I know that M. de ——'s daughters, who are held to be well dressed, have 25*l.* a-piece for their dress. In England you spend your money for the benefit of others. Here you spend it all on yourself.

Senior.—Not *you*, for Denantou belongs quite as much to the public as it does to you.

Haldimand.—It really belongs to the Lausanne public as much as Kensington Gardens belongs to the people of Kensington. My only privileges are, that I pay for keeping it up, and that I have the satisfaction of thinking that it is mine—that I can plant, and cut openings, and improve it as I like. But the use of it which I give to the public costs me nothing. They do no damage, and I should spend just as much in keeping it up—and with much less pleasure—if no one else ever entered it.

Friday, September 6th.—We crossed the lake in a steamer, going first to Thonon, a curious old Savoy town, where we had some delicious water from a natural fountain which rises in the kitchen of the hotel, then driving about seven miles along the side of the lake to Évian, whence a steamer took us back to Ouchy in the evening.

The Savoy side of the lake is far more pleasing than the Swiss side. Looking north it is less devoted to vine-culture, and the vines are treated on the Italian, not on the French system. They hang in festoons over dry trees, planted for the purpose, twenty or thirty feet high. There is a great deal of fine timber, not massed, as is usually the case in France and in the Pays de Vaud, in closely packed groves of long, branchless poles, but scattered over the fields and spreading its branches widely in search of air and sun. There is little, however, of Swiss neatness or prosperity. The towns are dirty, and the pretty villages, villas, and chalets are wanting. Savoy is French, not Swiss, in appearance and population.

Évian has a fine hotel, about 300 feet up the mountain, and a mineral water, said to be very useful in diseases of the bladder, but with no perceptible peculiarities. It is very bright and soft, pleasant to drink, and charming to bathe in. The inhabitants use it for all purposes. A pleasing, intelligent young American lady, a Miss Curtis, of Boston, whose family are living in the Beaurivage Hotel, joined us.

At Évian we found the Marquis Pallavicini, of Milan, the pro-dictator of the last Neapolitan revolution, under whose rule the popular vote for annexation to the kingdom of Italy was taken.

His earlier political life was less successful. He joined in the anti-Austrian conspiracy in 1821, and was imprisoned for fifteen years in Spielberg. For the first two, while the trial was going on, the treatment was tolerable, but after he had been convicted and sentenced to *carcere duro*, it was severe. He wore irons for ten years.

I asked what the climate was.

Pallavicini.—Not bad in itself. It is like all the centre of Germany,—cold in winter and hot in summer : but we, the prisoners, were unhealthy in consequence of our treatment. The Austrian Government, or rather the Emperor Francis, for he was the real manager of Spielberg, clothed us, but insufficiently ; we were not allowed gloves or great-coats. In winter we kept ourselves warm indoors, as we had stoves, but when we went into the open air for our hour's exercise, we were miserably cold ; and in summer our ill-ventilated cells were oppressively hot.

One merit I must concede to the Austrians,—they took good care of our property. Mine was given over to the management of my mother, and when I was released I found it greatly improved. One of our worst sufferings was the absence of information. For fifteen years I had no news respecting my family.

Senior.—Who were your companions?

Pallavicini.—For the first two years a malefactor; afterwards, state prisoners. I should have preferred solitude to the presence of a brute, which my first fellow-prisoner was; but I was very glad to have with me an educated man.

Senior.—You had no books, or writing materials?

Pallavicini.—None, lawfully; but I managed to get hold of a German and an English vocabulary. Partly as an exercise, and partly because I feared to lose my books, I cut all the important words with a nail on my wall, and in fact I taught myself to read tolerably, both in English and German, though of course my pronunciation, acquired only by the eye, is unintelligible to any one but myself. Then I tried to recollect all that I had read, and above all, I built castles in the air.

Senior.—Did you ever fancy that you would one day be sitting on this fine terrace, overlooking the lake, and talking over with an Englishman the prospects of the kingdom of Italy?

Pallavicini.—Never ; my boldest conjectures, even my most ardent hopes, never approached the reality. All that I hoped for was a kingdom of Upper Italy, composed of Piedmont, Lombardy, and Venetia, and perhaps of Parma and Modena, excluding the Austrian influence from the south, and liberalising, by its example, Tuscany, the States of the Church, and Naples. That these three great independent countries would be merged in the kingdom of Italy, I never thought possible.

Senior.—And do you believe now that the union will be permanent?

Pallavicini.—I do,—at least as long as the Austrians hold Venetia, Tuscany, Modena, and Parma may be relied on ; and so, I think, may those portions of the States of the Church which formed part of the old Viceroyalty of Italy. Even Naples, unless very great mistakes are made, will in time be reconciled to the loss of its individual nationality.

The *plébiscite* for annexation to the kingdom of Italy received 1,300,000 favourable votes, and only 10,000 adverse ones ; and I can assure you that it was fairly taken. When you deduct from 6,000,000 of Neapolitans, 3,000,000 for women, and deduct further the children and the very old, you will find that 1,300,000 is a considerable majority of the active citizens. And I repeat that the vote was fairly taken —neither solicitations nor threats were used. In fact, the only persons opposed to the Union are the priests, who are ignorant and devoted to the Pope—and the disbanded soldiers.

The reactionary party in Europe complains that those opposed to the Union are called 'brigands.' It calls their opposition 'a civil war,' and claims for them belligerent rights. But, in fact, the greater part of them, indeed almost all, except the priests, *are* brigands. They are men without political knowledge or political convictions, whose motives are the hope of plunder, and the bribes of the dethroned king. A strong proof that the Union is popular with the educated portion of the people is, that the Government ventures to employ the National Guards against the brigands, or, if I must not use that term, against the insurgents.

We talked of the two Cavours.

Pallavicini.—Of course they cannot be compared as to their powers. But Gustave de Cavour is not to be spoken of lightly. He is a man of great learning and of perfect honesty. You will be surprised, perhaps, when I say that I think him an honester politician than Camille. Camille's policy was not Italian but Piedmontese. He wished to make Piedmont the nucleus of a great kingdom. For that purpose it was necessary to give freedom to a portion of Italy; and he was glad to do so. But it was not his primary object. We all of us preferred Italy to Piedmont. He preferred Piedmont to Italy.

Senior.—What are the feelings of the Italians towards Louis Napoleon ?

Pallavicini.—Such as are the feelings of those who believe in magic towards a magician. We feel that he has enormous power : that from time to time he exercises that power by acts deeply affecting our welfare. But we cannot discover what are his motives. All that we can decidedly say is, that many of those which most influence other men are not among them. He obviously has no veracity, no honour, he is bound by no engagements. He seems to have no benevolence. He insults and betrays all whom he protects. He has some malignity, though it does not appear to be very strong. We suspect that intense selfishness is at the bottom of his character, but that does not much assist us in conjecturing his future conduct, since it is difficult to say what form his selfishness will take—whether it will be vanity, or ambition, or fear, or the mere love of excitement. The result is, that we thoroughly distrust him, that we feel no gratitude for the immense services which he has rendered to us, since we do not believe that our welfare was among his objects, that we look on him as an ill-tamed savage to be perpetually watched, and to be kept in order only by his fears. We believe that it is through his fears that we have got out of him what we *have* got ; and that it is by working on those fears, by constantly holding out to him the spectre of Orsini, that we shall get from him what more we want.

Here our visit was cut short by a summons from the boat, and we said good-bye to the Marquis.*

Miss Curtis.—There was something painful, as well as interesting in this conversation. I was thinking all the time how different would have been my feelings and those of the Marquis if we had met four years ago. Then he would have been looking at the prospects of his country with anxiety, almost with despondency: I should have been looking at those of mine with nothing but hope and confidence. In that short interval all has been changed. It is his turn now to be hopeful, and proud, and happy. It is mine to endeavour to turn my thoughts away from the misery and degradation of my country, to foresee nothing but calamity during the progress of this frightful contest, and nothing but calamity at its termination.

September 7th.—I had a long conversation this morning with Dr. Ricordon on the Lausanne Penitentiary.

Ricordon.—We have tried in our prison four different systems. Under the first, which lasted from 1803 to 1826, the prisoners were divided into two classes, according to their offences. Each class lived together and worked together. Silence was insisted on during their work, but not in their sleeping rooms, in which as many as sixteen were

---

* This was the General Pallavicini who took Garibaldi prisoner at Aspromonte.—ED.

together. Some were employed out of doors in the streets and the fields. The mortality was about four and a half per cent per annum, the recommittals were above fourteen per cent per annum. During the whole eighteen years there was only one case of madness, and the probability is that the prisoner was mad when she committed the crime. She had killed her husband in the presence of a neighbour whom she had called apparently as a witness.

There was no reformation. This want led to the adoption of the second system, that of cellular imprisonment. A large building was erected, provided with 104 cells, each ten feet long, seven wide, and nine high, containing, besides the necessary furniture, tools for shoemaking, joiner's work, and spinning, and also religious books. The prisoners worked in common, part of their work being the cultivation of the land round the prison, and received when they were discharged a portion of the value of their work. They were not allowed to speak, either during meals or at work ; but might converse during about two hours a-day, when allowed to walk in the prison-yard. The punishments were confinement in the cell, or in aggravated cases in a dark dungeon. At first all seemed to go on well, but in two or three years symptoms of failure showed themselves. The recommittals rose from fourteen per cent to fifteen. There was no reformation, but a degree of insubordination which rose to mutiny. There was much sickness, but scarcely any increase of mortality. During eight years there were only two cases of madness.

The failure of these attempts introduced a third system in 1834, which lasted about eight years. All conversation and all communication between the prisoners at any time, or under any circumstances, by word, by sign, even by a smile of recognition, was absolutely forbidden. The time for walking in the yards was reduced to one hour per day. Those who had been recommitted were not allowed to work in common. The punishments were confinement in the prisoner's own cell, in a light prison, and in a dark prison. In all these confinements the diet was bread and water for two days out of three. The result of the change during eight years was, as to mortality, little alteration, it was still four and a half per cent. Recommittals rose from fifteen to twenty-one per cent, and the cases of madness, of which there had been only three during the previous thirty-one years, rose in the eight subsequent years to thirty-one.

Senior.—What was the prevalent form of madness?

Ricordon.—What we call hallucinations. The patient is disturbed by voices. He hears jailors consulting how they shall poison him, or preparing to beat him. As the disorder of his brain increases, he thinks that he sees them. The visions which tormented the hermits of early Christianity—the saints of the Thebaide—with which the painters of St. An-

tony have amused themselves, were reproduced amon
our prisoners, changing only devils into *gens d'armes*
These, however, were the more active-minded pri
soners. The dull fell into torpor, ending in idiotcy.

Senior.—I suppose that the prisoners were allowe
to converse with the officers of the prison, and witl
the chaplain ?

Ricordon.—Yes; but with the officers only t
make complaints which led to nothing. As for th
chaplain, the majority of the prisoners despise hi
spiritual and moral exhortations, and hate him
because they believe that he has influence enougl
to improve their situation and refuses to exert it
Of course it is his duty to explain to them th
wickedness of their offences and the justice o
punishment. But when the mind is becomin
disordered this always fails. The prisoner generall
maintains that he is innocent, and raves against th
folly or the malevolence of his judges; or, if h
admits that he committed the act, refuses to admi
that it was blameable.

Senior.—Were there many cases of religious mad
ness ?

Ricordon.—Not many. The persons subject to
that sort of madness are to be found in convents,
not in prisons. I remember, however, the case of a
German from Baden, who had stabbed a man in a
quarrel. He was penitent from the beginning, and
read scarcely anything except the New Testament.
After he had been about six months in prison, he

told that us Jesus Christ appeared to him at night, forbade him to work, because his excellence as a workman excited his pride and promised him pardon if he would macerate his body. He accordingly refused to drink wine, or to consume more than a small portion of his rations, and tried even to do without sleep. He was removed to a lunatic asylum.

Senior.—How do you account for the number of recommittals under the severe system ?

Ricordon.—I can account for it only by supposing that that system so much weakened the mind, that the convicts when restored to the world were often unfit for its struggles, and unable to resist its temptations. Certainly there was nothing attractive in the severe system, and yet the recommittals increased.

Senior.—And what are the peculiarities of your present system ?

Ricordon.—One is that more time is allowed for recreation out-of-doors, and that during that time the prisoners are allowed to converse. Secondly, instead of practically limiting the work of prisoners to sedentary employments, such as weaving and shoemaking, we make them labour in the fields or in businesses which exercise the muscles, such as carpentering, stone-cutting, and cleaving firewood. Thirdly, we classify them, and keep the classes apart. Those who have been recommitted are always the most mischievous inmates of a prison. They keep up the tradition of vice and crime. We allow them to have no intercourse with the others. The other classes are distinguished at first by the nature of their sentences and afterwards by their conduct.

I cannot give you the present statistics of the prison, but I know that madness has almost disappeared, and that recommittals are less frequent.*

Dr. Alderson of London is here. He has been

---

* *Malvern, October 5th,* 1861.—I have just received a letter from Dr. Ricordon, inclosing one from M. Clavel, Controller of the Prison. He states that in 1843 enforced solitude was reduced to a period of three months, and that in 1844 it was abolished, except that the prisoners are alone in their cells during meal-times, the night, and on Sundays, except during divine service and exercise. The diet was at the same time changed, *café au lait* being given every day for breakfast, fish being frequently substituted for boiled beef, and more, and more varied, vegetables supplied. On the slightest appearance of mental disease the patient is removed to the infirmary, in which conversation is permitted. Silence is still kept during work. The result has been that insanity has become rare, and is quickly cured. There have been only six cases during the last six years, out of 886 prisoners, or about one in 147. This, compared with the insanity of the external world, is large. But it must be recollected, first, that insanity is common in the Pays de Vaud. It is probably connected with cretinism, which is prevalent throughout Switzerland; and secondly, that a large proportion of the prisoners have brains damaged by intemperance and minds embittered by a long and unsuccessful warfare against society. And these, perhaps, are reasons for thinking that in the Penitentiary of Lausanne the experiment of solitary imprisonment was not fairly tried.—N. W. SENIOR.

kind enough to meet Dr. Ricordon this evening in consultation, and they recommend me to give up all our intended visits in Switzerland and in France, to return to England, and to use the water-cure of Malvern. We quit Ouchy therefore to-morrow.

We have spent our last afternoon in driving to the Signal, a promontory of the Jorat just above Lausanne. As we were ordered to do, we saw the sun set. We were disappointed. The mountain view is not finer than that from M. Haldimand's garden, and the home view is not very superior to that from La Grangette. But it has one fine feature; it stands at the extremity of the Forest of Suava Bellin (Sylva Bellini), which was itself a part of the vast Hercynian forest. Some magnificent oaks form its entrance from the Signal. A happy accident has allowed them to stand and grow apart from one another. Farther on the forest degenerates into the mass of boughless poles which the French and the Swiss encourage.

My recollections of Ouchy are not pleasant. There are fine walks around Lausanne, but they are distant from Ouchy. I was not strong enough to do more than dawdle about M. Haldimand's grounds, which are exquisitely beautiful but small.

The inn is not well managed; the number of servants is far too small for that of the guests. They are generally young Germans, speaking and understanding little French, and less English. This has been an unusually hot and dry summer; the sun

and the reflection from the Lake have baked the
house. Using every means to exclude the sun and
even the light, we could not reduce the temperature
of our rooms below 78°; it often rose even in dark-
ness above 80°. The great size of the house, however, had one advantage; there were never less than
three or four families of our acquaintances in it. My
illness prevented our going much into any rooms
except our own and those of our friends, but we
were told that there was great fun in the common
drawing-room. The heroine of it was an American
young lady, very pretty and perfectly unrestrained.
Miss Curtis, our Boston acquaintance, said that the
training of this heroine had been the very worst
possible, since she had been born in a Georgian
plantation, educated in a New York boarding-school,
and brought out in Paris.

Senior.—I can easily believe that a Georgian
plantation and a New York seminary are bad schools,
but Paris is not; or rather its faults are only negative.
French girls seem to me to be too much kept back.
They dance a little, not nearly so much as the
married women; they seldom dine out, and when
they do you scarcely hear their voices. Now
Miss Z.'s faults are all positive; she is in a constant
state of representation, always showing off her beauty
—for which nature has done something and art
more—her talents and her originality.

Miss Curtis.—The world in which Miss Z. came
out though Parisian was not French; it was the

great American society of Paris. Rich, idle, frivo-
lous, vain, and differing little except by its idleness
from that of New York or Philadelphia. It contains
few English and few French, and is governed, like
the higher society on the other side of the Atlantic,
by the young people. You will admit, I think, that
it is not likely to be a good school.

If the weather be tolerable to-morrow we steam
to Geneva : but this morning it blew a hurricane.
The lake broke over our little pier, *fluctibus et
fremitu marino*. The boat had few passengers, and
could not take them up at the pier-head ; in such
weather sea-sickness is common on the lake.

Dijon, September 9th.—Yesterday was fine, and
we had a splendid voyage down the lake. M. De la
Rive met us at the Métropole, the new great inn of
Geneva. He tantalised us by telling us of the people
whom we should have met if we had been able to
pay him our promised visit. We reached Geneva
at eleven and started at three for Lyons. I was
struck still more than before by the wonderful beauty
of the road from Geneva to Ambèrieux. We did
not leave it till seven in the evening, so that for the
last hour and half while we were in shade the forests
or cliffs of the mountains above us were in bright
evening sunshine.

We slept at the Grand Hôtel de Lyon, a new
and very good hotel with baths on every floor.

At about twelve this morning we reached Dijon, and found the Hôtel du Parc good. The churches of Dijon appeared to me inferior to my recollection of them, and still more inferior to Murray's estimate. St. Michael's I thought overcharged, heavy, and barbarous, the Cathedral poor, and Notre Dame good, but not peculiarly interesting. The tombs, however, of Philippe le Hardi and Jean sans peur are equal to any praise. The figures justify Marochetti's admiration of painted statuary. The colouring, while it gives them life, does not diminish the dignity almost amounting to severity of their expression. There is something bold and very effectual in the interposition of the grand black marble slabs between the white marble cloister below and the recumbent figures above. They are among the very finest specimens of the monumental art of the fifteenth century.

There are few good pictures in the Musée ; the nine or ten worst are marked ' *Donné par l'Empereur Napoleon III.*'

Paris, September 10th.—We left Dijon at twelve at night and reached Paris at seven the next morning, and on the 11th returned to England.

END OF VOL. I.

LONDON:
Printed by STRANGEWAYS & SONS, Tower Street, Upper St. Martin's Lane.

Lightning Source UK Ltd.
Milton Keynes UK
UKHW011614160119
335572UK00012B/1129/P